GREEK AND ROMAN
SCULPTURE
IN AMERICA

GREEK AND ROMAN SCULPTURE IN AMERICA

MASTERPIECES IN PUBLIC COLLECTIONS IN THE UNITED STATES AND CANADA

Cornelius C. Vermeule

The J. Paul Getty Museum
Malibu, California

University of California Press
Berkeley Los Angeles London

UNIVERSITY OF CALIFORNIA PRESS

Berkeley and Los Angeles, California

UNIVERSITY OF CALIFORNIA PRESS, LTD.

London, England

LIBRARY OF CONGRESS CATALOGING IN PUBLICATION DATA

Vermeule, Cornelius Clarkson, III, 1925–
Greek and Roman sculpture in America.

Includes indexes.
1. Sculpture, Classical – United States.
I. Title
NB86. V47   733′074′013   81-3057
ISBN 0-520-04324-3   AACR2

PRINTED IN THE UNITED STATES OF AMERICA

1 2 3 4 5 6 7 8 9

CONTENTS

CATALOGUE

PREFACE

This publication illustrates the wealth of major Greek and Roman sculpture in American museums. The number of acquisitions by North American museums in the past half century has made such an appreciation long overdue. Cornelius C. Vermeule, curator of classical art at the Museum of Fine Arts, Boston, since 1957, has for the last thirty years attempted, in the midst of many other projects, to keep abreast of new acquisitions and collections. His continually updated manuscript "Checklist of Greek, Etruscan and Roman Sculpture in America" is consulted by foreign and American students of antiquity, typescripts being available in Boston, Malibu, and Cologne, Germany.

The selection of works of art in this book is personal, seeking to show the variety of classical holdings, including many masterpieces. Two limitations need to be defined. Any effort to include private collections or art market holdings would have produced a group too fluid for value, so they are omitted. On the other hand, the collections of the Museum of Fine Arts, Boston, and of the Metropolitan Museum of Art, New York, have been adequately, even widely published, so only some samples of their most recent acquisitions are included. Bibliographies of individual items are confined to major references.

The choice emphasizes on one side the older, comprehensive collections—like the Walters Art Gallery in Baltimore, the Cleveland Museum of Art, the University Museum in Philadelphia, the Royal Ontario Museum in Toronto—that are not well known except in publications for their local audiences. Next come museums in East and West that formerly did not possess large holdings in classical art but that in the past fifty years have developed substantial collections, often of superior masterpieces. Among these are the Virginia Museum of Fine Arts in Richmond, the Toledo Museum of Art, and the Houston Museum of Fine Arts. Some university collections, like the Fogg Art Museum of Harvard University, the Art Museum of Princeton University, the University of Indiana Art Museum (Bloomington), and the Kelsey Museum of Ancient and Medieval Archaeology of the University of Michigan (Ann Arbor) have been substantially increased by gifts and bequests. Last but not least is the J. Paul Getty Museum at Malibu (California) which had modest holdings of ancient art in 1950 but which in 1981 displays an important concentration of Greek and Roman sculptures, particularly portraits.

The foundations of scholarly interest in original works of Greek and Roman art in America were laid early in the twentieth century. The importance of the new collections did not escape A. Furtwängler, *Antiken in den Museen von Amerika* (Munich, Sitzungsberichte der K. Bayer. Akad. der Wissenschaft, vol. 3, 1905). More comprehensive were the studies of G. H. Chase, *Greek and Roman Sculpture in American Collections* (Cambridge, Massachusetts, Harvard University Press, 1924) and H. Philippart, *Collections d'antiquités classiques aux États-Unis* (Revue de l'Université de Bruxelles, Supplement, 1928). Several articles have appeared which embody the results of research on selected topics, including Dr. Vermeule's own "Roman Sarcophagi in America: a short inventory" in the *Festschrift für Friedrich Matz* (Mainz, 1962) and his "Greek and Roman Portraits in North American Collections" in the *Proceedings of the American Philosophical Society*, vol. 108 (April 1964). This volume hopes to bring the student, not only American but also European, and anybody interested in classical art some acquaintance with the history and fruits of American collecting.

Jiří Frel

ACKNOWLEDGMENTS

The first word of thanks must go to colleagues past and present—Mary B. Comstock, Collette Flynn (De Silver), and Florence Wolsky—in the Department of Classical Art, Boston, who helped with the initial formulation of the "Checklist of Greek, Etruscan and Roman Sculpture in North America" and with its continuous updating. This volume owes much to Sandra Knudsen Morgan who first became acquainted with and worked on the manuscript in the Department of Classical Art and whose support, with Dr. Jiří Frel's, at the J. Paul Getty Museum has brought it to publication. Special thanks are due to John A. Miles of the University of California Press for seeing the work through production.

Every museum approached has been extremely generous in supplying photographs and checking references to keep errors at a minimum. I would like to thank all the directors, curators, registrars, and photographers who have contributed over the last thirty years, most especially Dietrich von Bothmer of the Department of Greek and Roman Art of the Metropolitan Museum of Art in New York; Dorothy K. Hill and Diana Buitron of the Walters Art Gallery, Baltimore; Rollin Van N. Hadley of the Isabella Stewart Gardner Museum, Boston; Elaine K. Gazda of the Kelsey Museum of Archaeology, the University of Michigan; Bernard V. Bothmer and Robert S. Bianchi of the Department of Egyptian and Classical Art of the Brooklyn Museum; Thomas T. Solley of the University of Indiana Art Museum, Bloomington; Francis Robinson and William H. Peck of the Detroit Institute of Arts; Margaret E. Mayo of the Virginia Museum of Fine Arts; Kurt T. Luckner of the Toledo Museum of Art; Alan Shestack and Susan Matheson of the Yale University Art Gallery, New Haven; and Neda Leipen of the Greek and Roman Department of the Royal Ontario Museum.

C.C.V.

PART I

SCULPTURE IN THE
GREEK AND ROMAN WORLDS

Sculpture played a major part in the Classical civilizations of ancient Greece and Rome, chiefly in the centuries from shortly before 500 B.C. to the age of Constantine the Great in the fourth century of the Christian era. Statues, busts, sarcophagi, and decorative reliefs are found from Greek and Roman Spain to the heart of Syria, from the Alps in Europe to the upper reaches of the Nile in Africa.

Most of the sculptures illustrated in this book are fairly large and carved out of marble or, occasionally, limestone. Some monumental bronzes are also included, but statuettes in metal and fragments of metal vessels or furniture do not appear. The book offers a wide selection from many American public collections with riches in the field of Greek and Roman art (please see part two, p. 11 for an overview of the phenomenon of American collecting). The statues, heads, stelai, architectural sections, urns, sarcophagi, and portraits of various types reflect, of necessity, a personal choice, but all demonstrate that the ancients missed no opportunity to express themselves with sculptural forms. Individually, these carvings and castings represent every possible three-dimensional use available to the human, animal, or vegetable substance. As a unit, they give a comprehensive picture of the commemorative, biographical, funerary, and decorative arts of Greece and Rome.

The marbles involved in the creation of these sculptures came from the Luna (Carrara) quarries of northern central Italy, from mainland Greece (Pentelic), from the Aegean islands (Paros, Naxos), and from a number of sites in western Asia Minor, including Proconnesus (Marmara) in the Propontis. The limestones are Cypriote or Syrian or Egyptian. Carving was generally clean, precise, and done with careful hand-chisels in Archaic and Classical Greek times. There are exceptions, but sketchy undercutting and free use of the deep or running drills belonged to the period of the Roman Empire from about 70 of the Christian era onward, when illusionistic presentation of subjects and surfaces became fashionable, particularly in the Latin West, throughout much of the remainder of Antiquity. In the Greek East, traditional reverence for clearly defined figures against simple, neutral backgrounds lessened the influences of illusionism and hastened the flat frontality of major monuments in the Christian centuries of the Empire.

Roman monuments of pan-Mediterranean popularity, such as sarcophagi, had overtones of commercialism and mass production not unlike first-quality automobiles nowadays. Greek sculptors filling commissions for Roman officials and wealthy private patrons thus learned and applied varied techniques of sculpting commensurate with the widespread universal demands on their art.

Man was the center of the classical world, and representation of the human forms in sculpture began with the earliest civilization in Hellenic lands. The statuettes from the Cycladic islands of the Aegean (nos. 1 and 2) in the millennium from about 2400 B.C. are an isolated expression by a relatively small group of people very conscious of the superlative marbles available on the islands where they settled. During the Bronze Age, the Minoan civilization of Crete, and the Mycenaean of the Greek mainland, the story of sculpture as told by collections in North America must be illustrated by small bronzes, terracottas, and pottery of all sizes. Such continues to be the case in the Dark Ages, the Geometric and Orientalizing periods, and down to the revival of monumental sculpture in marble after about 640 B.C. The museums in New York, Boston, and Cleveland have long exhibited statues of Archaic youths (Kouroi) standing with their hands at their sides in a relatively free interpretation of the traditional Egyptian pose (see also no. 6). Along with these votive and funerary statues, mostly from Attica, are found splendid fragments of reliefs (no. 5) once used for similar purposes. Sculpture all over the Greek world from 640 to 480 B.C. was concerned with the evolution and technical perfection of the human figure in all forms. Animals, mythological and real (no. 11), and vegetable life, albeit always stylized, take part in these processes. Archaic developments from Attica eastward well into Asia Minor are called East Greek, Lydian, Ionian, Carian, Lycian, and otherwise according to geographical area. The Archaic sculpture of northern Greece centered around the island of Thasos at the top of the Aegean (see no. 8), where crystalline white marble was plentiful, just as a finer grade of the same stone had brought forth much sculptural activity on the islands of Naxos and Paros in the central Aegean. Athens dominated mainland or central Greece with styles increasingly influenced by Ionian Asia Minor, especially from 540 to the Persian Wars, 492 to 480 B.C. The Peloponnesus was conservative in art as well as politics and international outlook, the so-called Dorian region of the Greek world. Olympia in Elis was an international religious and, consequently, athletic center, but much of the sculpture found there was brought and dedicated by temporary visitors or overseas patrons. For almost the first century of the Archaic period, Corinth exceeded or at least rivaled Athens in many aspects of the arts; but much, as elsewhere in the Peloponnesus, was metalwork or pottery, and time has dealt harshly with the former.

The cities of southern Italy and Sicily took their character from the mainland areas which had colonized them and, later on, from the East Greek cities which sent them refugees from Persian expansion. Good marbles were rare, and sculptural stone had to be shipped from the Greek islands of the Aegean (no. 9 or no. 118 of terracotta). Altogether, however, cities like Tarentum, Naples or Capua, and Syracuse made their mark in the arts, and the first three spread their influences to the northwest to inspire local Etruscan sculpture in metal, terracotta, and volcanic stone. Southeast from Greece and just south of the Asia Minor coast, the island of Cyprus was an artistic crossroads with Egyptian, Phoenician, and Persian connections as well as a Hellenic heritage unbroken back to Minoan times (see nos. 43–47). The Archaic statues and reliefs of Cyprus were executed almost exclusively in white limestone. Costumes were borrowed from all the island cultures, but styles progressed from conservative Corinthian through the Attic and the Cycladic to the most elegant Ionian of the last two decades of the sixth century B.C. and the outset of the fifth.

By 510 B.C., near the end of the Archaic period, Greek sculpture had achieved several unified styles over a wide area from Sicily to the Egyptian Delta. That the island of Cyprus, Greek since about 1500 B.C., should contribute a splendid head of Aphrodite or a female votary (kore, no. 44) of late Archaic, Ionian or western Asia Minor style, is not unexpected. In the fifth and fourth centuries B.C. Archaic charm and elegance were replaced by the grandeur of the Classical styles in Athens and the Peloponnesus. Between the two, the Archaic and the Classical, came thirty years of transition (about 490 to 460 B.C.) during which Persian invaders were thrown out of Greece and Athens became generally supreme in the arts of Greece.

Classical Greece

The Greek world from 460 to 330 B.C. opened with the political and cultural hegemony of Athens, following several major Persian defeats, and closed with Alexander the Great about to complete his conquest of the Persian Empire. Perikles (no. 28), his architects, and his sculptural impresario Pheidias rebuilt the Athenian Acropolis, making the Parthenon and its cult-image the Athena Parthenos (see no. 29) marvels of human dignity and divine beauty throughout the ancient world. The Erechtheum with its Caryatid Porch of the Maidens followed shortly thereafter. Meanwhile, Pheidias had gone off to Olympia to complete the image of Zeus for the great new temple there. All this activity, combined with metalworking at Sikyon and artistic commissions for Hera at her shrine near Argos, brought Greek art, especially sculpture, through its High Classical period or Golden Age. The last generation of the fifth century was wasted in the great war between Athens and Sparta, but the arts flourished wherever the Athenians had been, from Syracuse to the Troad to Cyprus.

The earliest Attic funerary sculptures date to the decades after 440 B.C., when the Parthenon was begun. Grave reliefs, with single figures of heroic youths and contemplative ladies against neutral backgrounds (no. 63), and marble vases with figures carved in relief on their bodies (no. 65), represent the finest surviving original work of these Classical centuries made for Athens and its townships. As the years pass, these mortuary reliefs become more complicated, deeper in carving and filled with whole families framed by pilasters and pediments. The marble vases likewise appear larger and more numerous, also often portraying Athenian families in simple domestic actions or ornamental, ideal poses. Protective lions or dogs grow in physique and ferocity (no. 99). Sepulchral enrichment was thought to have gotten out of control in Attica in the decade of confusion following the death of Alexander the Great, and the art was dead in the city of Socrates by 310 B.C. The best Attic stelai, vases, and animals were undoubtedly produced under the eyes of the foremost sculptors.

Aside from grave stelai and their related vases or symbolic animals, collections in North America include a scattering of original statues, reliefs, and fragments fashioned in stone during the two heroic generations of Athens, from 460 to 400 B.C. There are also excellent Graeco-Roman copies of the famous athletic statues by Polykleitos of Argos (around 440 to 420 B.C., see nos. 23–26) or of the majestic cult-images (nos. 29, 31) by Pheidias, his contemporary who supervised the embellishment of the Parthenon and constructed the Zeus on his throne for the principal temple at Olympia. These copies in marble, often after originals in bronze or even gold and ivory, were mechanically faithful whether made at full scale or in reduced proportions. They were frequently imbued with all the nobility of human form for which the masters were famous in ancient literature. These creations influenced the divine and athletic sculptures produced in Greece and western Asia Minor in the sixty years from the end of the Peloponnesian wars to the hegemony of Philip II and the rise of his son Alexander the Great, roughly 400 to 340 B.C.

Wars continued throughout the first half of the fourth century, the Greek cities spending their military strength in local struggles and occasionally joining with their East Greek cousins in attacks on the aging Persian Empire. All this was to make way for Alexander the Great's father Philip II of Macedon, who saw respect for Greek culture as one of several ways to ease his domination of the Greek cities politically and then to proceed against the rich lands across the Hellespont and the Aegean. Philip was murdered in 336 B.C., and Alexander carried out the realities of this legacy. In the 380s to the 360s the shrine of Asklepios at Epidaurus was the scene of considerable sculptural activity. Just before the middle of the fourth century, great commissions were offered to Greek sculptors by the Ephesians, who were rebuilding their Temple of Artemis, and by the Carians of Halikarnassos, who ordered a great tomb or mausoleum for their King Mausolus and his Queen Artemisia, who died during the construction.

At the middle of the fourth century Praxiteles was giving softened, youthful forms to the Greek ideal of the human figure. One of the greatest sculptors of this century, Skopas, came back from jobs along the coast of Asia Minor at this time to complete pedimental sculptures for the Temple of Athena Alea at Tegea in the eastern central Peloponnesus. Skopas gave emotion to the traditional canons of sculptural perfection, gods or persons created in their images (no. 51). The travels of leading Greek sculptors and their ateliers stressed the international aspects of their art in the generation before the Hellenistic age. Another sculptor, Leochares, modeled and carved extensively at Halikarnassos and eventually fashioned a likeness of the young Alexander in marble. Finally, Lysippos, the court sculptor of Alexander, gave the human form a restless elongation consistent with the more scientific optic perceptions of Aristotle and the dawn of naturalism (see no. 59).

The Hellenistic World

The Hellenistic period embraced the ancient world from Italy to India in the wake of Alexander the Great's conquests and the rise of related kingdoms in the Adriatic area. Chronologically, the Hellenistic rulers held sway from Alexander's premature demise in 323 B.C. to the death of Cleopatra in Egypt in 31 B.C. This was the age of powerful sculptures and earthier subjects, such as the pedimental group of Pergamene type showing a lion pouncing on a bull (no. 120) or the muscular Herakles tottering along unsteadily after his drinking contest with Dionysos, the god of wine (no. 174). It was the era of famous personalities: the playwright Menander in the cosmopolitan context of Alexander's exploits (no. 104); Ptolemy III Euergetes (no. 108), who ruled Macedonian Egypt at the height of its power; or the stern but anonymous Roman officers of the late Republic who led the Italian peninsula on its ultimate conquest of East and West in the century from 130 to 30 B.C. (see no. 116).

Old artistic centers continued to be important in a world of powerful new clients and their farflung domains. Athens no longer dominated sculpture the way the city had in the fourth century B.C., but her craftsmen still traveled to influential commissions, from the Peloponnesus to the northern coasts of the Black Sea or to Egypt. At the end of the Hellenistic period, Athenian sculptors found renewed energy in creating academic reflections of older masterpieces for their Roman clients (nos. 156–166). Old cities hardly heard from artistically before the Hellenistic age became centers of sculptural activity: Smyrna and her neighbors in the earlier centuries, and Aphrodisias in Caria as the Romans shut down the last major Macedonian kingdoms. Pergamon in northwest Asia Minor has already been mentioned as a city which sprang to power as center of a new kingdom and of a "school" of powerful, baroque sculpture, centering around the groups of fighting Gauls in the second half of the third century and the great Gigantomachy of the Altar of Zeus the Savior in the second quarter of the second century B.C. (see nos. 176, 177). The altar commemorated Pergamon's defeat of the marauding Gallic tribes in western central Asia Minor, and the theme of the Olympians and their allies battling the giants near the beginning of mankind symbolized civilization's defeat of barbarism. Such heady subjects were repeated in the sculptural programs of other Asiatic cities in the Hellenistic age.

Alexander the Great was buried in Alexandria near the mouths of the Nile, and his Macedonian successors, the Ptolemies, made the great new metropolis a port of entry and a creative center for Greek art in Egypt and westward into Libya. By the end of the Hellenistic period, Greek sculptors were thoroughly versed in Egyptian veristic portraiture carved in the hard, colored stones of the pharaohs (see no. 109), and they found a ready market for these styles and materials all over the Roman world, especially around Rome itself. In southeast Asia Minor, in Syria, and beyond, Greek style and Greek iconography was often influenced by local traditions, and new forms of sculpture developed. Palmyra, on the caravan route from the Syrian coast to Mesopotamia, produced a Graeco-oriental sculpture destined to be significant and, ultimately, influential in Roman times. Funerary portraits and groups of figures with rich costumes and swirling, linear draperies which foreshadow the anticlassical, richly ornamental art of the Late Antique period and the Byzantine Middle Ages were a speciality of Palmyrene sculptors (nos. 329–336).

The Roman Empire

In the latter part of the third century B.C., Roman armies ranged up and down the Italian peninsula battling the Carthaginians, pacifying local tribes, and incorporating the old Greek colonies into the Roman Republic. This process was completed in the second century B.C., and the consular legions found themselves active in Spain, Punic North Africa, and, neither last nor least, the Hellenistic kingdoms and the old Greek city-states. The destruction of Corinth by the Roman general Mummius in 146 B.C. is reported to have brought countless cartloads of Greek art to Rome. In the last century of the Republic, from about 130 to 30 B.C., the latter date coinciding with the Roman conquest of all the major Hellenistic kingdoms of Alexander the Great's Macedonian successors, Romans displayed increased awareness of Greek art. The dictator Sulla around 80 B.C. incorporated Greek art and architectural details into his public, sacred, and municipal buildings from Rome through Praeneste to Pompeii. His successor thirty years later, Julius Caesar, turned to artists from Athens, from western Asia Minor, and (because of his infatuation with the Ptolemaic Queen Cleopatra) from Alexandria in Egypt. Virgil wrote that the Romans were destined to fight and rule, not to mold, carve, and paint; but Cicero in Julius Caesar's time had prosecuted unscrupulous Roman magistrate-collectors and had, himself, bought much Greek sculpture for his various villas.

The somewhat morbid, or at least ritual and factual, natures of the Etruscans and the rustic simplicity of the Romans as they absorbed Sabines, Latins, and others around them had produced a taste for naturalistic funerary portraiture and vigorous mythological scenes. Greeks from southern Italy and, later, from Athens, Asia Minor, and Alexandria were to help the Romans express their shrewd, no-nonsense faces in the arts and record great moments of their history on public buildings, in temples, in houses, and on tombs. Republican coinage shows us at an early date that the Romans could use mythology or allegory as the Greeks did to express historical events, but the descendants of Romulus and Aeneas preferred to record their past as nearly as possible as it had taken place. The elegance of Greek art thus aided and eventually enhanced these endeavors, especially as the Republic gave way to the Empire with the defeat of Mark Antony at the sea battle of Actium in 31 B.C., the suicide of Cleopatra shortly thereafter in Egypt, and the subsequent granting of the title Augustus to Octavian by the Roman Senate in 27 B.C.

Innovations in sculpture during the Roman Empire ranged from the heightened awareness of history through the commercial circulation of elaborate sarcophagi or marble coffins and the exploitation of classic Greek designs and motifs in the decorative arts to lifelike portraits often charged with emotion.

Romans from Bath to Beirut were not the only ones who filled their cities, their shrines, and their country estates with sculpture. The Greeks of the prosperous cities of Asia Minor, Syria, and North Africa made their marketplaces, fountain-façades, theaters, and temples into contemporary museums of Greek sculpture based on the art of every generation back through Pergamon to Praxiteles and Pheidias. Soldiers encamped near the frontiers ordered elaborate tombstones. Their generals put up triumphal monuments covered with statues and narrative reliefs. Client kingdoms and powerful neighbors, from the Crimea through Armenia to Arabia, built and carved in their own versions of the Hellenistic traditions and the Roman imperial innovations.

Roman imperial art was democratic to the extent that anyone with money could commission statues and reliefs for public or private settings. As "first among equals" with access to the treasury, the emperor ordered the most monuments of every sort, and additional commemorations were dedicated in his name by ambitious municipal magistrates all over the Empire. Free enterprise allowed local worthies to be sculptured in elaborate armor, in tasteful draperies, or even in the heroic nude, as flattering imitations of the Olympian emperors. Millionaires like Herodes Atticus in the second quarter of the second century A.D. put up buildings to the Antonine emperors, like the fountain-house at Olympia. He introduced his own wife and parents and others into the niches for statuary on a par with the families of Hadrian and Antoninus Pius in these sculptural honors. In Athens and on his country estates, notably at Marathon, Herodes commemorated himself more openly and, while not neglecting the ruling house, remembered his talented pupils Polydeukion (no. 274) and the black African Memnon.

In death the rich private citizen could rival the emperor with a great mausoleum, like those along the roads outside of Rome, and in the third century A.D. more than one private citizen went to rest in a huge, richly carved sarcophagus while the emperor was lucky enough if he escaped the sewers of the Tiber. The Roman copies of Greek statues and the carved furniture found in the ruins of the imperial palaces on the Palatine are often of above-average quality, but they can be matched by private possessions from all over the Empire. It is the quantity and diversity of statuary from Hadrian's Villa near Tivoli (including nos. 54 and 169) which impress us, not necessarily the superiority of these commercially produced works of art. The emperor Hadrian (117 to 138) was certainly aware of the quantitative effect he created, for he ordered several copies in marble of the same bronze original, like the Discobolus of Myron created about 450 B.C. in Attica, and he commissioned mirror-reversals of masterpieces (compare nos. 131 and 132) so that he could position the copies in unusual juxtapositions around curving colonnades or in banks of niches. Lesser mortals copied these imperial standards or eccentricities of taste for their own country estates.

The Hellenistic kings had used a few simple symbols to further their rule in the arts, motifs such as the Macedonian starburst, the Seleucid anchor, or the Ptolemaic eagle on thunderbolt. These appeared primarily on personal metalwork such as caskets or armor and on the coinage. The Romans carried the idea of imperial emblems from one end of the Empire to the other in a variety of forms and media. The oak wreath, the Wolf and Twins, the trophies of armor, the magistrates' symbols of office, the figure of

Victory in a host of poses, the goddess Roma with various Roman attributes, the Jovian thunderbolt, and numerous other designs were passed from the major to the minor arts and used over and over again by successive rulers. In employing art as a means of propaganda, the Roman state came to create an art of its own, one which marched well with the traditional expressions of Greek art, notably sculpture. It became commonplace to see motifs derived from a mythological battle of the fourth century B.C. used alongside vignettes of legionaries on the march or the emperor greeting faithful subjects at the gates of a provincial city. In short, Roman art was an expression manifest throughout a vast polity, and this art applied Roman symbols of power to peoples in all stages of Greek and Latin civilization.

Along with portraiture, the art form par excellence of the Roman imperial period was the marble sarcophagus or coffin (section XI, pp. 239–262). Cremation had been practiced by Romans of means in the late Republic and the Empire until the reign of the philhellene Hadrian (117 to 138), when inhumation became almost the universal rule, certainly in Italy, Gaul, and Hispania, also in Asia Minor, Syria, Egypt, North Africa, and much of Greece. The rectangular marble casket, or casket and vault combined, was enriched with decorative motifs, mythological scenes, and portraits of the deceased on the fronts and ends of the chest and on parts of the lid. Sometimes the cover of the sarcophagus was carved in the form of an elaborate couch with drapings, pillows, and the deceased reclining as if at an eternal banquet (no. 220). Sarcophagi with Christian themes were similarly fashioned, with reliefs on the chest and front of the lid; and there are examples in which the decorative repertory indicates the deceased was of the Jewish faith.

The twenty or more examples of sarcophagi included in this book span the great centuries of the later Empire from the Antonines in the second century through the house of Constantine after the middle of the fourth century. The older sarcophagi feature generalized series of designs, including various myths, appropriate either to paganism or the most Hellenized Judeo-Christian tradition. The later monuments include representations of the persons who commissioned the sarcophagus, the subject of the surrounding carving sometimes indicating a Christian occupant. Otherwise, the date in the period when most religions were tolerated and the frequent use of general symbols of the seasonal cycle often give no specific indication of the career or religious beliefs of the occupant. What becomes evident, however, is that, as the Roman world began to disintegrate politically and regroup spiritually, people in all walks of life poured their wealth and artistic energies into tombs of every size and description. Where commissions for public monuments such as triumphal arches or reliefs in theaters were no longer available, sculptors perpetuated their art in the carving of coffins.

After the sarcophagi, the Romans seemed to care most for carved furniture, chiefly trapezophoroi or table-supports, sculpture set up in connection with fountains, and small statues of secondary divinities such as Tyche-Fortuna. Elaborate theater-masks were also popular, both on stage-buildings and in the garden-courtyard of Pompeiian-type villas. Sometimes they too served as waterspouts. The small statues of every conceivable decorative subject were placed in household or garden shrines, or they could have served as secondary offerings in larger temples and municipal buildings of the type found in every city or town of the Empire.

The Roman world was also dominated by portraiture and monumental decoration in the glyptic arts. The Julio-Claudian emperors from Augustus (no. 239) through Nero can be seen as they intended the public to admire their perfected images in the temples, market places, theaters, and baths of the ancient world. The wives and mothers of the Julio-Claudian rulers look out at us with an idealized severity at variance with what we read in the lives of Suetonius, the annals of Tacitus, or the romances of Robert Graves. The Flavian emperor Vespasian (no. 256) led the Roman legions to the walls of Jerusalem in 69 and began the Colosseum in Rome. His sons Titus and Domitian witnessed the volcanic destruction visited on Pompeii and Herculaneum in the year 79.

The emperor Trajan (98 to 117) conquered Dacia (Rumania), undertook vast building programs in Rome and the provinces, and left the Roman Empire at its greatest territorial extent. Fashions of portraiture shifted from the naturalistic to the factual overlaid with idealism during almost a century of sane and sober emperors who brought the ancient world to its pinnacle of unified prosperity, the *pax Romana*. Hadrian (117 to 138, no. 266) grew a beard like those of elders on Athenian grave stelai half a millennium in the past and tried to combine the harmonies of Attic art with the demands of Roman action. Antoninus Pius (138 to 161) and Marcus Aurelius (161 to 180) saw the Empire move from peace and vast prosperity to wasting wars abroad and unrest, triggered by disappointments and inflation, in East and West. Portraiture progressed to the extremely baroque, rich locks and curls framing meaningless emotion. The weak features of the emperor Lucius Verus (161 to 169) and of Marcus Aurelius's monstrous son Commodus (180 to 192) catch these currents with extreme artistic sensitivity.

Commodus was murdered in the last hours of 192, civil war followed, and Septimius Severus (193 to 211, no. 297), a North African in origin, led the armies of the European frontiers to imperial power. At first his portraits try to suggest the dynastic fiction that he was a son and grandson of the two great and good Antonine Emperors. He even named his evil son "Caracalla" (211 to 217) Marcus Aurelius Antoninus, a name also borne by his wife Julia Domna's grand-nephew, the priestly little pervert Elagabalus (218 to 222, no. 305). By that time, however, portraits were imbued with the melancholy harshness of a new century. Large, soulful eyes gaze out from veristic faces, framed by close-cropped scalps and often set off by stubby beards.

In the Roman and Greek worlds during the century from the Severans to Diocletian (no. 322) and the Tetrarchs, portraiture mirrored the anxious souls of both soldier-emperors and their often confused subjects. The most penetrating likenesses belong to the anonymous Romans of all ages (nos. 294, 314), often persons of intellect and substance, who had to stand by powerless, except in rare moments of crisis, while semi-barbarians up from the ranks wasted the fortunes of the Empire or sought patchwork military solutions for depopulation, decay, and alien invasions on the frontiers. The most sympathetic portraits were usually those of Greek imperial priests, magistrates, and men of intellect who retreated from this unrewarding world into the reborn philosophies of Plato or Christianity. After the Empire became Christian under Constantine the Great's family, portraiture (see no. 325) wavered between the demands of a failing imperium and the concerns of a world strong in spirituality.

Greek and Roman sculpture did not "die" with the fall of the western Roman Empire in 476 nor with the iconoclastic controversies of the early Middle Ages in the Byzantine East. So-called "Coptic" or Christian sculpture had a long life in Egypt, even after the Islamic conquests of the seventh century. The decorative motifs and narrative figures on Roman sarcophagi continued in the monumental ecclesiastical sculpture of the Middle Ages in the Latin West. With the Classical revivals of the thirteenth century and the grand Renaissance of the Quattrocento, the sculpture considered here came to enjoy a renewed afterlife, in creative work and in collections open to the public, which has persisted to the last quarter of the twentieth century.

PART II

AMERICAN
COLLECTIONS AND COLLECTORS

Private citizens and public institutions in the United States have actively collected Greek and Roman art for over a century. Isolated examples of Graeco-Roman statuary reached the young Republic early in the 1800s, notably in Philadelphia, where the iconography of our government originated; but museums began assembling masterpieces of classical sculpture from the 1840s on and, most determinedly, about the time of the United States Centennial. In 1870 the Metropolitan Museum of Art in New York and the Museum of Fine Arts in Boston were both founded. The Centennial Exposition at Philadelphia in 1876 brought art from all over the world to the international pavilions. Consul Louis di Cesnola had arrived in New York from Ottoman Cyprus with his vast collection of statues, vases, terracottas, bronzes, and jewelry, making evident to a wide public that ancient art could come as easily to the United States as it had to the kingdoms and principalities of northern Europe.

The Greek and Roman sculptures illustrated here represent a small fraction of what has entered public and permanent private collections since 1870. It would be easy to choose several hundred fine statues, heads, and reliefs just from the collections in the Metropolitan Museum of Art, the Museum of Fine Arts, Boston, the Walters Art Gallery in Baltimore, or the J. Paul Getty Museum in Malibu. A selection combining the best from these four institutions would rank with the best in any museum of the world, including the national museums of the Mediterranean. But masterpieces representing only the four or five largest museums do not give a fair picture of the wealth and extent of Classical art in America. The collections in Philadelphia, Cleveland, Toledo, Cambridge–Dumbarton Oaks, Brunswick (Maine), or Bloomington (Indiana) come to mind as following closely behind the titans, but there are a dozen others. There are also institutions with only one or two Greek and Roman sculptures, but these works of art are examples worthy of inclusion in this conspectus.

Generally, even small American museums have succeeded in buying a Cycladic idol, an Attic Greek grave stele, a Hellenistic torso of athletic male or ideal female type, one or two Roman portraits from the first century B.C. to the fourth century of the Christian era, a Roman mythological or decorative sarcophagus, and probably a Romano-Egyptian or a Palmyrene relief. Allegedly high prices often account for the growth of American collections, but many unsung "bargains" have reached the New World, and many a major historical discovery has been made in the galleries and basements of American museums. In addition, classical antiquities such as the mosaics of Antioch are scattered around North America as a result of licensed excavations in Mediterranean lands.

The most careful, successful assembling of masterpieces doubtless has been carried out by museum directors and general curators responsible for spending bequeathed and donated funds. Greek and Roman sculpture of quality can only be collected with care. There are many forgeries, recut sculptures, clever restorations, and misplaced attributions. The roll of Greek and Roman masterpieces in a half dozen or more United States institutions testifies to the success of dedicated art historians in bringing the glyptic beauty of the ancients across the Atlantic.

Early Travelers, Missionaries, and Naval Commanders

As was the case in the 1870s after the founding of museums of art in Boston and New York, the first acquisitions of the federal period in the United States were plaster casts. The founding fathers and their young disciples were, naturally, oriented toward Paris, supporter of the colonies in their struggle for independence and the center of neoclassic "republican" culture. Napoleon's cultural as well as political triumphs afforded the opportunity to collect replicas in plaster of all the great marbles of Graeco-Roman antiquity, chiefly the ancient copies dug up in and around the eternal city.

Most of the marbles brought to the United States before the Civil War, with the exception of the group of fragments acquired by C. C. Perkins in Rome or Florence, came from Greece, Asia Minor, and Syria, the heart of the Ottoman Empire (for instance, no. 275). The presence of missionaries and the Mediterranean squadron led to chance acquisitions which eventually reached educational, historical, and artistic institutions along the Atlantic seaboard. Turkish authorities were liberal about export; Greece was in the process of winning her own independence; and Italy was filled with local collectors (like the Torlonia family or the papal archaeologists) bent on redressing the balance of exports to France and England in the fifty years before Waterloo.

Highlights of the first century, exclusive of the activities of the brothers Cesnola on Cyprus, can be documented chronologically.

1803. Robert R. Livingston, as first purchasing agent in Paris, obtained a collection of casts for the New York Academy of Fine Arts (chartered in February, 1808, as the American Academy of Arts). These seem to have included a dozen or more of the showpieces of the Vatican, the Borghese collection, and the Louvre as united in the French capital under Napoleon. Shortly thereafter, the painter John Vanderlyn was commissioned to proceed to Paris, Florence, Rome, and elsewhere in Italy "to procure casts from antique statues and other pieces of sculpture. . . ." After a fire in April 1839, the casts were sold to the National Academy of Design, remaining in use in that institution's school until destruction by another fire in 1905.

1822. Augustus Thorndike presented, according to a letter of Ralph Waldo Emerson, "the institution [the Boston Athenaeum] with a beautiful collection of casts of the ancient statues, which attract the eye in every corner from the tedious joy of writing and reading." Of the selection, eight were full-size and three were "small." They are a perfect index of contemporary taste, and the institution was said, in the report of January 6, 1823, to possess "casts (with the exception of one) of all the most celebrated statues of antiquity. . . ." The eight full-scale statues were Apollo Belvedere, Laocoon, Venus de Medici, Venus of the Capitol, Gladiator Borghese, the Torso, Diana, and Hermaphroditus. The three small figures were Diskobolos, the Little Apollo, and Antinous of the Capitol. The statue needed to complete this pantheon could have been the Faun of the Capitol or the Silenus with the infant Bacchus, the latter among the casts evidently in Robert Livingston's shipment for the Academy in New York.

1827. Elnathan Gridley of Yale and the Andover Theological Seminary (1796–1827) collected two marble tombstones of the third century A.D. near Philadelphia (Alashehir) and Kula in Lydia. They are of a well-known type with figures of the deceased and lengthy texts in Greek. Another relief in this series, a votive stele to Artemis Anaïtis and Men Tiamu dated A.D. 196–197 in the Sullan era, came to Boston in the 1840s or early 1850s and was long to be seen at the old "Boston Museum," a hall attached to a theater.

1828. "Over the main door outside [of the Pennsylvania Academy of The Fine Arts] is the colossal, mutilated statue of Ceres in marble (referred to in the opening paragraph) brought from Melagra, Greece, and presented by Commodore Daniel F. Patterson in 1828." In 1806 the Academy had purchased a selection of over fifty casts of famous antiquities then in the Musée Napoleon; Nicholas Biddle enlisted Houdon's advice for the transaction.

1834. Matthew Calbraith Perry (1794–1858) presented the marble portrait of a young man of about 130 to 140 to the U.S. Naval Lyceum in Brooklyn (no. 275). It is in the pure proto-Antonine style of western Asia Minor, reportedly came from Ephesus, and was evidently collected by the future Commodore when he was with the Mediterranean squadron from 1825 to 1832.

1837. Jesse D. Elliott (1792–1845), when commander of the Mediterranean Squadron, acquired two marble sarcophagi at Beirut in the summer of 1837. They are of the garland type from Asia Minor and were evidently from the same tomb, of clients or freedpersons of the empresses Julia Domna, Julia Maesa, Julia Soemias, and Julia Mamaea (all Syrians) about A.D. 225. One went to Girard College, Philadelphia, as the intended tomb of the founder, and the other was consigned to Washington, to serve a like function for President Andrew Jackson. The victor of New Orleans felt that a sarcophagus with

Roman imperial connections was too grand for his republican tastes. It can be seen on the terrace outside the Museum of History and Technology in Washington, D.C.

1843. Charles Callahan Perkins (1823–1886) visited the sculptor Thomas Crawford in Rome and acquired a large number of Graeco-Roman relief-fragments from a palazzo or villa wall. These were donated to the recently founded Museum of Fine Arts, Boston, in 1876.

1845–1846, the winter. The two sarcophagi of 330 to 300 and 300 to 280 with couples reclining, as if in bed, on the lids were found at Vulci. They came into the possession of the Princess of Canino at Musignano, where they were much admired by travelers. They were brought to Boston for an International Exhibition at the Mechanics' Building in 1883 and were lent to the Museum of Fine Arts in 1884 by their owners, Messrs. J. J. Jarvis and George Maquay of Florence. In 1886 Mrs. Gardner Brewer helped the Museum of Fine Arts to buy one, and the Boston Athenaeum bought the other. George Dennis saw these sarcophagi in 1846 to 1847. In 1854 the villa of Prince Lucien "passed into the hands of Prince Torlonia, and it has now lost its attractions."

1870. The first gift (accession number 70.1) to the newly founded Metropolitan Museum of Art in New York was a large Proconnesian garland sarcophagus of the first half of the third century A.D. It was found at Tarsus in Cilicia and was donated by Abdo Debbas, U.S. vice-consul, reaching New York about a year before the U.S. Centennial. The ensemble, body and triangular lid with akroteria and friezes, is like the larger of the two sarcophagi brought from Beirut by Commodore Jesse D. Elliott.

1880–1883. In the fifteen years after the Civil War, a Graeco-Roman head of Juno or a major personification, over lifesize and restored as a bust, was on display in the Philadelphia Academy of Art. It had come to America at an earlier date and passed into the collection of the numismatists and antiquarians S. H. and H. Chapman. Charles E. Barber copied its profile for the United States five-cent piece of 1884.

The Era of the Titans and Beyond

The Americans who controlled the wealth of the continent in the last decade of the nineteenth century came to appreciate masterpieces of Classical sculpture. Isabella Stewart ("Mrs. Jack") Gardner purchased several major sculptures in Rome for the courtyard of her Renaissance palace in the Fenway, Boston. She bought statues, sarcophagi, and reliefs on the advice of a number of distinguished historians of art. Her main interest at the beginning of the present century, however, was in old-master paintings, and she regarded even the best Roman copies of Greek sculptures as essentially decorative adjuncts to her Italianate architectural undertaking. In these respects, Mrs. Gardner followed the tastes of her noble and wealthy predecessors in Rome, the Alban Hills, and Florence. When she did buy something important, it was predictably what an Italian nobleman would have added to his palazzo or villa in Rome at any time from the Renaissance to the rise of modern Italy. The Gardner Peplophoros (no. 14), perhaps her prime piece, falls into this category, a Roman imperial version of a draped female in the severe style of about 465 B.C. Thus, Mrs. Gardner could have Greek modesty and dignity combined with Graeco-Roman polish and facility of finish.

Edward W. Forbes of Cambridge (Gerry's Landing) was the son of a Civil War leader who backed Alexander Graham Bell's most celebrated invention. As a student he fell under the spell of Charles Eliot Norton, founder of the discipline of the history of art in the United States. His life was occupied with collecting for the Fogg Museum of Harvard University, at which he was both director and teacher of generations of museum personnel later prominent throughout North America. Edward Forbes collected excellent examples of the type of Graeco-Roman sculpture available in the 1890s and early 1900s, the time when Mrs. Gardner also acquired ancient marbles. Like Isabella Stewart Gardner, however, E. W. Forbes found his greatest love in Italian painting of the Renaissance. His most important Classical acquisition was the impressive early Roman imperial copy of the Meleager of Skopas found in the ruins of an ancient villa along the coast just northwest of Rome. The marble head of Augustus which he gave to the Museum of Fine Arts, Boston, in 1906 has always been recognized as one of the most sensitive surviving likenesses of the first emperor.

The gifts and bequests of William Randolph Hearst, his family, or his business organizations have made the Los Angeles Museum of Art an important center for monumental Graeco-Roman sculpture in marble (including nos. 48, 49, 58, 155). The Hearst estate at San Simeon contains the residue of the antiquities, mostly sarcophagi and architectural reliefs, assembled for Mr. Hearst by his agents in England, France, and Italy. W. R. Hearst's mother, Phoebe Apperson Hearst, was concerned with archaeology in Egypt and the eastern Mediterranean. At the time, early in the twentieth century, her advisors acquired the important Greek and Roman sculptures now in the R. H. Lowie Museum of Anthropology at the University of California in Berkeley. Mrs. Hearst's agents generally chose the most tried and true route, that of purchases from the dealers around the Piazza di Spagna in Rome.

Domestic and funerary sculptures of first quality (see nos. 224, 227) were also acquired for the Villa Vizcaya (Deering) from European decorators much in the way Mrs. Gardner had ordered antiquities for her showplace in Boston's Back Bay. James Deering sought works of art, furnishings, and the Graeco-Roman decorative marbles suitable for an Italian post-Renaissance villa on the bay just south of Miami.

Several important, smaller American collections were founded on the same principle, the initiative of one director or teacher backed by the good advice of friends and colleagues, including donors who had acquired a statue or relief with the needs of the institution in mind. Certain museums owe their masterpieces of Greek and Roman sculpture almost entirely to the generosity of one man. For example, the taste and initiative of Wright S. Ludington have shaped the collections in the Santa Barbara Museum of Art (see no. 55). Walter Chrysler has made Norfolk, Virginia, a rival to Richmond in diversity and unusualness of Greek, Roman, Etruscan, and Late Antique sculpture of all sizes and in a variety of materials. Norton Simon has brought masterpieces of Attic funerary sculpture of the fourth century B.C. to Pasadena (no. 72).

Collectors of Greek and Roman sculpture at the outset of the 1980s fall into several general categories. There are those who collect with an institution in mind, making gifts in their lifetime, leaving their sculptures to the museum in question after death, and, finally, providing funds with which, with support from their families, their aims can be continued by understanding curators. Professor Benjamin Rowland, Jr., of Harvard University, collected in this fashion for the Museum of Fine Arts, Boston, from the late 1950s to the early 1970s. Another group of collectors are those owning one or two sculptures as adjuncts to other works of art, while providing funds on a regular basis to institutions desirous of building permanent collections. And, of course, there are the major private collectors whose collections are shown from time to time in different museums but who have not promised their holdings to an institution on a permanent basis.

That major private holdings continue to come on the market and become available for public institutions and other private collectors was demonstrated late in 1979 when the Greek and Roman sculptures belonging to the late Ernest Brummer were sold in Zurich. Until his death in 1964, Ernest Brummer had been an antiquarian in Paris and New York. In the decade before the sale, his widow Mrs. Ella Brummer had kept the collection in her home in Durham, North Carolina, lending important objects to the several leading museums of the Raleigh–Durham–Chapel Hill area. The sculptures and other antiquities might have seemed destined to pass to one or another of these institutions on a permanent basis, but they were sold over a four-day period by Galerie Koller A.G. and Spink and Son at the Grand Hotel Dolder. Some of the most significant Greek sculptures illustrated in this book were brought to America through his brother Joseph Brummer, who died in 1947, and two Attic funerary monuments of the years around Alexander the Great's death have been included here from the October 1979 auction (nos. 87, 96).

Collectors of Egyptian and Cypriote Art

The honor of being the first United States citizen to collect Egyptian antiquities of both ancient Egypt and the Graeco-Roman periods seems to have belonged to John Lowell (1799–1836). Walter Muir Whitehill has written in his epic *Museum of Fine Arts Boston: A Centennial History* that

> he, after the death of his wife and daughters from scarlet fever, had in 1831 abandoned the textile business, and set out for the Mediterranean and the East. At Luxor, in Upper Egypt, he bought granite sculptures from the ruins of the great temple of Karnak; there also he fell ill and made a will establishing the Lowell Institute, which became effective when he died at Bombay. Although he never returned to New England, his cumbersome purchases safely arrived. In 1875

his heirs gave the museum—with, one suspects, some pleasure and relief—a great black granite seated statue of the goddess Sekhmet, two fine fragments from the broken red granite obelisk of Queen Hatshepsut, and a colossal royal head of the Eighteenth Dynasty from Karnak.

Otherwise, the systematic collections of Egyptian art which reached the United States before the Civil War were formed by Britishers in Egypt, the Abbott antiquities in the New-York Historical Society (now in the Brooklyn Museum), and the Hay (Way) objects in Boston. Six Egyptian sculptures, ranging in date from the Eighteenth to the Twenty-Ninth Dynasty (the latest a headless statue of King Haker, dating from just prior to the Ptolemaic period), were acquired by a Yankee ship-captain at Alexandria during the American Civil War. Confederate forces captured his vessel and placed the sculptures in the New Orleans customs house, from which they were brought to the Boston area by the Reconstruction port collector. In 1929 the Union official's son sold them from his garden in Lowell, Massachusetts, to the Museum of Fine Arts, where they have long been favorites of those interested in the bizarre modern migrations of ancient works of art.

Colonel Horatio Blake Reed ("Reed Pasha"), chief of artillery to the Khedive of Egypt, Ismail Pasha, and from a Hudson River family, collected small antiquities on an expedition up the Nile in the winter of 1874 and 1875. His acquisitions were confined to various shawabtis, bronzes, glass, coins, and terra cotta lamps of the Ptolemaic and Graeco-Roman or Roman imperial periods. Colonel Reed took up his official career in Egypt after command of the Twenty-Second New York Cavalry under General Philip Sheridan in the Civil War. His activities in Egypt were chronicled in connection with those of a number of Union and Confederate officers, who found active duty in the Ottoman Empire preferable to retirement or the poverty of defeat at home. On their way back to New York, Colonel Reed and his wife acquired other antiquities in Italy.

Cesnola and Other American Military Collections

Although Italian rather than American in origin, Colonel (or "General") Luigi (or Louis) Palma di Cesnola was another collector of Egyptian antiquities. Working on Cyprus after the Civil War, he assembled works of art imported from Egypt to Cyprus in antiquity or derived closely from Egyptian models of several periods. Nearly all his collection came to the United States, notably to the Museum of Fine Arts, Boston, in 1872, and the far larger portion to the Metropolitan Museum of Art in New York a year later. Colonel Cesnola was director of the Metropolitan Museum for three decades.

What General Cesnola admired most of Egyptian art were not the purely Egyptian imports which he collected all over Cyprus, but the limestone statues clothed in Egyptian garb and carved in a vaguely Egyptian style, Cypriote Archaic sculptures of the sixth century B.C. from the great inland sites of Idalion and Golgoi. Among the "Bronzes from Dali" (Idalion), on plate IV of Louis Palma di Cesnola's *Cyprus: Its Ancient Cities, Tombs, and Temples*, appears the upper half of a mutilated (forearms from above the elbows missing) royal Egyptian bronze statuette of presumably the Ptolemaic period. Among the antiquities purchased by the Museum of Fine Arts with the large group in 1872 from Louis Palma di Cesnola were two shawabtis, Osiris in mummy form, of fine style and bearing interesting inscriptions. These faience objects and fifteen green and blue glass (glazed) amulets must assuredly have been excavated on Cyprus.

Luigi Palma di Cesnola was, of course, best known for his collecting of Cypriote art, meaning every possible artifact from the Neolithic through the Byzantine periods in the island. The fame of his holdings in the Metropolitan Museum of Art and elsewhere (the antiquities having been scattered chiefly as a result of a major sale in 1928) centers around the monumental late Archaic statues, stelai, and sarcophagi carved in white limestone. But the island produced good examples of Hellenistic and Roman ideal statuary in imported marbles, and the original Cesnola collection included specimens of these. At the sale in 1928, major purchases were made for the Ringling collections in Sarasota, Florida, and now no study of Cypriote Archaic sculpture in America is complete without recourse to the riches of the Ringling Museum.

Alexander Palma di Cesnola worked on Cyprus from 1873 until 1879, and part of the collection which he formed (with funds furnished by Edwin Henry Lawrence of London) ultimately reached institutions in Canada and the United States. It included many small Egyptian or Egyptianizing antiquities (notably scarabs and jewelry), but Alexander never had the connections with the United States enjoyed by Luigi (or Louis, as he named himself when he settled permanently in the New World). Louis Palma di Cesnola's career, in a way, formed a pattern of the military (the Civil War), archaeology (work in the Eastern Mediterranean), and administration (direction of a major museum in the United States) which was paralleled by the activities of Major-General Charles Greely Loring (1828–1902), Curator of the Museum of Fine Arts from 1876, the institution's chief executive, and, finally, Director from 1886 to 1902. General Loring had studied Egyptian art and archaeology along the Nile in the early to middle 1850s and had returned to these pursuits in Egypt in 1868 and 1869.

General Loring may have collected, since so many of his contemporaries did, but the only record is in the donation of plaster casts to the Museum of Fine Arts. One of these, arriving with the general in America's Centennial year and a gift in July of 1876, is a cast of the Rosetta Stone. This "Reproduction Sculpture" is still carried on the museum's records, having found its way to the Children's Room. As footnote to this increase in systematic collecting of Egyptian artifacts at the end of the first century of American independence, the Egyptian Commissioner to the Centennial Exposition at Philadelphia in 1876, Emil Brugsch, presented a coarse, hard, redware two-handled jar to the Museum of Fine Arts. This household pot is of a type which could have been fashioned in Egypt in the Roman or early mediaeval periods.

The other recorded pre-Civil War "collections" of Egyptian antiquities, notably that of Colonel Mendes I. Cohen of Baltimore, assembled at Thebes in 1832, were of a nature similar to what was gathered in Egypt by the officers from the Union and former Confederate armies. These objects ranged from wooden mummy-cases to minor sculptures. Colonel Cohen was also remembered as one of the first systematic collectors of United States coins by type and date. His Egyptian artifacts were given to Johns Hopkins University after his death.

Collecting in the United States

Cycladic idols, Attic grave stelai, Attic funerary lions, Roman sarcophagi, marble urns, some architectural fragments, and especially portraits of all periods provide the majority of sculptures collected by American institutions in the twentieth century. This is partly because such antiquities have been plentiful and have always formed the core of great post-Renaissance and modern collections in Mediterranean lands and northern Europe. Sarcophagi and portraits came from Italy in the nineteenth century, where many of them had been known in papal and princely surroundings since the early Renaissance. With the building programs in Athens and its suburbs from about 1900 on, and chiefly between the two World Wars, good Attic funerary sculpture of the late Archaic period through the fourth century B.C. (kouroi, korai, stelai, lekythoi, and lions) entered the European art markets and migrated to the growing collections of America.

Since the Second World War, a variety of sculptures have crossed the Atlantic. Many of these have come from old princely or ducal collections on the Continent and from their equivalents in the British Isles. Cycladic idols, once considered decorative pieces when present in the older collections, have appealed in recent decades to the European and American taste for pure form in modern sculpture. The fashion for such figures has increased with touristic exploitation of the central Aegean islands. Unfortunately, a large number of the so-called Cycladic idols sold in western Europe and the Americas are forgeries, since such ancient works of art are not difficult to imitate and since they are so like what many contemporary sculptors are carving as original examples of their own creativity. As one critic remarked, in many instances these latter-day "Cycladic" creations are as handsome (and as useful for teaching purposes) as their currently favored ancient prototypes, which are often mutilated or ruined by corrosive patinas.

Other, peripheral or provincial, sculptures have reached America through the accidents of discovery or the changing politics of the modern Mediterranean world. Upheavals in Lebanon and Syria have sent new collections of funerary sculpture in limestone to the United States. These statues and reliefs vary from the masterpieces of Palmyrene portraiture to less attractive, cruder pieces with unclassical proportions, often carved of inferior, pitted limestone. The sculpture of the Nabatean Arabs and their relatives, either in limestone or in a material resembling alabaster, enjoyed a flurry of fashion in the 1950s and 1960s and, as a result, had found its way into a number of American museums. Canonical Greek and Roman marbles reaching America, however, were now the choicest pieces from famous palaces, castles, and country houses.

Character of the Collections

Consul Luigi Palma di Cesnola at the beginning of the great century of collecting and J. Paul Getty at the end stand out as the most colorful figures in the processes of classical acquisition in America. Biographies of both men have been written by their contemporaries and by their successors in the arts, journalistic or curatorial. With few other exceptions, the big collectors associated with holdings now in museums have been retiring men and women more associated with the collective decisions of the boardroom than the individuality of the chase in European lands. From the quiet tone and financial guidance set forth by a Libbey in Toledo, a Nelson in Kansas City, or a Davis in Seattle, not to overlook what Mr. Henry Walters did for Baltimore, came the contemporary ability of museum directors and curators to select and recommend purchases the way investment advisors indicate growing stocks and sound bonds.

Administrators of American museums are very conscious that they are often the sole custodians of monumental interior beauty available to the public in an urban environment. These directors and curators have to buy and exhibit only the worthwhile. In their programs for the arts and education, Greek and Roman sculpture continues to play an essential part. The departments devoted to public education in the museums of the United States and Canada have always built their programs on the ancient Mediterranean world around the original works of Egyptian, Greek, and Roman art available in their galleries. By way of compensation for the distance from North America to actual archaeological sites in the Old World, teachers from the beginning grades to adult education for senior citizens have made Greek and Roman sculpture part of the avid quest for knowledge characteristic of citizens in the New World. When a major new museum comes into being in Fort Worth, Malibu, or Pittsburgh, the result is that students in yet another urban center have access to the best in ancient art and modern education.

The Future in America

There are a number of major private collections in New York, Texas, California, and elsewhere which undoubtedly will pass to universities or public museums. In addition, enough museums possess such considerable funds for acquisition as to insure the growth of holdings in classical sculpture for decades to come. Along with the J. Paul Getty Museum in Malibu, Ann Arbor, Baltimore (The Walters Art Gallery), Brooklyn, Cambridge (Fogg Art Museum), Cleveland, Detroit, Toledo, Worcester, and others, not to mention Boston (Museum of Fine Arts) and New York (Metropolitan Museum of Art), all include specialists in ancient art on their curatorial staffs. The presence of such personnel guarantees that these collections will grow, according to the fortunes of the marketplace or the wills of benefactors and donors. And, while Mr. Getty was the titan of our age, there are other collectors capable of founding their own museums or, like Mr. Norton Simon, of upgrading and transforming an existing institution into a major new private museum.

Major Collections of Ancient Sculpture

The Art Institute in Chicago purchased a major Greek figure from an Attic funerary monument of about 350 B.C. and an equally important Late Antique portrait, probably of Constantia, wife of Licinius I, at the outset of the 1960s. These masterpieces keep good company with another, larger Attic grave stele and the famous late Hellenistic or Neo-Attic relief of a fallen Greek, based ultimately on the Amazonomachy on the shield of the Athena Parthenos by Pheidias, about 435 B.C. In the 1970s other marbles were acquired by gift and purchase, a (headless) statue of the Skopasian Meleager, an athletic child in the traditions of Hellenistic funerary sculpture, and a portrait of the 260s, seemingly the emperor Gallienus as Dionysos. The Museum of Art in Toledo has built a splendid collection of Greek painted vases and Etruscan or Graeco-Roman bronzes in recent decades, but no single monumental sculpture in the collections can approach the magnificent Polykleitan bronze youth acquired in the mid-1960s, a statue of the second century A.D. based in imaginative fashion on a work of about 435 B.C. Good Roman portraits and a number of masterpieces in sculptured silver have broadened Toledo's holdings in recent years.

Wellesley College pioneered in the acquisition of a single important statue (rather than an already assembled collection) at the beginning of the present century, when it accepted the gift of a major Graeco-Roman marble copy of the athlete with a discus by Polykleitos (no. 19). This statue was formerly the showpiece of the Odescalchi collection in Rome. Among Palmyrene reliefs of the second and third centuries A.D., a woman laden with jewelry is exceptional not only as a work of quality but because this funerary monument stands out in the small but choice collection of Greek, Etruscan, and Roman sculptures at Mount Holyoke College. Although a statuette and therefore beyond the scope of this book, the bronze youth or young god of about 460 B.C. from the Peloponnesus is alone worth the effort of a visit to South Hadley. The Mead Art Museum at Amherst College has always displayed handsome objects from all periods of ancient art; and additional Greek sculptures at the end of the 1970s, notably a major Attic stele of the fourth century B.C., have heightened the visual quality of an educational institution.

Some collections have come on the horizon only in the last several decades, since the Second World War. Purchase of a complete collection, gifts, and selected single acquisitions have placed the Museum of Art of the Indiana University at Bloomington among the best college and regional collections in North America. The pair of busts of Septimius Severus and Julia Domna (nos. 297 and 298), made in Rome in the first quarter of the third century A.D., are as fine as any such imperial portraits in the museums of Europe. That the University of Pittsburgh should possess an excellent Roman symbolic and mythological sarcophagus only exemplifies the effort of universities and smaller urban museums to acquire good works of art from all periods.

Using funds raised from communal energies, the Museum of Art of the Carnegie Institute has acquired several excellent Graeco-Roman copies of famous Polykleitan to late Hellenistic statues. In the last twenty-five years, under the initiative of Professor and Mrs. Saul Weinberg, the University of Missouri at Columbia has become the custodian of a comprehensive collection of ancient art from the Minoan and Mycenaean periods through to the Middle Ages and Renaissance. An early Archaic stele of a warrior from Crete, a class of carvings hardly to be found outside of Greece, and an imperial portrait in marble from Roman Egypt, the young Nero or Titus, illustrate the diversity of holdings in the Museum of Art and Archaeology at the University of Missouri.

The Francis W. Kelsey Museum of Archaeology at the University of Michigan received numerous works of art from the Michigan excavations in Graeco-Roman Egypt (notably Karanis in the Fayum and Terenuthis near the head of the Delta) and Mesopotamia (Seleucia-on-the-Tigris) before the Second World War. One of these sculptures, a second-century-A.D. Graeco-Egyptian head in green stone of the god Serapis (Hades-Osiris) is illustrated in this book. The artistic importance of the Graeco-Egyptian collections at Ann Arbor has only become known to a wide audience in recent years, although scientific catalogues of certain finds (glass, terracottas, coins) appeared in the decade following the excavations. In the 1970s the curators of the Kelsey Museum have purchased important Graeco-Roman copies and Roman imperial portraits.

The largest, richest collection developed since World War II, and most extensively since 1970, is the J. Paul Getty Museum in Malibu, California. The combination of unlimited finances, flawless taste, and the advice of the late Jean Charbonneaux of the Louvre and of Professors Bernard Ashmole and Jiří Frel has built a collection of Greek and Roman sculpture equaling that of the Metropolitan Museum in New York, the Museum of Fine Arts in Boston, and Walters Art Gallery in Baltimore. Hellenistic statuary, Greek marble portraits, and portraits of private citizens of the Roman Empire in various media represent the greatest areas of strength. The sculptures chosen here to illustrate ancient sculpture from Mr. Getty's collection and that of the J. Paul Getty Museum span the centuries from 500 B.C. to A.D. 300 or later. Since the Getty collections are growing at an amazing pace, the statues, heads, and reliefs discussed and illustrated in this volume stress works of Greek and Roman art not yet widely known, certainly not in their location in a pseudo-Roman villa on the southern-California coast.

At the time of this writing, the sculptures in the J. Paul Getty Museum fall into three categories. The first comprises those marbles collected by Mr. Getty before his museum became a professional reality. The second group represents the marbles and bronzes sought out by Mr. Getty's curators and advisors and purchased with his approval. Finally, there are and there will continue to be, in increasing numbers, those masterpieces bought from the fortune with which J. Paul Getty endowed his museum on his death in June 1976. Since it is the only museum in the greater Los Angeles area actively acquiring Greek and Roman art, the J. Paul Getty Museum has received numerous gifts from private collectors with no special links to the Getty family or their business interests.

Further Reading: American Collections and Collectors

Cesnola, Louis Palma di. *Cyprus: Its Ancient Cities, Tombs, and Temples.* New York: Harper and Brothers, 1878.

Comstock, Mary B., and Cornelius C. Vermeule. *Sculpture in Stone: The Greek, Roman and Etruscan Collections of the Museum of Fine Arts, Boston.* Boston: Museum of Fine Arts, 1976.

Dennis, George. *The Cities and Cemeteries of Etruria.* 2 vols. Revised edition. London: John Murray, 1878. (Quotation about the sarcophagi: pp. 470, 472; the first edition appeared in 1848.)

Dinsmoor, William B. "Early American Studies of Mediterranean Archaeology," *Proceedings of the American Philosophical Society*, vol. 87, no. 1 (1943). (Mendes I. Cohen: pp. 94–99, figs. 17–20.)

Dow, Sterling. *A Century of Humane Archaeology.* New York: Archaeological Institute of America, 1979.

Dunham, Dows. *Recollections of an Egyptologist.* Boston: Museum of Fine Arts, 1972.

Henderson, Helen W. *The Pennsylvania Academy of the Fine Arts and Other Collections of Philadelphia.* Boston: L. C. Page, 1911. (Quotation on the Ceres from Greece: pp. 188 and 10.)

Hesseltine, William B., and Hazel C. Wolf. *The Blue and the Gray on the Nile.* Chicago: University of Chicago Press, 1961.

Howe, Winifred E. *A History of the Metropolitan Museum of Art, with a Chapter on the Early Institutions of Art in New York.* New York: Metropolitan Museum of Art, 1913.

Oliver, Andrew, Jr. *Beyond the Shores of Tripoli: American Archaeology in the Eastern Mediterranean 1789–1879.* Washington, D.C.: Archaeological Institute of America, 1979.

Swan, Mabel Munson. *The Athenaeum Gallery, 1827–1873: The Boston Athenaeum as an Early Patron of Art.* Boston: The Boston Athenaeum, 1940.

Vermeule, Cornelius. *Numismatic Art in America: Aesthetics of the United States Coinage.* Cambridge, Mass.: Belknap Press, 1971.

Whitehill, Walter Muir. *Museum of Fine Arts, Boston: A Centennial History.* 2 vols. Cambridge, Mass.: Harvard University Press, 1970. (Quotation on John Lowell: vol. 1, p. 32.)

" . . . the Second Greatest Show on Earth." *The Making of a Museum. An Exhibition of Works of Art, Documents, & Photographs, Sponsored Jointly by the Archives of American Art–Smithsonian Institution & the Museum of Fine Arts, Boston, November 8, 1977–January 15, 1978.*

Colorplates

Colorplate 1. HARP PLAYER. *The Virginia Museum of Fine Arts, Richmond, Virginia.* Catalogue no. 1.

Colorplate 2. FRAGMENT OF AN ATTIC GRAVE RELIEF. *The J. Paul Getty Museum, Malibu, California.* Catalogue no. 5.

Colorplate 3. PEPLOPHOROS. *Isabella Stewart Gardner Museum, Boston, Massachusetts.* Catalogue no. 14.

Colorplate 4. RELIEF OF A WOUNDED WARRIOR. *The Art Institute of Chicago, Chicago, Illinois.* Catalogue no. 18.

Colorplate 5. YOUNG ATHLETE. *The Toledo Museum of Art, Toledo, Ohio.* Catalogue no. 24.

Colorplate 6. ATHENA PARTHENOS. *Museum of Fine Arts, Boston, Massachusetts.* Catalogue no. 29.

Colorplate 7. COLOSSAL HEAD OF A GODDESS. *Worcester Art Museum, Worcester, Massachusetts.* Catalogue no. 44.

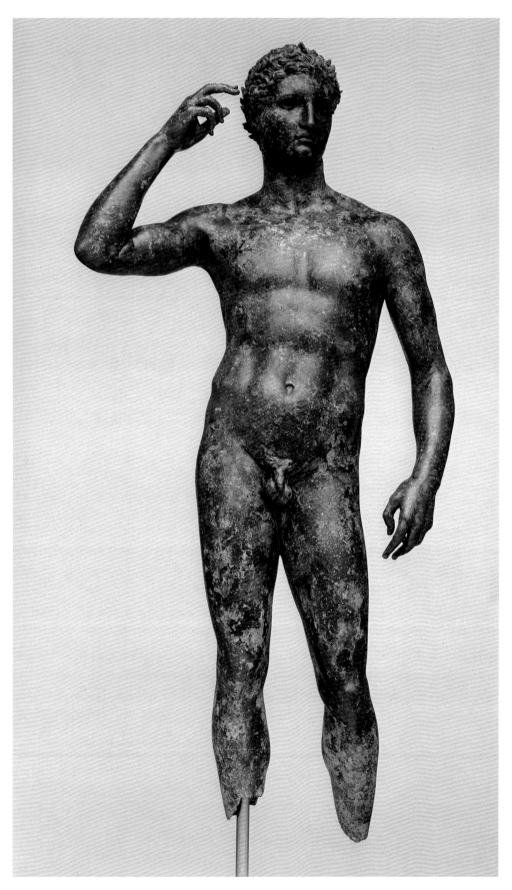

Colorplate 8. ATHLETE CROWNING HIMSELF. *The J. Paul Getty Museum, Malibu, California.* Catalogue no. 59.

Colorplate 9. HEAD OF A LADY. *The Ackland Art Museum, The University of North Carolina at Chapel Hill, Chapel Hill, North Carolina.* Catalogue no. 60.

Colorplate 10. FRAGMENT OF THE GRAVE STELE OF KALLISTRATE. *The St. Louis Art Museum, St. Louis, Missouri.* Catalogue no. 69.

Colorplate 11. FUNERARY STATUE OF A SERVANT GIRL. *Kimbell Art Museum, Fort Worth, Texas.* Catalogue no. 82.

Colorplate 12. PORTRAIT OF A NUBIAN. *The Brooklyn Museum, Broooklyn, New York.* Catalogue no. 113.

Colorplate 13. ARTEMIS HUNTING. *Albright-Knox Art Gallery, Buffalo, New York.* Catalogue no. 136.

Colorplate 14. INFANT HERAKLES (?). *The St. Louis Art Museum, St. Louis, Missouri.* Catalogue no. 149.

Colorplate 15. RELIEF WITH PROCESSION OF GODS. *Yale University Art Gallery, New Haven, Connecticut.* Catalogue no. 161.

Colorplate 16. WEARY HERAKLES. *The Detroit Institute of Arts, Detroit, Michigan.* Catalogue no. 175.

Colorplate 17. BARBARIAN QUEEN OR GEOGRAPHICAL PERSONIFICATION. *Fogg Art Museum, Harvard University, Cambridge, Massachusetts.* Catalogue no. 177.

Colorplate 18. JONAH SPAT OUT; ONE OF A GROUP OF EARLY CHRISTIAN SCULPTURES. *The Cleveland Museum of Art, Cleveland, Ohio.* Catalogue no. 189.

Colorplate 19. SECTION OF THE BASE OF A TRIUMPHAL MONUMENT. *The University Museum, University of Pennsylvania, Philadelphia, Pennsylvania.* Catalogue no. 192.

Colorplate 20. SARCOPHAGUS WITH ORESTES AND THE FURIES. *The Cleveland Museum of Art, Cleveland, Ohio.* Catalogue no. 200.

Colorplate 21. SARCOPHAGUS WITH EROTES AND VICTORIAE. *The Walters Art Gallery, Baltimore, Maryland.* Catalogue no. 201.

Colorplate 22. TOGATE STATUE OF THE EMPEROR CALIGULA. *The Virginia Museum of Fine Arts, Richmond, Virginia.* Catalogue no. 249.

Colorplate 23. PORTRAIT STATUE OF THE EMPRESS VIBIA SABINA. *Museum of Fine Arts, Boston, Massachusetts.*
Catalogue no. 270.

Colorplate 24. PORTRAIT HEAD OF POLYDEUKION. *Kelsey Museum of Archaeology, University of Michigan, Ann Arbor, Michigan.*
Catalogue no. 274.

Colorplate 25. VEILED PORTRAIT STATUE OF A WOMAN. *Dallas Museum of Fine Arts, Dallas, Texas.* Catalogue no. 280.

Colorplate 26. BUST OF A LADY. *Worcester Art Museum, Worcester, Massachusetts.* Catalogue no. 289.

Colorplate 27. PORTRAIT HEAD OF A LADY. *Cincinnati Art Museum, Cincinnati, Ohio.* Catalogue no. 296.

Colorplate 28. BUST OF THE EMPEROR SEPTIMIUS SEVERUS. *Indiana University Art Museum, Bloomington, Indiana.* Catalogue no. 297.

Colorplate 29. BUST OF THE EMPEROR ELAGABALUS. *Museum of Fine Arts, Boston, Massachusetts.* Catalogue no. 305.

Colorplate 30. BUST OF A LADY. *The Metropolitan Museum of Art, New York, New York*. Catalogue no. 328.

I Early Greek and Archaic Sculpture

1 ← (See colorplate 1.)
HARP PLAYER
The Virginia Museum of Fine Arts,
Richmond, Virginia
The Glasgow Fund (65–42)
Marble, H: O.165 m.
Cycladic idol from the Greek islands, ca.
2400–2000 B.C.

   Ancient Art in the Virginia Museum (1973) 62–63,
no. 71.

2
FEMALE FUNERARY FIGURE
Kimbell Art Museum, Fort Worth, Texas
Gift of Ben Heller (AG 70.2)
From the Greek islands
Marble, H: 0.412 m.
Cycladic idol, ca. 2500–2000 BC.

   Thou Shalt Have No Other Gods before Me,
The Jewish Museum, New York, New York
(1964) no. 220; *KAM Catalogue* (1972) 2–3;
KAM Handbook of the Collection (1981) 5.

3

HORSE HEAD

The Metropolitan Museum of Art,
New York, New York

Bequest of Walter C. Baker (1972. 118.106)

Found at Eleusis

Marble, H: 0.325 m.

First half of the sixth century B.C.

W. Deonna, *RA* 11 (1908) 195, fig. 4; *Baker Collection* no. 54, ill.; *American Private Collections* no. 145, pl. 38; F. Eckstein, *Gnomon* 31 (1959) 643; *New York Private Collections* 26, no. 107, pls. 32, 33; *The Horses of San Marco*, checklist (1980) no. 5.

4

LAMP

*The Metropolitan Museum of Art,
New York, New York*
Rogers Fund (06.1072)
and *Museum of Fine Arts, Boston, Massachusetts*
H. L. Pierce Fund (01.8212)
Said to have come from Thebes; formerly in
the E. P. Warren collection
Fine-grained Greek (Pentelic?) marble,
H (max.): 0.13 m.

The Boston and New York fragments were
rejoined and are currently on display in the
Metropolitan Museum. The motifs reflect
strong Ionian influences on the art of Attica
in the late sixth century B.C.

MMA Handbook of the Classical Collection (1927)
79, fig. 48; J. D. Beazley, *JHS* 60 (1940) 40, 42–43,
fig. 21, pl. 7; Richter, Metropolitan Museum, *Greek
Sculptures* 6, no. 8, pl. 11; W. H. Schuchhardt,
Gnomon 30 (1958) 482; Gabelmann, *Löwenbild* 59,
115, no. 57; D. von Bothmer, in Metropolitan,
Chase, Capture 122; Comstock, Vermeule, *Sculpture
in Stone* 16, no. 24; I. Scheibler, *Griechische Lampen*
(Kerameikos 11, 1976) 174, n. 10; J. R. Mertens,
AK 22 (1979) 35, n. 70.

5 (See colorplate 2.)

FRAGMENT OF AN
ATTIC GRAVE RELIEF

The J. Paul Getty Museum, Malibu, California
(79.AA.1)

Finest Parian marble, H: 0.50 m.; preserved
W: 0.575 m.

The left youth fastens a bandage around
the head of another whose closed eyes indicate that he is dying. Two other Attic
grave reliefs appear to be by the same hand
(G. M. A. Richter, *Archaic Attic Gravestones*
[1961] no. 59, figs. 151–153, and no. 74,
fig. 166). Ca. 530 B.C.

JPGM Checklist of Antiquities 1 (1979) no. 3;
JPGM Guidebook (1980) 24, ill.

6 →

HEAD OF A YOUTH

*William Rockhill Nelson Gallery of Art–Atkins
Museum of Fine Arts, Kansas City, Missouri*

Nelson Fund (38-7)

Said to have been found in Attica

Marble, H: 0.188 m.

Included by Richter early in her group of
Ptoon 20, ca. 510 B.C.

J. Sieveking, *Pantheon* 23 (1939) 36–38; P. E.
Arias, *Istituto d'Archeologia e Storia d'Arte* 1 (1952)
245, fig. 5; G. M. A. Richter, *Kouroi* (1960) 139,
no. 164, pls. 485–488; J. D. Cooney, *Apollo* 96
(1972) 13, pl. 13; *Handbook* 1 (1973) 34, ill.

7

YOUTH CONTROLLING A HORSE,
PART OF A VOTIVE RELIEF
The J. Paul Getty Museum, Malibu, California
(78.AA.59)
From central Greece, via Cottenham near
Cambridge, England, the Fitzwilliam
Museum, and the collection of Professor
A. B. Cook, Cambridge
Hymettan marble, H: 0.275 m.
Ca. 500 B.C.

A. B. Cook, *JHS* 37 (1917) 116–125; J. D.
Beazley, *Lewes House* 15; Picard, *Manuel* 2.1, 20;
Fuchs, *Skulptur* 504–505, fig. 586; M. Moore, Getty
MJ 2 (1975) 37–50, figs. 1–7; *JPGM Checklist of
Antiquities* 1 (1979) 3, no. 7; *JPGM Guidebook* (1980)

8

GODDESS (CYBELE OR APHRODITE)
IN A SHRINE AND ATTENDANTS
The J. Paul Getty Museum, Malibu, California
(55.AA.13)
Found in 1913 on the acropolis of Thasos;
formerly in the Wix de Zsolnay collection,
Vienna
Thasian marble, H: 0.36 m.; W: 0.65 m.
Ca. 500–490 B.C.

C. C. Vermeule, N. Neuerburg, *Catalogue of the Ancient Art* (1973) 3, no. 1; *JPGM Checklist of Antiquities* 1 (1979) 3, no. 8.

9 ←
FRAGMENT OF VOTIVE RELIEF
WITH HEROIC BANQUET
The Museum of Fine Arts, Houston, Texas
Laurence H. Favrot Fund (72-25)
From southern Italy, allegedly near Meta-
pontum, via a private collection near Naples
Greek-island marble, H: 0.61 m.; W: 0.55 m.
Note the holes in the hair for attaching a
bronze wreath. Late archaic period in
southern Italy, ca. 490–480 B.C.

Exhibited at the Amsterdam Historisch Museum, 1970; *Bulletin* 3 (Winter 1973) 109, ill.;
A Guide to the Collection (1981) 10, no. 14, pl. 2.

10
UNFINISHED HEAD OF A MAN
FROM A RELIEF
*Fogg Art Museum, Harvard University,
Cambridge, Massachusetts*
Gift of Mr. and Mrs. Norbert Schimmel
(1969.175)
From western Asia Minor
Marble, H: 0.185 m.; W: 0.16 m.
ca. 500 B.C.

Acquisitions 1969–1970 (1971) 131; H. Hoffmann, *Collecting Greek Antiquities* (1971) 10, fig. 10.

11
HEAD OF PAN (?)
The Cleveland Museum of Art, Cleveland, Ohio
Gift of Leonard C. Hanna, Jr. (26.538)
Said to have been found on the north slope of
the Acropolis
Limestone with traces of polychromy,
H: 0.345 m.
Attic work of ca. 480 B.C.

R. Howard, *CMA Bulletin* (March 1927) 36, ill.;
M. Bieber, *Art in America* 31 (1943) 112–126, fig. 2;
Handbook (1966) 20; H. S. Robinson, *CMA Bulletin*
64 (1977) 231–241; Ridgway, Archaic Style 162, 180,
fig. 50.

II Classical Sculpture
Of the
Fifth Century B.C.

12

PEPLOPHOROS

The J. Paul Getty Museum, Malibu, California
(70.AA.114)

From Attica or the Aegean Islands; formerly in the collection of the Earl of Elgin,
Broom Hall

Grey island (?) marble, H: 0.71 m.

Ca. 470 B.C.

A. Michaelis, *JHS* 5 (1884) 145, no. 2; C. C.
Vermeule, *AJA* 59 (1955) 132; C. C. Vermeule,
N. Neuerburg, *Catalogue of the Ancient Art* (1973)
3–4, no. 2; B. S. Ridgway, *Hesperia* 38 (1969)
213–222; Fuchs, *Skulptur* 183–184, fig. 190; *JPGM
Checklist of Antiquities* 1 (1979) 4, no. 9; *JPGM
Guidebook* (1980) 23, ill.

13
PEPLOPHOROS
Santa Barbara Museum of Art,
Santa Barbara, California
Gift of Wright S. Ludington (78.4.2)
From Sicily
Marble, H: 1.105 m.
Roman copy of a type created about 470 B.C.

M. A. Del Chiaro, *The Collection of Greek and Roman Antiquities at the SBMA* (1962) no. S-3; Ridgway, *Severe Style* 73 (identified as the Candia-Kisamos-Ludovisi type).

14 (See colorplate 3.)
PEPLOPHOROS
Isabella Stewart Gardner Museum,
Boston, Massachusetts
(S5c2)
Discovered in 1901 in the Gardens of Sallust
on the Pincian Hill, Rome; the statue resided
in the American Academy in Rome until 1936
Marble, H: 1.48 m.
Roman copy of a Greek type of ca. 465 B.C.

S. Reinach, *Rép. stat.* 3 (1904) 185, no. 10;
MAAR 1 (1915–16) frontis. and foreword; *Sculpture in the Isabella Stewart Gardner Museum* (1977)
6–7, no. 10 (with previous bibl.); *The Connoisseur*
(May 1978) 44–45, colorplate.

15
HEAD OF A GIRL OR SPHINX
The Cleveland Museum of Art, Cleveland, Ohio
Gift of J. H. Wade (24.538)
From the island of Amorgos
Pentelic (?) marble, H: 0.115 m.
Ca. 460 B.C.

CMA Handbook (1958) fig. 14; Ridgway, *Severe Style* 59 ff., figs. 88–91.

16

HEAD OF APOLLO

The Brooklyn Museum, Brooklyn, New York

Gift of A. Augustus Healy (18.166)

From Italy

Marble, H: 0.323 m.

Roman copy after the so-called Omphalos

Apollo, ca. 460–450 B.C.

Stefano Bardini Sale (American Art Association, New York, 25–27 April 1918) no. 412, ill.; E. Paribeni, *Museo Nazionale Romano, Sculture greche* (1953) 20, under no. 16 (list of replicas, this no. 24); Ridgway, *Severe Style* 61–62, 71 (the types and variants).

17
HEAD OF APOLLO
Honolulu Academy of Arts, Honolulu, Hawaii
Gift of Mrs. Charles M. Cooke (3604)
Formerly in the collection of Hatchik
Sevadjian
Marble, H: 0.292 m.
Early Antonine copy after an original asso-
ciated with the Kassel Apollo of ca. 460 B.C.
and perhaps by Kalamis.

Honolulu Academy of Art (1937) 62; J. Frel,
Getty *MJ* 1 (1974) 55–60, figs. 3–4.

18 (See colorplate 4.)
RELIEF OF A WOUNDED WARRIOR
The Art Institute of Chicago, Chicago, Illinois
Gift of Alfred E. Hamill (1928.257)
Found at Piraeus, the port of Attic Salamis,
in 1925
Marble, H: 0.47 m.; W: 0.83 m.
Second-century-A.D. version of the figure of
"Kapaneus" from the reliefs on the shield of
the Athena Parthenos by Pheidias, type of ca.
438 B.C.

International Studio 84 (1926) 31 (discovery);
AIC Bulletin 21 (1927) 9–10; D. C. Rich, *ibid.* 23
(1929) 102–103; *AIC Brief Illustrated Guide* (1935)
8; A. D. Fraser, *AJA* 43 (1939) 447–457, fig. 2; *AIC
Brief Guide* (1948) 6; G. Becatti, *Problemi Fidiaci*
(1951) 114, p. 67, fig. 202; V. M. Strocka, *Piräus-
reliefs und Parthenosschild* (1967) 40, 69 ff., 82, 92,
Abb. 27 (relief XIII) (with previous bibl.);
M. Robertson, *A History of Greek Art* (1975)
316, 671 n. 55.

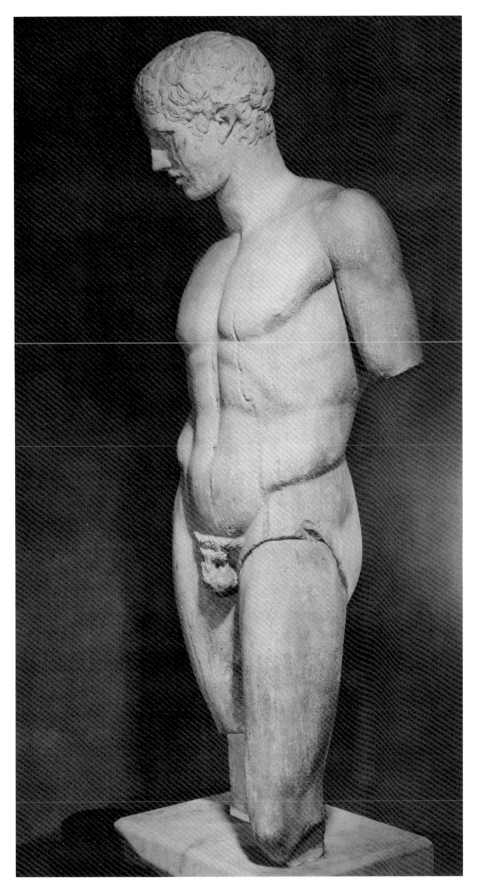

19
DISKOPHOROS
Wellesley College Museum, Jewett Arts Center,
Wellesley, Massachusetts
Gift of Hannah Parker Kimball (1904.1)
Formerly in the Odescalchi collection, Rome
Marble, H: 1.32 m.
Roman copy after the type by Polykleitos.

S. Reinach, *Rép. stat.* 5 (1924) 293, no. 3; P. E. Arias, *Policleto* (1964) 134–135, pl. 8; Vermeule, *Polykleitos* 13, 22, fig. 14; *Antiquity in the Renaissance,* Smith College Museum of Art (1978) no. 31.

20
DIADOUMENOS TORSO
The J. Paul Getty Museum, Malibu, California
(79.AA.146)
Greek marble with big crystals, H: 0.71 m.
The arms were attached separately in antiq-
uity. Second-century-B.C. adaptation after the
Polykleitan original.

J. Frel, Getty *MJ* 8 (1980) 92–95.

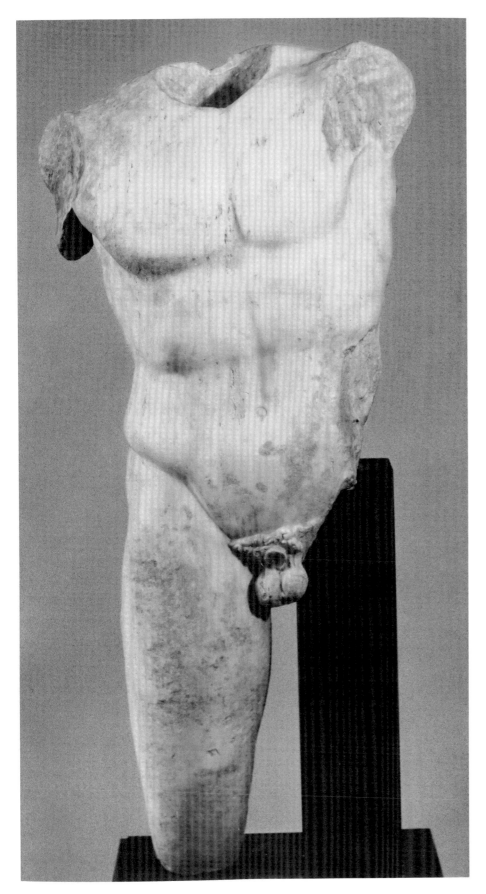

21
DIADOUMENOS
Rhode Island School of Design, Museum of Art,
Providence, Rhode Island
(26.159)
Marble, H: 1.14 m.
Roman copy after the Diadoumenos of
Polykleitos.

B. S. Ridgway, *Catalogue of the Classical Collection,*
Classical Sculpture (1972) 39, 156–158, no. 13.

22
HEAD OF PAN
Seattle Art Museum, Seattle, Washington
Norman Davis collection (71.1)
Marble, H: 0.17 m.
Copy after a statue type attributed to a student
of Polykleitos. Compare Arnold, *Polykletnach-
folge* 247, pl. 1.b, 2.a,b. Late fifth century B.C.

23

POLYKLEITAN HERMES
The Metropolitan Museum of Art,
New York, New York
Gift of the William Randolph Hearst Foundation (56.234.15)
Presumably from Italy, formerly in the Lansdowne collection, London
Marble, H: 1.75 m.
Roman copy after a type of the mid-fourth century B.C.

J. Dallaway, *Anecdotes of the Arts in England* (1800) 364 ff. (found in a swamp near Hadrian's Villa), 368, no. 19; Clarac, *Musée de Sculpture* (1841) pl. 946, no. 2436A; Michaelis *AZ* (1874) 36, no. 30; idem, *Marbles in Great Britain* 446, no. 35; Christie's (March 5, 1930) 68, no. 104, ill.; *EA* 213–215; C. C. Vermeule, D. von Bothmer, *AJA* 63 (1959) 330, pl. 77, figs. 3–5; C. Blümel, *Der Diskosträger Polyklets* (90. Winckelmannsprogramm, 1930) 12, fig. 7, 15; D. von Bothmer, *MMA Bulletin* 16 (1958) 187, 189, ill.

24 (See colorplate 5.)
YOUNG ATHLETE
The Toledo Museum of Art, Toledo, Ohio
Gift of Edward Drummond Libbey (66.126)
From western Asia Minor
Bronze, H (max.): 1.43 m.
Hadrianic to early Antonine work after a
Polykleitan type of ca. 440 B.C.

TMA Museum News 12 (1969) ill.; Vermeule,
Polykleitos 23 ff., figs. 20 A–F, cover; D. T. Owsley,
Carnegie Magazine 46 (1972) 21, fig. 7; R. V.
Nicholls, review of Arnold, *Polykletnachfolge, JHS* 93
(1973) 266; P. Zanker, *Klassizistische Statuen* (1974)
37, no. 33, 67, Taf. 33, 5.

25
POLYKLEITAN YOUTH
Carnegie Institute, Museum of Art,
Pittsburgh, Pennsylvania
(71.16)
Presumably from Italy, via France
Marble, H: 0.965 m.
Greek imperial version of ca. A.D. 140.

ArtQ 35 (1972) 318, 327; *Carnegie Magazine*
(May 1974) 203.

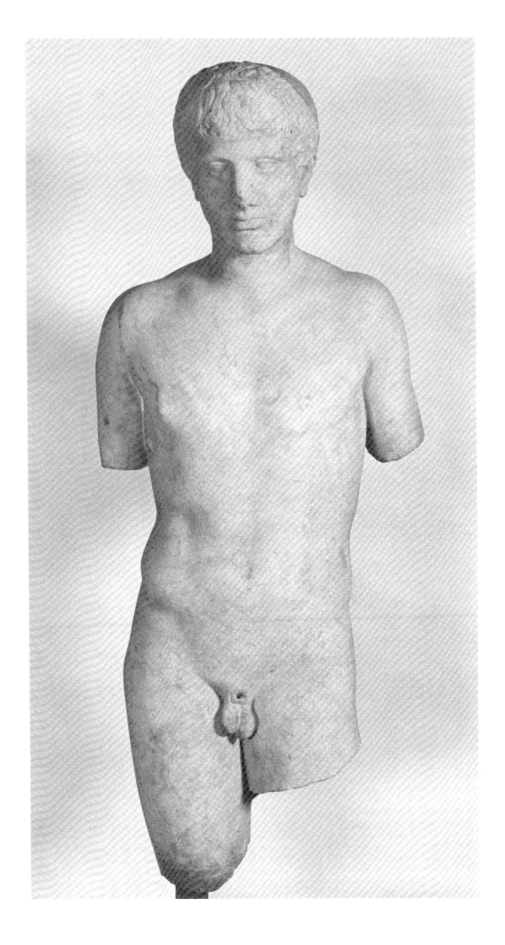

26
TORSO
University Gallery, University of Minnesota,
Minneapolis, Minnesota
Anonymous gift (69.8)
White Parian (?) marble, H: 0.838 m.
Variation of the Apollo from Centocelle now
in the Vatican of ca. 400 B.C.

W. D. E. Coulson and D. S. Furmanik, *AntPl* 17
(1977) 71–72; W. D. E. Coulson and S. McNally,
Archaeology 32 (1979) 61–63, ill.

 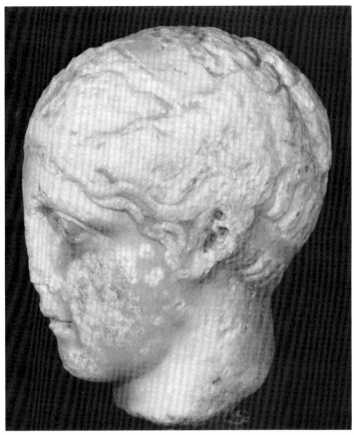

27

HEAD OF A WOMAN

Albright-Knox Art Gallery, Buffalo, New York

Gift of Mrs. Seymour H. Knox, Sr. (26:5)

Said to have been found in Athens near the
Acropolis

Greek, slightly grained marble, H: 0.2413 m.;
W: 0.1651 m.

Late-fifth-century-B.C. work.

   Buffalo Artist's Register (1926) 55, ill.; M. Bieber,
Art in America (July 1943) 114, fig. 7; A. C. Ritchie,
Catalogue of the AKAG (n.d.) 213, no. 238.

28

PORTRAIT OF PERIKLES

The Art Museum, Princeton University,
Princeton, New Jersey

Alden Sampson collection, presented by
Edward Sampson, Class of 1914 (62–132)
From Rome; formerly in the Hartwig
collection

Pentelic marble, H: 0.29 m.; W: 0.18 m.

A good Roman copy of the type attributed to
Kresilas in Athens about 430 B.C. or slightly
later.

   Lippold, *Vaticanischen Skulpturen* 3.1 (1936) 88
(in the list of variations); F. F. Jones, *Record of the
Art Museum* (1962) 47–48, 52, figs. 4–6; Richter,
Portraits of the Greeks 103, no. 5, figs. 442–443;
Ackland, *Ancient Portraits* no. 1.

29 (See colorplate 6.)
ATHENA PARTHENOS
Museum of Fine Arts, Boston, Massachusetts
Classical Department Exchange Fund
(1980.196)
"African" marble, H: 1.54 m.
Roman copy of the early third century A.D.
after Pheidias' original. The head, of different
marble, was worked separately for insertion
but belongs without any question. Arms and
shield were also attached separately. Nose,
lower lip, and chin restored.

Unpublished.

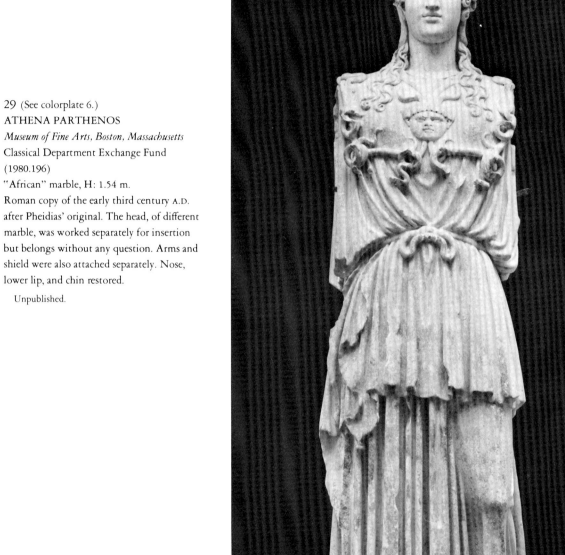

30

ARTEMIS

The J. Paul Getty Museum, Malibu, California
(73.AA.5)

Marble, H: 1.38 m.

The quiver originally attached to her right
shoulder identifies the goddess. The prototype lies somewhere between the Artemis
from Ariccia (Lippold, *Handbuch* 3.1, pl. 62,
no. 4) and the Demeter of Eleusis (pl. 70,
no. 1). She could come from a group by
Kresilas. Roman reduced copy of a statue of
Ca. 420 B.C.

Unpublished.

31

ATHENA

Los Angeles County Museum of Art,
Los Angeles, California
William Randolph Hearst Collection
(51.18.12)
Found at Ostia in 1797; formerly in the Hope
collection, Deepdene
Carrara marble, H: 2.18 m.
The eighteenth-century restorations, includ-
ing the arms, were removed recently. After
a fifth-century original from the school of
Pheidias.

Michaelis, *Marbles in Great Britain* 290–291,
no. 39; Christie's (23–24 July, 1917) lot 258; Picard,
Manuel 2.2 (1939) 550; D. Mustilli, *Museo Mussolini*
(1939) 136, no. 13.1; C. C. Vermeule, *AJA* 59
(1955) 135; Lippold, *Handbuch* 3.1, 190, n. 10
questions head.

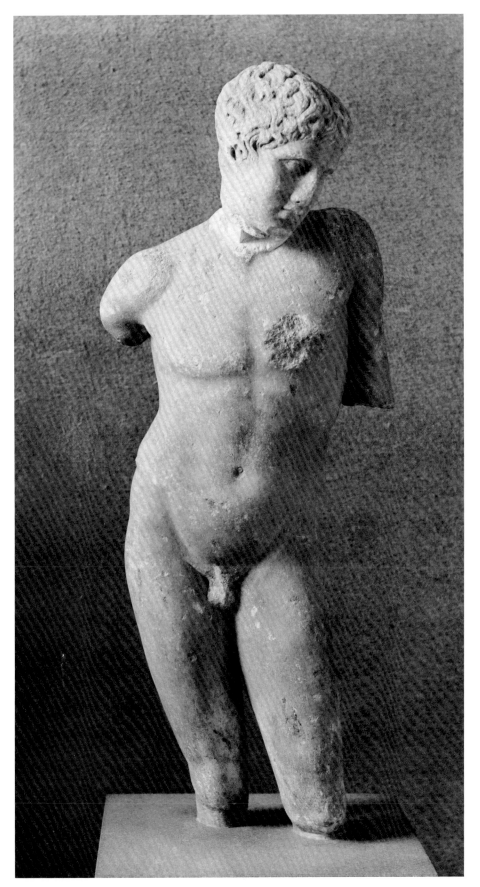

32
ATHLETE
Fogg Art Museum, Harvard University,
Cambridge, Massachusetts
Gift of E. W. Forbes (1902.10)
From Megara in Attica, via Scotland; formerly
in the S. Pozzi collection, Paris
Marble, H: 0.535 m.
Roman copy of a votive or funerary statue
(the so-called "Narcissus") by a follower of
Polykleitos of ca. 400 B.C.

Burlington Exhibition 14, no. 13, pl. 13; Chase,
American Collections 63 ff., fig. 68; Fogg, Catalogue
of Exhibition of Ancient Sculpture (1950) no. 33;
A. Furtwängler, Antiken in den Museen von Amerika
(1905) 280; Picard, Manuel 2.2 (1939) 705; Vermeule, Polykleitos fig. 15.

33

RELIEF OF DAEDALUS AND ICARUS
The Metropolitan Museum of Art,
New York, New York
Bequest of Walter C. Baker (1972.118.115)
Probably from Rome where it was sketched in
1826 by Horatio Greenough; formerly in the
Botkin collection
Marble, H: 0.675 m.; W: 0.533 m.
The subject is known in two replicas, both in
the Villa Albani, Rome. Classicizing work
after a Greek original of the early fourth cen-
tury B.C.

J. Pijoan, *Summa Artis* 5 (1934) 191, fig. 255;
Baker Collection no. 63, ill.; F. Eckstein, *Gnomon* 31
(1959) 644; *New York Private Collections* no. 119, pl. 38.

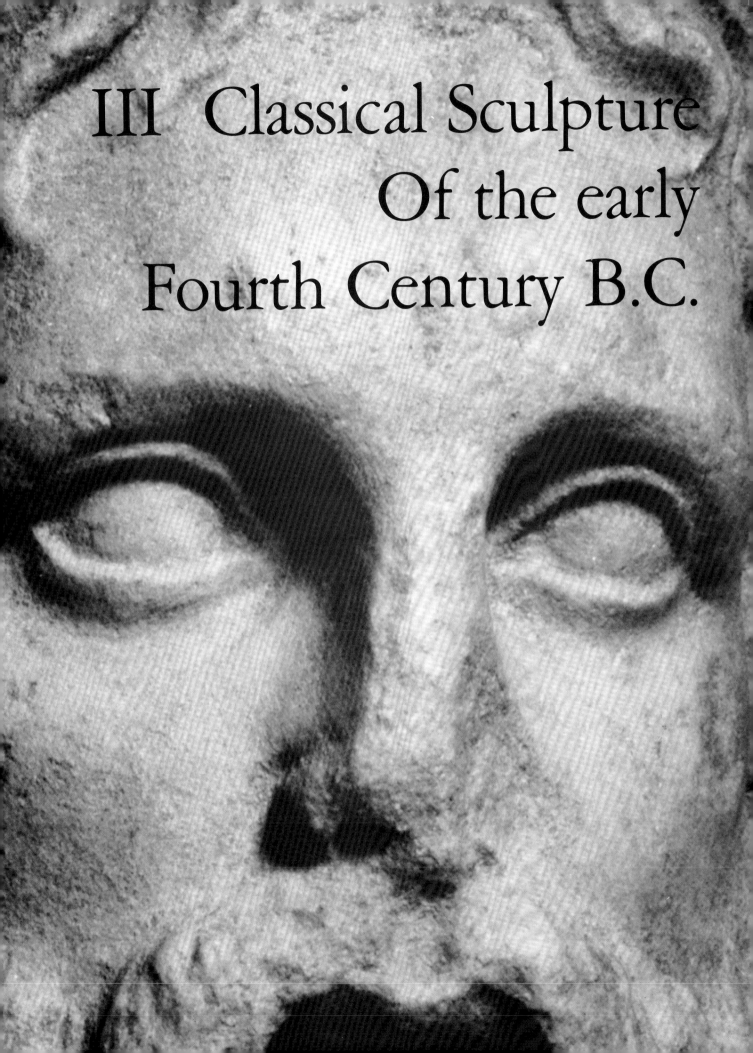

III Classical Sculpture
Of the early
Fourth Century B.C.

34

HEAD OF A GODDESS, PERHAPS DEMETER

Los Angeles County Museum of Art,
Los Angeles, California

Gift of the Hearst Foundation (46.36.1)

Marble, H: 0.36 m.

The type traces back through Agorakritos or
Alkamenes (compare Berlin: C. Blümel,
Kopien 4, no. K173) to the Lemnia of Pheidias, especially the replica in the Ashmolean
Museum, Oxford (P. Gardner, *JHS 43* [1923]
50–52, pl. 1). A Roman copy of the Trajanic
period after an original of the early fourth
century B.C.

 LACMA Illustrated Handbook (1965) 29.

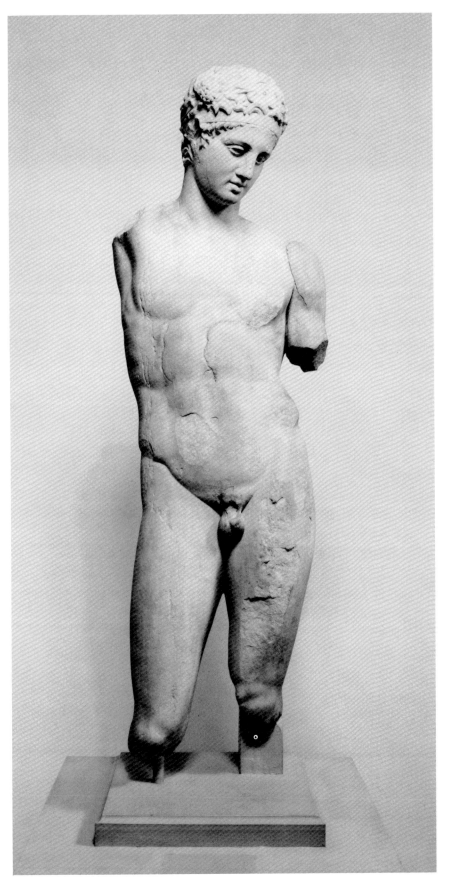

35

YOUNG SATYR POURING WINE

The Walters Art Gallery, Baltimore, Maryland
(23.22)

Found at Porto d'Anzio; formerly in the
Mengarini collection

Marble, H: 1.065 m.

Roman copy after an original identified as by
Praxiteles, about 360 B.C.

W. Klein, *Praxiteles* (1898) 192, no. 12; F. Weege,
89 *Ber. Winckelmannsprogramm* (1929) *passim*;
G. E. Rizzo, *Prassitele* (1932) 17–20, pls. 24–25;
Handbook (1936) 30, ill.; Picard, *Manuel* 3 (1948)
416 ff., figs. 170 ff.; *Archaeology* 10 (1957) 21, ill.;
P. Gercke, *Satyrn des Praxiteles* (1968) 188, no. At. 1.

36

EROS WITH BOW AND ARROW
Museum of Fine Arts, Boston, Massachusetts
Classical Department Exchange Fund
(1979.477)
Said to have been found in the Levant
Greek island marble, H: 0.63 m.
A copy, made ca. A.D. 150 to 175, of a small
statue perhaps created about 50 B.C. after an
original of about 360 B.C., a work of Praxiteles
just before the height of his career. The type is
known as the "Eros from Centocelle" after a
copy of the Praxitelean original from near
Rome and now in the Vatican.

Kunstwerke der Antike, Schweizerische Kunst und
Antiquitatenmesse 1979 (Basel, 1979) 3, fig. 5.

37
HEAD AND TORSO
OF THE YOUTHFUL DIONYSOS
Royal Ontario Museum, Toronto,
Ontario, Canada
(925.23.24)
Formerly in the Donaldson collection
Marble, H: 0.67 m.
Roman copy of a creation after the pose of the
Lycian Apollo.

Sotheby's (July 6–10, 1925).

38

TORSO OF DIONYSOS

Isabella Stewart Gardner Museum,

Boston, Massachusetts

(S8e9)

Probably from Italy

Coarse-grained marble, H: 0.92 m.

Roman copy of a Praxitelean type of ca.

340 B.C.

  Sculpture in the Isabella Stewart Gardner Museum
(1977) 22, no. 27; *The Connoisseur* (May 1978) 45.

39

TORSO OF A FLUTE-PLAYING SATYR

*Kelsey Museum of Archaeology, The University of
Michigan, Ann Arbor, Michigan*

(76.1.1)

Marble, H: 0.787 m.

Roman copy after a Greek original of the late
fourth century B.C.

J. G. Pedley, *Greek Sculpture in Transition*, Checklist (1981) no. 16, ill.; *Bulletin, Museums of Art and
Archaeology, The University of Michigan*, forthcoming.

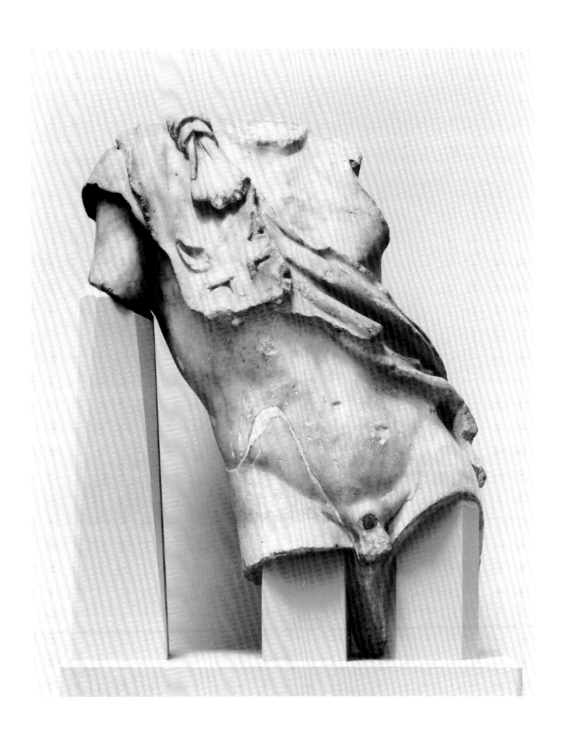

40

TORSO OF A RESTING SATYR

The Bowdoin College Museum of Fine Arts,
Brunswick, Maine

E. P. Warren collection (1923.110)

Marble, H: 0.834 m.

Graeco-Roman work of the first or second
century A.D. after the famous Resting Satyr
of Praxiteles.

K. Herbert, *Ancient Art in Bowdoin College* (1964)
38, no. 86, pl. 12.

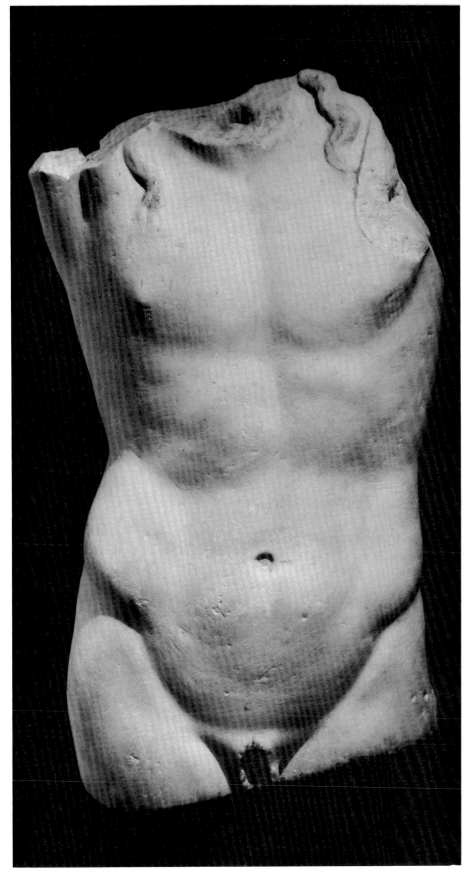

41

TORSO OF DIONYSOS

Stanford University Museum of Art,
Stanford, California

Gift of Benjamin F. Vaughn III in memory of
Dr. Hazel D. Hansen (63.60)

Marble, H: 0.95 m.

Or, less likely, Apollo. Roman copy in the
Praxitelean tradition of ca. 365 B.C.

Unpublished.

42

BEARDED HEAD OF A GOD (?)

University of Illinois, Krannert Art Museum,
Champaign, Illinois

Mrs. Herman C. Krannert Fund (70-11-1)

From Attica

Pentelic marble, H: 0.235 m.

Ca. 330 B.C.

  Kunstwerke der Antike, Auktion 26, Münzen
und Medaillen A. G. (Basel, 5 October 1963) 93,
no. 178, pl. 63; Sotheby's (London, 1 July 1969) 62,
no. 117, ill.

IV Cypriote Sculpture

43
BEARDED VOTARY
The Art Institute of Chicago, Chicago, Illinois
Waller Fund (1926.437)
From the "temple" at Golgoi on Cyprus
Limestone, H: 0.30 m.
In the Ionian tradition, ca. 530 B.C. Perhaps
by the same hand as a similar votary in the
M. H. de Young Museum, San Francisco,
and definitely by the same sculptor as a votary
in the Royal Ontario Museum, Toronto,
also from Golgoi (T. A. Heinrich, *Treasures
of the ROM* [1961] 94).

AIC Bulletin 20 (September 1926) 85, 99; C. C.
Vermeule, *AJA* 78 (1974) 289, pls. 61, 62.

44 (See colorplate 7.) →
COLOSSAL HEAD OF A GODDESS
Worcester Art Museum, Worcester, Massachusetts
(1941.49)
From Cyprus
Limestone, H: 0.51 m.
A Dionysiac procession of satyrs and maenads
on the crown; ca. 510 B.C.

WAM Bulletin 7 (December 1941) no. 3, ill.;
Art through Fifty Centuries, WAM (1948) 13, fig. 10;
E. Neumann, *The Great Mother* (1955) 145, 299;
WAM Handbook (1973) 13, ill.

45
WREATHED MALE HEAD
Kimbell Art Museum, Fort Worth, Texas
(AP 72.5)
From Cyprus
Limestone, H: 0.16 m.
Compare the sculptures found at Vouni of the
high Ionian style (G. Hill, *A History of Cyprus*
[1940] 218, frontis.). Ca. 500 B.C.

   KAM Catalogue (1972) 3-4; *KAM Handbook of
the Collection* (1981) 7.

46 →
WREATHED HEAD
OF A BEARDED VOTARY
*Dartmouth College Museum and Galleries,
Hanover, New Hampshire*
Bequest of the widow of Hiram Hitchcock,
"intimate friend and advisor of L. P. di
Cesnola" (12-1-324)
From Cyprus
Limestone, H: 0.37 m.
Extensive traces of color survive (red on
eyes, green on wreath, blue on beard); ca.
480 B.C. (cf. Toledo 28.165 and Metropolitan
74.51.2461).

   D. F. Jordan, *Report for the Years 1947–1948* 16,
no. 1.

47
FUNERARY RELIEF OF A COUPLE
The Art Institute of Chicago, Chicago, Illinois
Gift of Mr. Armen Avedisian in memory of
Karokin Der Avedisian (1971.457)
From the necropolis at Golgoi in Cyprus
Limestone, H: 0.572 m.
Ca. 350 B.C.

L. P. di Cesnola, *A Descriptive Atlas of the Cesnola
Collection of Cypriote Antiquities in the Metropolitan
Museum of Art, New York* 1 (1885) no. 633, pl. 94;
*Cypriote and Classical Antiquities, Duplicates of the
Cesnola and other Collections*, The Anderson Galleries,
Sale No. 2253 (New York, 30–31 March 1928)
71–72, no. 287, ill.

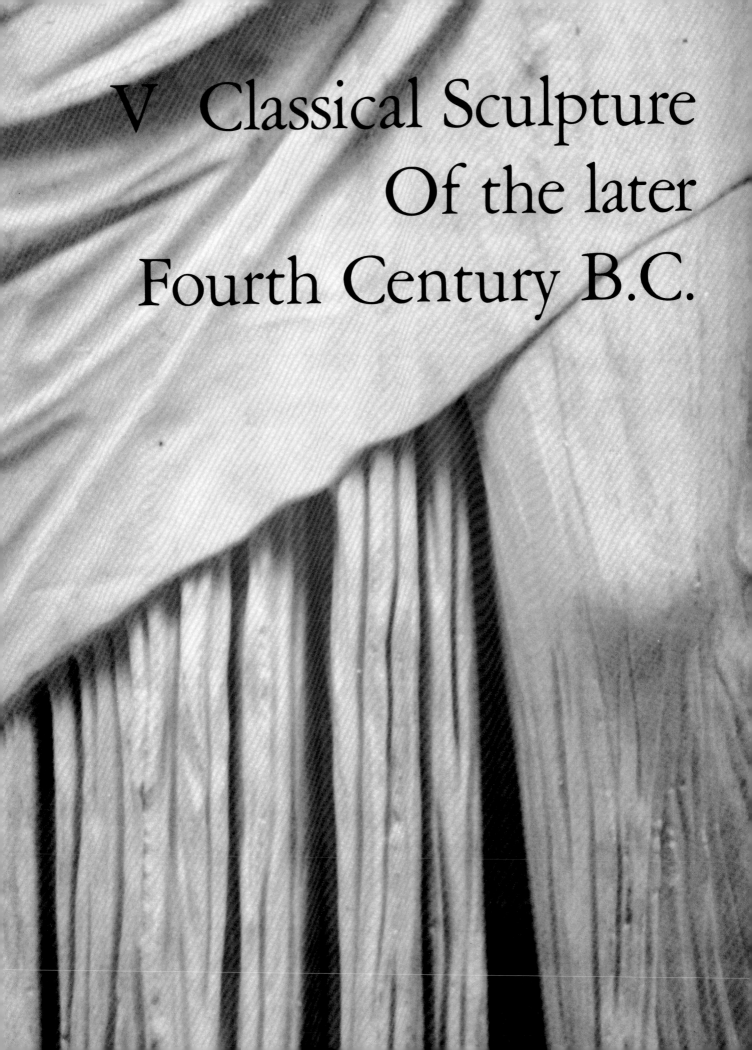

V Classical Sculpture
Of the later
Fourth Century B.C.

48

HYGIEIA

Los Angeles County Museum of Art,
Los Angeles, California

William Randolph Hearst collection
(50.33.23)

Found at Ostia in 1797; formerly in the Hope
collection, Deepdene

Italian marble, H: 1.88 m.

Roman copy of a work of ca. 360 B.C., sometimes attributed to Skopas.

Michaelis, *Marbles in Great Britain* 282–283,
no. 7; A. Lawrence, *Greek and Roman Sculpture*
(1972) pl. 46 c–d; Christie's (23–24 July 1917)
lot 252; B. Ashmole, *PBSR* 10 (1927) 1–11; P. E.
Arias, *Skopas* (1952) 122–124, M 12, no. 2; C. C.
Vermeule, *AJA* 59 (1955) 139; idem, *ibid.* 60
(1956); A. Stewart, *Skopas of Paros* (1977) 83, 111.

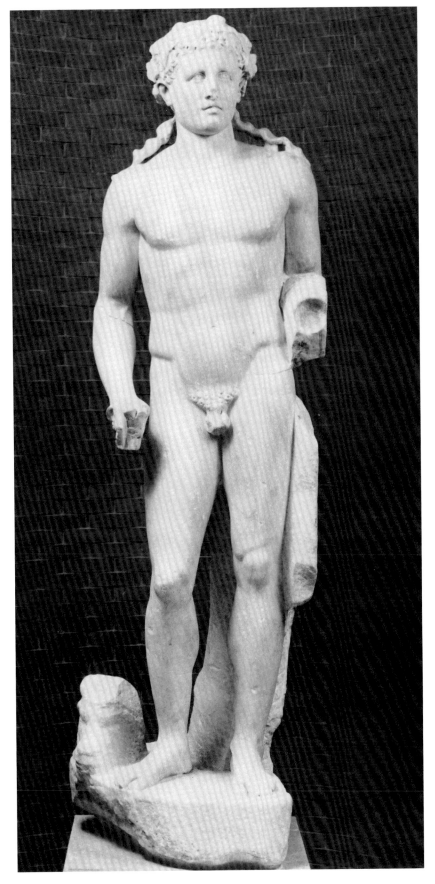

49

STATUE OF HERAKLES

Los Angeles County Museum of Art,
Los Angeles, California

William Randolph Hearst collection
(50.33.22)

From Italy; formerly in the Arundel and Hope
collections

Marble, H: 1.943 m.

Roman copy of the second century A.D. after
the Skopaic type of ca. 350 B.C., possibly the
statue set up in the gymnasium at Sikyon.

S. Reinach, *RA* 6 (1917) 460 f.; idem, *Rép. stat.* 5
(1924) 81, no. 6; C. C. Vermeule, *AJA* 59 (1955)
134 (not recorded by Michaelis); S. Lattimore, Getty
MJ 2 (1975) 17–21, figs. 1–5; A. Stewart, *Skopas of
Paros* (1977) 90 f., 139 f., pl. 31; S. Howard, *The
Lansdowne Herakles* (1978) 29–30, n. 51, figs. 86–88
(for complete bibl.).

50

HEAD OF ACHILLES

The J. Paul Getty Museum, Malibu, California
(79.AA.7)

From the west pediment of the temple of
Athena Alea in Tegea, completed ca. 350–
340 B.C.; formerly in the de Bry collection
Doliana marble, H: 0.185 m.

Probably the head of the central figure of the
west pediment: Achilles. Upper lip and some
details recut in antiquity to repair damage; a
hole in the middle of the neck was made for
remounting the head on the body. (J. Frel)

F. Chamoux, *BAntFr* (1978) in press; idem,
MonPiot, in prep.; *JPGM Checklist of Antiquities 1*
(1979) 6, no. 19; *JPGM Guidebook* (1980) 25, ill.
J. Frel, Getty *MJ* 8 (1980) 90–93; A. Stewart, *The
Head of Achilles* (forthcoming 1982).

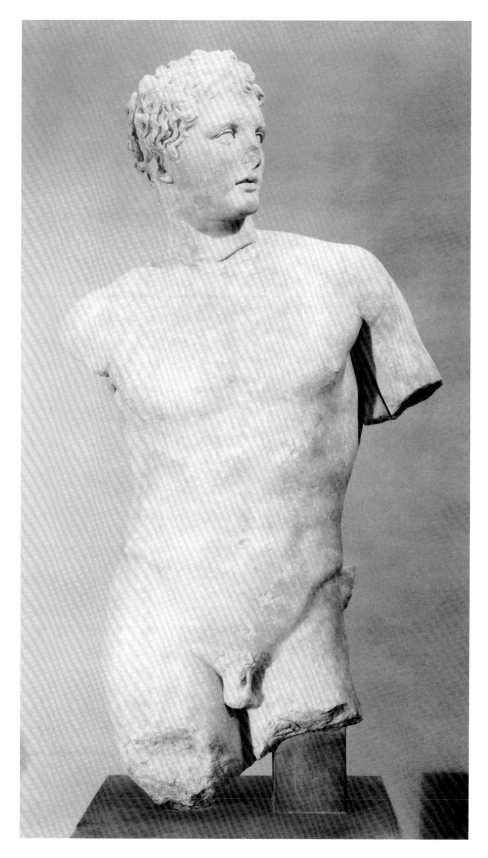

51

MELEAGER

Fogg Art Museum, Harvard University,
Cambridge, Massachusetts
Bequest of Mrs. K. G. T. Webster (1926.48.7)
From a Roman villa at Santa Marinella near
Civitavecchia
Marble, H: 1.17 m.
Roman copy after Skopas's original of ca.
340 B.C.

G. H. Chase, *American Collections* 86 ff., figs. 97
and 101; Bieber, *Sculpture* 24 f., figs. 54, 56–57;
G. M. A. Hanfmann and J. G. Pedley, *AntPl* 3
(1964) 61 ff., pls. 58–72; J. Charbonneaux et al.,
Classical Greek Art (1972) fig. 403; A. F. Stewart,
Skopas of Paros (1977) 104–107, 110, 122, 144;
G. M. A. Hanfmann and D. Mitten, *Apollo* 107
(1978) 362–363, fig. 1. pl. 44a (with full bibl.).

52 ←

HEAD OF MELEAGER

Kimbell Art Museum, Fort Worth, Texas
(AP 67.10)

Marble, H: 0.298 m.

Copy made ca. A.D. 50 of the Skopaic original
of ca. 350 B.C.

Münzen und Medaillen A. G., *Auktion 34* (Basel,
6 May 1967) 105, no. 201, pl. 69; *KAM Catalogue*
(1972) 10–11; *KAM Handbook of the Collection* (1981)
11.

53

HEAD OF MELEAGER

Fogg Art Museum, Harvard University,
Cambridge, Massachusetts

Van Rensselaer Fund (1913.28)

Marble, H: 0.33 m.

Reversed Roman copy made ca. A.D. 150 of
the Skopaic original.

G. H. Chase, *ArtBull* 3 (1917) 113, fig. 3; C. C.
Vermeule, MFA *Bulletin. Boston* 65 (1967) 175,
177, fig. 2; H. Hoffmann, *Collecting Greek Antiquities*
(1971) 32, fig. 28; *Greek Sculpture in Transition*,
Checklist, Kelsey Museum no. 3.

54
STATUE OF HERAKLES

The J. Paul Getty Museum, Malibu, California
(70.AA.109)
Excavated at Hadrian's Villa near Tivoli in
1790; formerly in the Lansdowne collection,
London
Pentelic marble, H: 1.935 m.
Eighteenth-century restorations removed
in 1978. Roman copy of an original in the
Skopaic tradition of about 340 B.C.

Michaelis, *Marbles in Great Britain* 451, no. 61;
C. C. Vermeule, N. Neuerburg, *Catalogue of the Ancient Art* (1973) 6–8, no. 9; S. Lattimore, Getty *MJ* 2
(1975) 17ff.; A. F. Stewart, *Skopas of Paros* (1977)
98–99, 142, pl. 42; S. Howard, *The Lansdowne
Herakles*, 2d ed. (1978) (with previous bibl.).

55

TORSO OF APOLLO KITHAROEDOS
Santa Barbara Museum of Art,
Santa Barbara, California
Gift of Wright S. Ludington (71.51.1)
Fine-grained marble, H: 1.53 m.
Augustan or Julio-Claudian copy after a
Greek type of the fourth century B.C.

M. A. Del Chiaro, *AJA* 78 (1974) 68–69, pls.
18–19, figs. 1–5.

56

PERSEPHONE

Indianapolis Museum of Art,
Indianapolis, Indiana

Gift of J. Anton Scherrer in memory of
Josephine Turner Scherrer and Adolph
Turner Scherrer (61.34)

Formerly collection von Matsch, Vienna

Marble, H: 0.475 m.

An original of about 340–330 B.C.

Schefold, *Meisterwerke* 250, 260, no. 336; C. C.
Vermeule, *Bulletin, Art Association of Indianapolis*
(1961) 39–46; idem, *Greek Art* 13–14, 117, fig. 14A.

57

PERSEPHONE (?)

Isabella Stewart Gardner Museum,
Boston, Massachusetts

(S5c1)

Purchased in Rome

Greek-island marble, H: 1.515 m.

First-century-B.C.-or-A.D. version of a Praxitelean type of 340 B.C.

Reinach, *Rép. stat.* 4 (1913) 412, no. 3; *Sculpture in*
the Isabella Stewart Gardner Museum (1977) 10–11,
no. 12; Vermeule, *Greek Art* 13, 117, fig. 14.

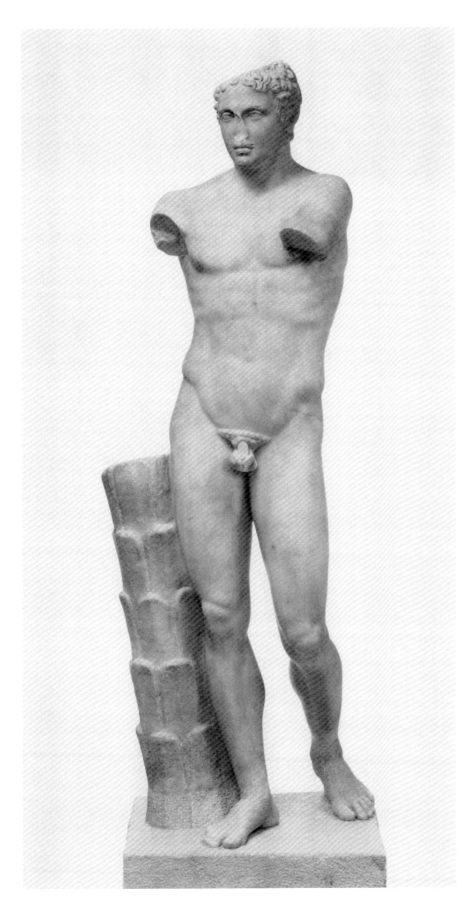

58
ATHLETE
Los Angeles County Museum of Art,
Los Angeles, California
William Randolph Hearst collection
(49.23.12)
From Italy, formerly in the Lansdowne
collection
Marble, H: 1.91 m.
Second-century-A.D. Roman copy after an
early creation by Lysippos. Recent conser-
vation has removed the modern restorations
and reset the head.

Clarac, *Musée de Sculpture* pl. 856; Michaelis,
Marbles in Great Britain 446, no. 36; Christie's, 5
March 1930, lot 103, ill. p. 66; J. Dörig, *AntPl* 4
(1965) 39, fig. 5; J. Podany, Getty *MJ* 9 (1981)
forthcoming.

59 (See colorplate 8.)
ATHLETE CROWNING HIMSELF
The J. Paul Getty Museum, Malibu, California
(77.AB.30)
From the Adriatic Sea
Bronze, H: 1.515 m.
Original fourth-century-B.C. sculpture by
Lysippos, ca. 320 B.C.

Time (December 12, 1977) 22, ill.; H. Herzer,
Artemis Annual Report (1977–78) 10–13; J. Frel,
The Getty Bronze (1978); *JPGM Checklist of Antiquities* 1 (1979) 12, no. 50; Vermeule, *Greek Art*
23–24, 96, 120, fig. 28.

60 (See colorplate 9.)

HEAD OF A LADY WEARING A FILLET
AND HIMATION

The Ackland Art Museum, The University of
North Carolina, Chapel Hill, North Carolina
Ackland Fund (67.24.1)
From Asia Minor
Bronze, H: 0.289 m.
Type of ca. 325 B.C.

S. A. Immerwahr, *Hesperia* 38 (1969) 150–156,
pls. 42–44; Ackland, *Ancient Portraits* no. 2; *Cata-*
logue (1971) no. 1; C. Mattusch, *Ackland Note*
(1975) no. 10.

61
VEILED FEMALE HEAD
William Rockhill Nelson Gallery of Art–Atkins
Museum of Fine Arts, Kansas City, Missouri
Nelson Fund (33-3/4)
Marble, H: 0.345 m.
Third quarter of the fourth century B.C.,
probably Tarantine.

Handbook 1 (1973) 36, ill.

62

VOTIVE RELIEF TO APOLLO (?)
AND ARTEMIS
Museum of Fine Arts, Boston, Massachusetts
Gift of Mr. and Mrs. Cornelius C. Vermeule III
(1977.171)
From Attica
Pentelic marble, H: 0.545 m.; W: 0.71 m.
Ca. 325 B.C.

    The Museum Year: 1976–1977, 25, fig., 40;
Vermeule, *Greek Art* 34–35, 123, fig. 48.

VI Classical
Funerary Sculpture

63

GRAVE STELE OF A WARRIOR

Worcester Art Museum, Worcester, Massachusetts
(1936.21)
Found near Megara in Attica; formerly in the
collection of Colonel C. T. Gordon, Cairness
House, Aberdeenshire
Pentelic marble, H (with base): 2.197 m.;
W: 0.95 m.
Ca. 420–410 B.C.

O. Stackelberg, *Die Gräber der Hellenen* (1836) 38,
pl. 3,2; H. Diepolder, *MJb* 5 (1928) 15–19; J. D.
Beazley, *JHS* 49 (1929) 1–5; H. Diepolder, *Die
attischen Grabreliefs* (1931) 21, 22, ill.; Sotheby's
(London, 28 July 1936) 12, lot 70; *WAM Bulletin* 2
(October 1936) 1–2, ill.; F. H. Taylor, *AJA* 41
(1937) 6, 7, no. 1, ill.; H. Möbius, *JdI* 64 (1949) 52,
fig. 4; G. M. A. Hanfmann, *Classical Sculpture*
(1967) 314, fig. 106; *WAM Handbook* (1973) 27,
ill.; R. Vasić, *AK* 19 (1976) 27, pl. 6,3; Vermeule,
Greek Art 27–28, 121, fig. 32.

64

GRAVE STELE OF A LADY
WITH A SERVANT
The J. Paul Getty Museum, Malibu, California
(73.AA.115)
Pentelic marble, H: 0.715 m.
The upper right corner with the bust of the
servant is restored (thanks to the identifi-
cation of the piece in the Kanellopoulos
Museum, Athens). From the last ten years
of the fifth century B.C.

JPGM Guidebook (1976) 47, ill.; M. A. Zagdoun,
BCH (1978) 291, fig. 5; *JPGM Checklist of Antiquities*
1 (1979) 16, no. 63.

65

FUNERARY LEKYTHOS WITH
RELIEF SCENE OF LEAVETAKING
*The Ackland Art Museum, The University
of North Carolina, Chapel Hill, North Carolina*
Ackland Fund (76.24.1)
Marble, H: 0.40 m.; W: 0.254 m.
Ca. 390 B.C.

   Unpublished.

66
ATTIC FUNERARY LION
Rhode Island School of Design, Museum of Art,
Providence, Rhode Island
Gift of Mrs. Gustav Radeke (15.003)
From Spata, near Athens
Marble, H: 0.467 m.
This animal belongs to a group that includes a
complete lion in the Museum of Fine Arts,
Boston, one in a private collection in New
York, one in North Carolina, and several
others. Ca. 390 B.C.

B. S. Ridgway, *Catalogue of the Classical Collection,*
Classical Sculpture (1972) 32–33, 147–148, no. 10.

67

FRAGMENT OF THE STELE
OF XENOCRATES

Honolulu Academy of Arts, Honolulu, Hawaii
Gift of Mrs. Charles M. Cooke (3605)
From Attica; formerly in the Dresnay collection, Paris
Pink (?) marble, H: 0.355 m.; W: 0.44 m.
Early fourth century B.C.

P. Perdrizet, *Antiquités grecques de la collection du Vicomte du Dresnay* (1918), unpaged.

68
HEAD OF A MAN FROM
A LARGE ATTIC GRAVE STELE
The Minneapolis Institute of Arts,
Minneapolis, Minnesota
William Hood Dunwoody Fund (70.9)
From Attica
Pentelic marble, H: 0.29 m.; W: 0.185 m.
Compare H. Diepolder, *Die attischen Grab-*
reliefs (1931) pls. 14, 24.1, 30, and 42.2
Ca. 375 B.C.

  ArtQ 33 (1970) 319, cover; J. Frel, B. Kingsley,
GRB Studies 11 (1970) 211, no. 49, pls. 12, 17
("Sculptor of Pheidylla"); *MIA Bulletin* (1970) 59.

69 ← (See colorplate 10.)
FRAGMENT OF THE GRAVE STELE
OF KALLISTRATE
The St. Louis Art Museum, St. Louis, Missouri
(4:1933)
From Attica
Pentelic marble, H: 0.84 m.
Another inscription is above the epistyle on
the lower part of the pediment. Ca. 370 B.C.

SLAM *Bulletin* 18.2 (April 1933); G. E. Mylonas,
Art Bull 18 (1936) 103–105; *SLAM Handbook*
(1975) 12, ill.; Furtwängler, Oikonomides, *Master-pieces* 421, fig. LXXVIII; I. Jucker, *Festschrift Karl Schefold*
(1967) 139, Abb. 48.1.

70
HEAD OF A MAN
FROM A LARGE STELE
*Amherst College Museum of Art, Mead Art
Gallery, Amherst, Massachusetts*
(S 1940.1)
Said to have come from Attica
Pentelic marble, H: 0.38 m.
Ca. 360 B.C.

C. H. Morgan, *Archaeology* 20 (1967) 4, ill.;
Catalogue of the Amherst Sesquicentennial Exhibition,
Hirschl and Adler Galleries, New York (1972) 71,
no. 37, ill. p. 60; F. Trapp, ed., *The Classical Collection
at Amherst College* (1979) 3, no. G; Vermeule, *Greek
Art* 28–29, 121, fig. 33.

71

STELE OF PHILOMELOS

The Minneapolis Institute of Arts,
Minneapolis, Minnesota

Ethel Morrison Van Derlip Fund (31.4)

Pentelic marble, H: 0.86 m.; W: 0.34 m.

Attic work of ca. 360 B.C.

    MIA Bulletin (March 7, 1931); *MIA Guide*
(1970) 52-53, ill.

72 →

GRAVE STELE OF PHILOKYDIS

Norton Simon Museum, Pasadena, California

From Attica; formerly in the collection of the
Cranbrook Academy of Art, Bloomfield Hills,
Michigan

Pentelic marble, H: 0.962 m.; W: 0.608 m.

The metric inscription on the architrave states
that the monument belongs to Philokydis,
daughter of Aristokles and Timagora.

Ca. 360 B.C.

    C. Clairmont, *Gravestone and Epigram* (1970)
169-70, pl. 37; *The Cranbrook Collections*, Sotheby
Parke-Bernet (New York, May 4, 1972) 126-127,
no. 326.

73
YOUNG MAN
FROM A FUNERARY MONUMENT
The Art Institute of Chicago, Chicago, Illinois
Gift of Silvain and Arma Wyler Foundation
(1960.70)
From Attica, allegedly the Kerameikos
cemetery, by way of a northwest-European
collection
Marble, H: 0.81 m.
Ca. 350 B.C.

C. C. Vermeule, *AIC Quarterly* 54 (December
1960) 6–9; Furtwängler, Oikonomides, *Masterpieces*
pl. U1.

74

ARTEMIS, OR A LADY
FROM A FUNERARY MONUMENT
Rhode Island School of Design, Museum of Art,
Providence, Rhode Island
Gift of Mrs. Gustav Radeke (13.1478)
Probably from Athens
Pentelic marble, H: 0.437 m.
Head broken off but original. Close to the
Dresden Artemis attributed to the early
career of Praxiteles, ca. 350 B.C.

B. S. Ridgway, *Catalogue of the Classical Collection,*
Classical Sculpture (1972) 43–44, 162–163, no. 15.

75
FUNERARY LEKYTHOS
OF ARISTONICE
Seattle Art Museum, Seattle, Washington
Gift of Mr. Norman Davis in memory of his
brother Mr. Ellis Davis (55.204)
From Attica
Marble, H: 1.295 m.
Base and neck are modern restorations.
Ca. 350 B.C.

Sotheby's (31 July–1 August 1939) lot 43; *ArtQ*
19 (1956) 201; B. Schmaltz, *Untersuchungen zu den
attischen Marmorlekythen* (1970) 25, 45–47, 56, 59,
95, 142; Vermeule, *Greek Art* 31–32, 36, 122, fig. 41.

76 (top)
FUNERARY LION
Cincinnati Art Museum, Cincinnati, Ohio
J. J. Emery Fund (1946.40)
From Attica
Marble, H: 0.838 m.; L: 1.95 m.
Ca. 345 B.C., probably from a funerary
monument.

C. C. Vermeule, P. von Kersburg, *AJA* 72 (1968)
100; idem, *ibid.* 76 (1972) 50, pl. 11; *Sculpture
Collection of the CAM* (1970) 42.

77
GREEK FUNERARY RELIEF
The Walters Art Gallery, Baltimore, Maryland
(23.185)
Marble, H: 0.48 m.; W: 1.80 m.
Mid-fourth century B.C.

IG II–III², 11646; A. Brueckner, *AA* (1926)
274–276, fig. 4; B. Schmaltz, *AM* 93 (1978) 90–91,
pls. 30–31, 1.

78
GRAVE STELE OF A WOMAN
The Museum of Fine Arts, Houston, Texas
Annette Finnigan collection (37–25)
Pentelic marble, H: 0.432 m; W: 0.508 m.
The standing woman holding an infant
may indicate that the seated deceased died
in childbirth. Mid-fourth century B.C.

H. Hoffmann, *Ten Centuries That Shaped the West:
Greek and Roman Art in Texas Collections* (1970)
22–23, no. 6, ill.; *A Guide to the Collection* (1981) no. 15.

79
HEROIC BANQUET RELIEF
The Walters Art Gallery, Baltimore, Maryland
(23.222)
Presumably from Attica; long in England
Marble, H: 0.305 m.; W: 0.56 m.
Ca. 340 B.C.

ArtQ 31 (1968) 205, 209, ill.; D. K. Hill, *WAG Bulletin* 20.4 (1968) 1; *Octagon* (Spink and Son, London, Winter, 1966), unpaged; *Illustrated London News* (19 November 1966) 29.

80

FRAGMENT OF A GRAVE STELE
WITH A SEATED WOMAN
Royal Ontario Museum,
Toronto, Ontario, Canada
(948.229.2)
Marble, H: 0.65 m.
Attic work of ca. 340 B.C.

Unpublished.

81

FUNERARY STELE
Amherst College Museum of Art, Mead Art
Gallery, Amherst, Massachusetts
Adela Wood Smith Trust in memory of
Harry de Forest Smith (1978.67)
From Attica
Fairly coarse Pentelic marble, H: 1.26 m.;
W: 0.395 m.
A scene of family farewell on the body of a
loutrophoros, ca. 340 to 335 B.C.

F. Trapp, ed., *The Classical Collection at Amherst*
College (1979) 4, no. H.

82 (See colorplate 11.)
FUNERARY STATUE
OF A SERVANT GIRL
Kimbell Art Museum, Fort Worth, Texas
(AP 72.3)
Marble, H: 1.169 m.
Ca. 340–330 B.C.

KAM Catalogue (1972) 4–6; *KAM Handbook of the Collection* (1981) 9.

83 ←

GRAVE STELE OF A WARRIOR
The Cleveland Museum of Art, Cleveland, Ohio
Bequest of Leonard C. Hanna, Jr. (70.82)
Marble, H: 1.10 m.; W: 0.675 m.
Boeotian work showing Attic influence.
Compare E. Pfuhl, *Malerei und Zeichnung
der Griechen* 3 (1923) figs. 633, 634.
Ca. 335–325 B.C.

Unpublished.

84

ATTIC FUNERARY LION
*The Minneapolis Institute of Arts,
Minneapolis, Minnesota*
Ethel Morrison Van Derlip Fund (25.25)
Said to have come from Athens, just north of
the Acropolis, in 1913
Pentelic marble, H: 0.64 m.; L: 1.24 m.
Displayed without the restored legs, tail, and
plinth. Ca. 330 B.C.

S. Reinach, *Rép. stat.* 6 (1930) 149, no. 1;
F. Willemsen, *Die Löwenkopf-Wasserspeier am Dach
des Zeustempels* (1959) 53, 131, pl. 63; *Guide* (1970)
52–53, no. 12; C. C. Vermeule, P. von Kersburg,
AJA 72 (1968) 100; idem, *ibid.* 76 (1972) 50.

85
YOUNG MAN FROM A GRAVE STELE
Dallas Museum of Fine Arts, Dallas, Texas
Gift of Mr. and Mrs. Cecil H. Green (1966.26)
Presumably from Attica
Pentelic marble, H: 1.613 m.
From a large Attic funerary monument
Ca. 330 B.C.

H. Hoffmann, *Ten Centuries That Shaped the West:
Greek and Roman Art in Texas Collections* (1970)
12–17, no. 4; C. C. Vermeule and J. Ternbach,
Archaeology 25 (1972) 216–221.

86
ATTIC GRAVE STELE
The Art Institute of Chicago, Chicago, Illinois
Alexander White collection (28.162)
Evidently from Attica, vicinity of Athens
Marble, H: 1.35 m.; W: 1.05 m.
Ca. 330–325 B.C.

D. C. Rich, *AIC Bulletin* 22 (1928) 114–116, ill.;
AIC Brief Illustrated Guide (1935) 8; M. Bieber, *Art in America* 30 (1942) 104–109, ill.

87

FRAGMENT OF A GRAVE STELE
WITH A SEATED WOMAN
Museum of Fine Arts, Boston, Massachusetts
Classical Department Exchange Fund
(1979.510)
Formerly in the E. Brummer collection,
Pentelic marble, H: 0.75 m.; W: 0.56 m.
Probably 330–320 B.C.

The Ernest Brummer Collection 2 (1979) 206–207,
no. 615.

88
GRAVE STELE OF IOSTRATE
Royal Ontario Museum,
Toronto, Ontario, Canada
(956.108)
Pentelic marble, H: 1.35 m.
Ca. 330–320 B.C.

Art Treasures from the ROM (1961) 98–99, ill;
J. W. Graham, *Bulletin ROM* 26 (December 1957)
2–4, no. 26, pl. 1.

89
HEAD OF A MOURNING WOMAN
Cincinnati Art Museum, Cincinnati, Ohio
(1945.66)
From Chalkis on Euboea
Marble, H: 0.34 m.
From a funerary or votive monument. Com-
pare W. Fuchs, *Die Skulptur der Griechen*
(1969) 269–271, fig. 297. In the style of
Praxiteles, ca. 325 B.C.

O. J. Brendel, *ArtQ* 6 (1943) 10, 13; *Sculpture
Collection of the CAM* (1970) 42; Vermeule, *Greek
Art* 32–33, 122, fig. 45.

90
HEAD OF A VEILED WOMAN
The St. Louis Art Museum, St. Louis, Missouri
(57.1941)
Perhaps from the island of Rhodes or its
vicinity
Marble, H: 0.395 m.
From a statue of a goddess, ca. 325 B.C.

ArtQ (Winter 1943) 3–16; O. Brendel, *CAM
Bulletin* 27 (1942) 22–26; *Art News* (Dec. 15–31,
1941) 8; *AJA* 47 (1943) 338–339; *SLAM Handbook*
(1975) 11, ill.

91

HEAD OF A SERVANT GIRL
FROM A GRAVE STELE
Museum of Art and Archaeology, University of
Missouri, Columbia, Missouri
Gift of Mr. H. W. Prentis, Jr. (59.17)
Said to be from an old collection in Athens
Marble, H: 0.17 m.
Ca. 320 B.C.

   Missouri Alumnus 48 (December 1959) 2–3, ill.

92

STELE OF POLYSTRATE OF HALAI
William Rockhill Nelson Gallery of Art–Atkins
Museum of Fine Arts, Kansas City, Missouri
Nelson Fund (31–65)
From Attica
Marble, H: 1.37 m.; W: 0.76 m.
Ca. 320 B.C.

  Handbook (1973) 36; Vermeule, *Greek Art* 31,
122, fig. 40.

93
HEAD OF A GIRL
Royal Ontario Museum,
Toronto, Ontario, Canada
(959.17.1)
Formerly in the Ludwig Curtius collection;
acquired in Athens in 1906
Fine-grained Parian marble, H: 0.206 m.
Compare the Brunn head in the Munich
Glyptothek, no. Gl.210, and related monu-
ments of ca. 320 B.C. after a prototype attrib-
uted to the school of Praxiteles.

N. Leipen, *AK* 17 (1974) 103–106, pl. 22.

94
FRAGMENT OF A GRAVE STELE:
FIGURE OF AN OLD MAN
Worcester Art Museum, Worcester, Massachusetts
(1932.2)
From Attica, said to come from the
Kerameikos
Marble, H: 1.874 m.; W: 0.63 m.
Ca. 320 B.C.

F. H. Taylor, *WAM Bulletin* 23 (April 1932)
17–27, ill.; Faison, *New England* 186; D. von Bothmer, *AJA* 57 (1953) 296; *Handbook to the WAM*
(1973) 28, ill.; Vermeule, *Greek Art* 32, 122, fig. 43.

95

HEAD OF A WOMAN
FROM A FUNERARY MONUMENT
The Metropolitan Museum of Art,
New York, New York
Bequest of Walter C. Baker (1972.118.112)
Marble, H: 0.375 m.
The bust was worked separately for insertion
in a statue, ca. 320–315 B.C.

G. M. A. Richter, *BABesch* 24–26 (1949–51)
42–45, fig. 1; *Baker Collection* no. 60; *American
Collections* no. 161, pl. 45; F. Eckstein, *Gnomon* 31
(1959) 643–644; *New York Private Collections* 28,
no. 113, pls. 32, 36.

96
GRAVE STELE
WITH LOUTROPHOROS IN RELIEF
Museum of Fine Arts, Boston, Massachusetts
(1979.511)
Formerly in the E. Brummer collection
Greyish-white marble, H: 0.82 m.; W: 0.46 m.
The metallic shape and rich ornament of the
loutrophoros suggest a date in the last
quarter of the fourth century B.C.

   The Ernest Brummer Collection 2 (1979) 196–197,
no. 609.

97

UPPER PART OF A STELE

The Walters Art Gallery, Baltimore, Maryland

(23.174)

Marble, H: 0.545 m.; W: 0.496 m.

Late fourth century B.C.

　IG II–III², 11865a.

98
ATTIC FUNERARY LION
The J. Paul Getty Museum, Malibu, California
(73.AA.121)
From Marathon; formerly in the van Bran-
teghem collection
Pentelic marble, H: 1.04 m.
Probably from a funerary monument of the
late fourth century B.C.

    M. Collignon, *Les statues funéraires dans l'art grec*
(1911) 230, fig. 150; F. Willemsen, *Die Löwenkopf-
Wasserspeier am Dach des Zeustempels* (1959) 69,
pl. 66; *JPGM Guidebook* (1976) 38, ill.; *JPGM Checklist of Antiquities* 1 (1979) 16, no. 62.

99

PAIR OF ATTIC FUNERARY LIONS

The Wadsworth Atheneum, Hartford, Connecticut

J. P. Morgan collection (1917.224 and
1917.225)

From the vicinity of Athens

Marble, H: 0.736 m.; L: 1.385 m.

Ca. 317 B.C.

   Handbook (1958) 13; C. C. Vermeule, P. von
Kersburg, *AJA* 72 (1968) 101.

100

STELE OF THEAGENES

Dayton Art Institute, Dayton, Ohio

Gift of Mr. Jefferson Patterson (30.110)

From Istanbul

Marble, H: 0.675 m.; W: 0.385 m.

To be dated in the second century B.C.; the
iconography is unusual in Greek funerary art.

N. Firatli, *Les stèles funéraires de Byzance gréco-
romaine* (1964) 129, no. 220, pl. 68.

VII Hellenistic Portraits

101

HEAD OF ALEXANDER

The J. Paul Getty Museum, Malibu, California
(73.AA.27)

From the Aegean region

Pentelic marble, H: 0.28 m.

From a large commemorative or funerary
monument, ca. 320 B.C. Goes with no. 102
below.

B. Fredericksen, ed., *The J. Paul Getty Museum*
(1975) 26–27, ill.; *JPGM Checklist of Antiquities* 1
(1979) 7, no. 20; Vermeule, *Greek Art* 55, 59, 126,
fig. 71A; *JPGM Guidebook* (1980) 20, ill; *Search for
Alexander* 101, no. 6, color pl. 2.

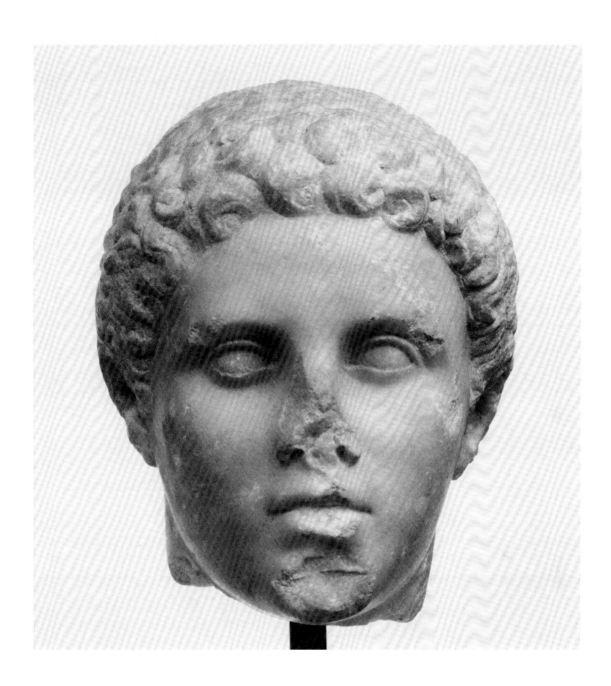

102
HEPHAISTION
The J. Paul Getty Museum, Malibu, California
(73.AA.28)
From the Aegean region
Pentelic marble, H: 0.26 m.
From a large commemorative or funerary
monument, ca. 320 B.C. Goes with no. 101
above.

B. Fredericksen, ed., *The J. Paul Getty Museum*
(1975) 26–27; *JPGM Checklist of Antiquities* 1
(1979) 7, no. 21; Vermeule, *Greek Art* 55, 59, 126,
fig. 71B; *Search for Alexander* 105, no. 13, color pl. 2.

103
HEAD AND TORSO OF
ALEXANDER THE GREAT
The Brooklyn Museum, Brooklyn, New York
Charles Edwin Wilbour Fund (54.162)
From Egypt
Egyptian alabaster, H: 0.109 m.
From a draped statuette. Early third century B.C.

Five Years of Collecting, The Brooklyn Museum
(1956) 20–21, no. 23, pls. 41–42; M. Bieber, *Alexander the Great* (1964) 86 f., figs. 80–85; Richter,
Portraits of the Greeks 3 (1965) 256, no. 6, fig. 1740;
M. Bieber, *Greece and Rome* 12 (1965) 186, pl. 8,
fig. 15; *Search for Alexander* 118–119, no. 39.

104
BUST OF MENANDER
The J. Paul Getty Museum, Malibu, California
(72.AB.108)
From Syria
Bronze, H: 0.17 m.
The inscribed pedestal was the first confirmation of the identity of the portrait.

B. Ashmole, *AJA* 77 (1973) 61, pl. 11–12; *JPGM Checklist of Antiquities* 2 (1979) 9, no. G24; Vermeule, *Greek Art* 70, J. Frel, *Greek Portraits in the JPGM* (1982) no. 34.

105

HERM BUST OF A PHILOSOPHER

Isabella Stewart Gardner Museum,
Boston, Massachusetts

(S27w54)

Found near S. Saba on the Aventine Hill,
Rome

Pentelic marble, H: 0.52 m.

Roman copy of an original of ca. 320–280 B.C.
The likeness is close to portraits of Epicurus
and Metrodorus.

   V. Poulsen, *BurlMag* 92 (1950) 196, figs. 12, 15;
Greek and Roman Portraits, Museum of Fine Arts,
Boston (1959) no. 7; Richter, *Portraits of the Greeks*
1, 96, no. 7*, figs. 388–389; *Sculpture in the Isabella
Stewart Gardner Museum* (1977) 34, no. 44.

106
METRODOROS OF LAMPSAKOS
Sir Charles Nuffler Foundation,
Cambridge, Massachusetts
(On loan to the Museum of Fine Arts, Boston)
Formerly in the collection of the earls of
Pembroke, Wilton House, England
Marble, H: 0.375 m.
Roman copy of a bronze statue of ca. 275 B.C.

Richter, *Portraits of the Greeks* 2 (1965) 201, no. 9,
figs. 1244–1245; Münzen und Medaillen A.G. *Auktion* 34 (Basel, 6 May 1967) 107, no. 204, pl. 70;
Comstock, Vermeule, *Sculpture in Stone* 79, no. 124.

107

HEAD OF A GODDESS

The University Museum, University of
Pennsylvania, Philadelphia, Pennsylvania
(30-7-1)
Formerly in the Arundel and Hope collections
Marble, H: 0.385 m.
Nose restored. Early Hellenistic.

E. H. Dohan, *Bulletin* 2 (1931) 150–151; Vermeule, *Greek Art* 69, 128, fig. 87.

108
PORTRAIT HEAD OF
PTOLEMY III EUERGETES
Duke University Classical Collection,
Durham, North Carolina
Gift of Women's College Class of 1966 and
Lambda Chi Alpha Fraternity (1966.1)
Probably from Egypt
Marble, H: 0.16 m.
The identification is suggested by comparison
with the portrait in the Ny Carlsberg
Glyptotek (3270).

   Ackland, *Ancient Portraits*, no. 7; C. R. Mack,
Classical Art from Carolina Collections (1974) no. 45;
I. Jucker, *AK* 18 (1975) 21–22, pls. 4,4; 5,4;
Kyrieleis, *Bildnisse der Ptolemäer* 33, C5, pl. 22.1, 2.

109
PORTRAIT HEAD OF BERENIKE II
Indianapolis Museum of Art,
Indianapolis, Indiana
Gift of Joseph J. Daniels in memory of
Alexander R. Holliday (52.26)
Said to have been in the collection of Baron
Andrassy, Hungary
Jet, H: 0.15 m.
Alexandrian work of about 240 B.C. The
sharply cut top and back of the head
were probably for insertion into a veiled
statue body.

   O. J. Brendel, *Bulletin of the Art Association of*
Indianapolis/John Herron Art Institute 40 (1953) 5–8.

110

PORTRAIT HEAD OF A PTOLEMAIC
QUEEN, PERHAPS ARSINOE II
The Brooklyn Museum, Brooklyn, New York
Charles Edwin Wilbour collection
(16.580.82)
From Egypt
Pentelic(?) marble, H: 0.21 m.
Third century B.C.

J. D. Cooney, *Late Egyptian and Coptic Art*,
Brooklyn Museum (1943) 16, pl. 7; V. M. Strocka,
JdI 82 (1967) 128, no. 59.

111

PORTRAIT OF A HELLENISTIC RULER

*Peabody Museum of Natural History, Yale
University, New Haven, Connecticut*

Barringer collection (4.1.1953) (on extended
loan to Yale University Art Gallery)

From Egypt

Basalt, H: 0.37 m.

Contemporary portrait, perhaps of Ptolemy III
Euergetes in Egyptian guise. Ca. 221–204 B.C.

M.I. Rostovtzeff, *Social and Economic History of the
Hellenistic World* (1947) 872, pl. 26.1; W. Needler,
Berytus 9 (1949) 129–142; B. V. Bothmer, *Egyptian
Sculpture of the Late Period, 700 B.C. to A.D. 100*,
The Brooklyn Museum (1960) 131–133, no. 103, pl.
96, figs. 257, 258; Kyrieleis, *Bildnisse der Ptolemäer*
41, C16, pl. 28.1–3; W. K. Simpson, *The Face of
Egypt: Permanence and Change*, Dallas Museum of
Fine Arts (1977) 49, no. 47 (called Augustus).

112
STATUETTE OF SELEUCUS IV
PHILOPATOR AS HERAKLES
William Rockhill Nelson Gallery of Art–Atkins
Museum of Fine Arts, Kansas City, Missouri
Nelson Fund (46-37)
Found at Benevento
Bronze, H: 0.568 m.
Roman miniature after a Hellenistic statue of
the second century B.C.

Hellenistic Art in Asia, Fogg Art Museum
(1954–55) no. 2; *Handbook* (1969) 34; Vermeule,
Greek Art 75, 129, fig. 92A.

113 (See colorplate 12.)
PORTRAIT OF A NUBIAN
The Brooklyn Museum, Brooklyn, New York
Charles Edwin Wilbour Fund (70.59)
Probably from Asia Minor
Dark grey marble, H: 0.28 m.
Second century B.C.

    B. V. Bothmer, *Apollo* 93 (1971) 126 f.; idem,
Connoisseur 176 (1971) 131; *BM Annual* 11
(1969–70) 20 ff.; D. Kiang, *Archaeology* 25 (1972)
4–7, cover; *The Image of the Black in Western Art*
(1976) 194, 197–199, figs. 251–252; A. Adriani, *AM*
93 (1978) 119–131, *passim*.

114

HEAD OF A YOUTH

The Brooklyn Museum, Brooklyn, New York
Charles Edwin Wilbour Fund (63.184)
From Egypt, an old collection in Alexandria
Marble, H: 0.155 m.
Compare the boy boxer from Tralles in Istan-
bul and similar ideal portraits of the post-
Pergamene period in western Asia Minor
and the Greek islands (M. Bieber, *The Sculp-
ture of the Hellenistic Age* [1961] 163–164, figs.
698, 699). Ca. 100 B.C.

   BM Annual 5 (1963–64) 159, frontis.; J. L.
Keith, *JARCE* 6 (1967) 157–162.

115

HEAD OF A HELLENISTIC RULER

William Rockhill Nelson Gallery of Art–Atkins Museum of Fine Arts, Kansas City, Missouri

Nelson Fund (45–67)

Marble, H: 0.26 m.

The head is typical of a class of romantic likenesses from western Asia Minor and the Aegean islands of about 100 B.C.

C. C. Vermeule, *Apollo* 99 (1974) 312–313, no. 1, fig. 1.

116

HEAD OF A ROMAN GENERAL

The J. Paul Getty Museum, Malibu, California
(73.AB.8)

Bronze, H: 0.28 m.

Eyes and lips originally inlaid. An early first-
century-B.C. portrait in the Hellenistic style.

B. Fredericksen, ed., *The J. Paul Getty Museum*
(1975) 37, cover; *JPGM Guidebook* (1980) 35, ill;
Roman Portraits in the JPGM, Philbrook Art Center
(1981) 12–13, 120, no. 1.

117
HEAD OF A WOMAN
Yale University Art Gallery,
New Haven, Connecticut
Bequest of Adra M. Newell (1967.34.24)
Marble, H: 0.30 m.
Hellenistic work of the late second century
B.C., perhaps from Alexandria.

   Unpublished.

VIII
Hellenistic Sculpture

118

ORPHEUS AND TWO SIRENS

The J. Paul Getty Museum, Malibu, California
(76.AA.11)

From southern Italy

Terracotta, H (siren 1): ca. 1.40 m.; H (Orpheus): ca. 1.04 m.; H (siren 2): ca. 1.40 m.

Late fourth century B.C.

JPGM Checklist of Antiquities 1 (1979) 25–26, nos. 99–101; *JPGM Guidebook* (1980) 34, ill.; detailed publication in progress.

151

119
GIRL WITH GARLAND
Colby College Museum of Art,
Waterville, Maine
Gift of Adeline and Caroline Wing (60-S-3)
Marble, H: 0.205 m.
From a funerary or votive relief, third
century B.C.

Selections from the Colby College Art Collection, Vose
Galleries, Boston (15–25 November 1961) 6.

120

LION ATTACKING A BULL

Allen Memorial Art Museum, Oberlin College,
Oberlin, Ohio

R. T. Miller Jr. Fund (48.28)

Said to be from Pergamon; formerly in the
S. Pozzi collection, Paris

White marble, apparently from Asia Minor,
H: 0.445 m.; W: 0.711 m.

From a small pediment. Greek original sculpture of the second century B.C.

Collection S. Pozzi, G. Petit (25–27 June 1919) no.
364, ill.; C. W. Lunsingh Scheurleer, *Oudheidkundig
Jaarboek* 3 (1923) 201 ff.; W. Stechow, *AMAM
Bulletin* 5 (1948) 25; M. Sturgeon, *AMAM Bulletin*
33 (1975–76) 28–43; L. Budde, *AntPl* 2 (1963) 59,
71, fig. 6; *AMAM Catalogue of Paintings and Sculpture* (1967) 189, 190, 334, fig. 223; Vermeule, *Greek
Art* 79, 131, fig. 101.

121
BEAR
The J. Paul Getty Museum, Malibu, California
(72.AA.125)
White-grained Thasian marble, L: 1.207 m.
Roman copy of a Hellenistic creation.

C. C. Vermeule, N. Neuerburg, *Catalogue of the
Ancient Art* (1973) 13, 14, no. 24; *JPGM Checklist of
Antiquities* 2 (1979) 37, no. V79; Vermeule, *Greek
Art* 99, 136, fig. 139.

122
RAM
The Toledo Museum of Art, Toledo, Ohio
Gift of Clement O. Miniger (26.9)
Presumably from Italy; formerly in the Hope
collection, Deepdene
Marble, H (at head, without modern base):
1.14 m.; L: 1.35 m.
Roman copy, possibly after a Hellenistic creation showing Odysseus escaping from the
cave of Polyphemus. Alternatively, the ram
and the palm tree may indicate it came from a
shrine dedicated to Jupiter Ammon. Ca. first
century A.D.

Reinach, *Rép. stat.* 5 (1924) 447, no. 2; 6 (1930)
161, no. 1; Anderson Galleries, New York (26–27
January 1921) 141, lot 792, ill.; *TMA News* (September 1928) 658, cover; M. Bieber, *AJA* 47
(1943) 378 ff.; *EA* 5100; *TMA Guide* (1959) 7, ill.;
M. Bieber, *Sculpture* 100, fig. 401; B. Fellmann, *Die
antiker Darstellungen des Polyphemabenteuers* (1972)
98; Vermeule, *Greek Art* 99, 137, fig. 140.

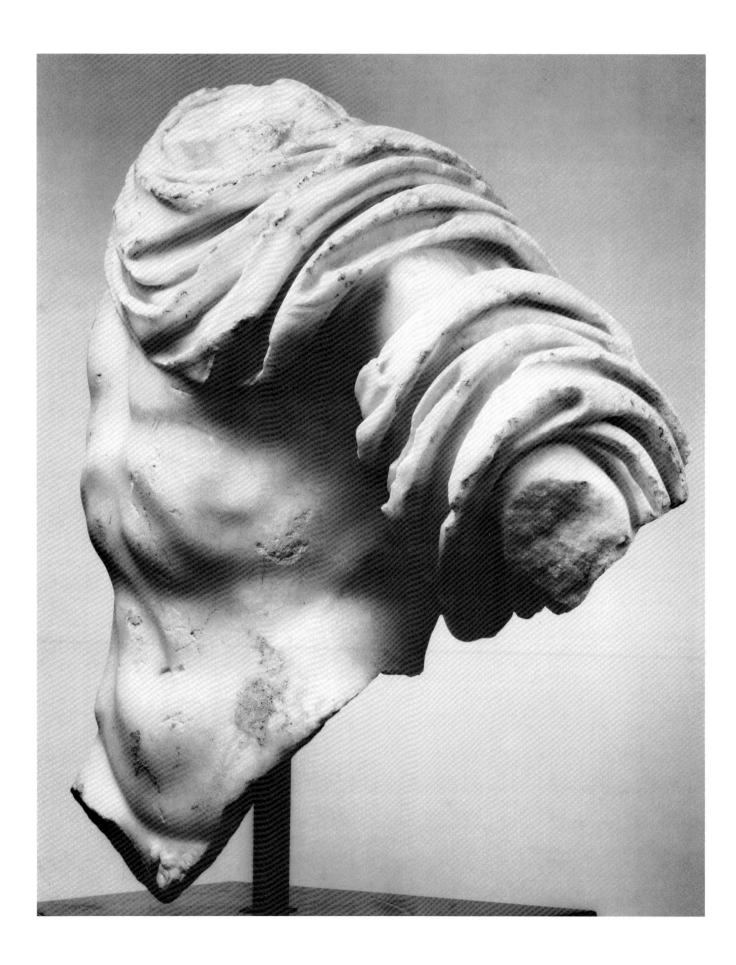

123 ←
TORSO OF A HERO
The J. Paul Getty Museum, Malibu, California
(72.AA.110)
From Italy
Marble, H: 0.638 m.
Compare the statue of Antinous as Androkles,
boar-hunting hero of Ephesus, in Izmir
from the Gymnasium of Vedius at Ephesus
(Inan–Rosenbaum, *Portrait Sculpture* 73–74,
no. 37, pl. 24). Perhaps Meleager or Adonis, or
Antinous in heroic guise. Graeco-Roman
creation after an early Hellenistic statue.

Unpublished.

124
HEAD OF ZEUS (?)
Williams College Museum of Art,
Williamstown, Massachusetts
Gift of the Greylock Foundation (63.34)
Probably from one of the towns on the
Syro-Phoenician coast
Marble, H: 0.31 m.
Late Hellenistic, perhaps ca. 50 B.C.

S. L. Faison, *Handbook of the Collection* (1979)
no. 4.

125

TORSO OF A DANCING SATYR

William Rockhill Nelson Gallery of Art–Atkins
Museum of Fine Arts, Kansas City, Missouri

Nelson Fund (34–135)

Probably from Italy; formerly in the collection of Marbury Hall, Cheshire

Marble, H: 0.585 m.

Graeco-Roman replica after the Hellenistic
original in a group of a satyr inviting a
nymph to dance.

Michaelis, *Marbles in Great Britain* 510, no. 22;
C. C. Vermeule, *AJA* 59 (1955) 142.

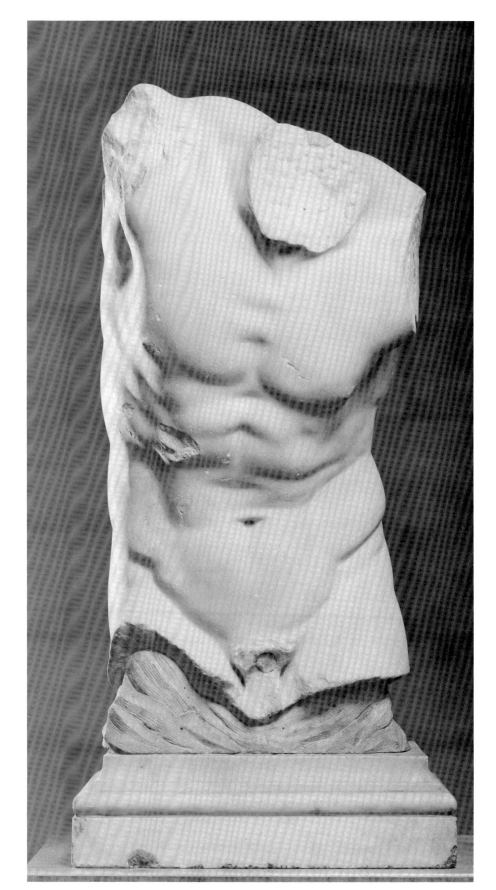

126
HEAD OF A SATYR
Honolulu Academy of Arts, Honolulu, Hawaii
Gift of Daphne Damon in memory of Violet
D. Putnam (2300.1)
Marble, H: 0.225 m.
Hadrianic copy after a type of the third cen-
tury B.C.

Unpublished.

127
STATUE OF A SMILING SATYR
Smith College Museum of Art,
Northampton, Massachusetts
(1919:15-1)
Marble, H: 0.674 m.
An architectural or decorative support,
Graeco-Roman, ca. first century B.C.

Reinach, *Rép. stat.* 6 (1930) 28, no. 5; *Catalogue*
(1937) 31, ill.; Vermeule, *Greek Art* 93, 135, fig. 130.

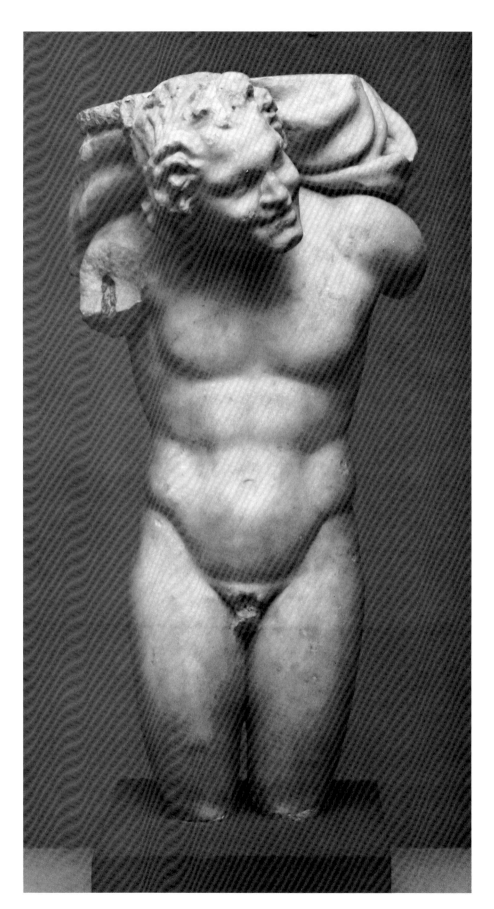

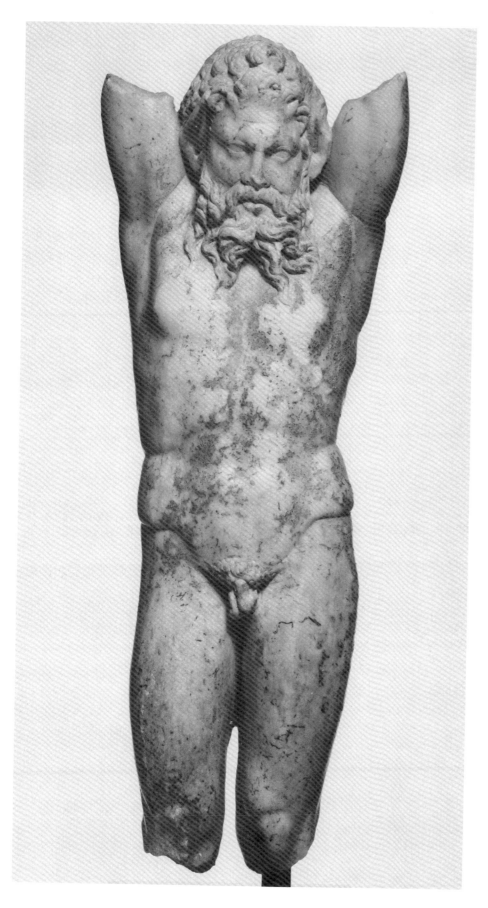

128
SATYR AS AN ATLAS-TYPE SUPPORT
The J. Paul Getty Museum, Malibu, California
(72.AA.107)
Fine-grained marble, H: 0.432 m.
First century B.C.

C. C. Vermeule, N. Neuerburg, *Catalogue of the
Ancient Art* (1973) 14, no. 25; *JPGM Checklist of
Antiquities* 1 (1979) 27, no. 106.

129
SATYR
Elvehjem Museum of Art, University of Wisconsin,
Madison, Wisconsin
Max W. Zabel Fund (70.1)
Formerly in the collection of Hon. Brecken-
ridge Long
Marble, H: 0.61 m.
Graeco-Roman copy after a Hellenistic orig-
inal showing a satyr bending to his left to
play with a small panther.

    Bulletin (1970–71) 45, ill.; C. C. Vermeule, *Burl-
Mag* 110 (1968) 556, fig. 19; idem, *Roman Taste*
34, fig. 37.

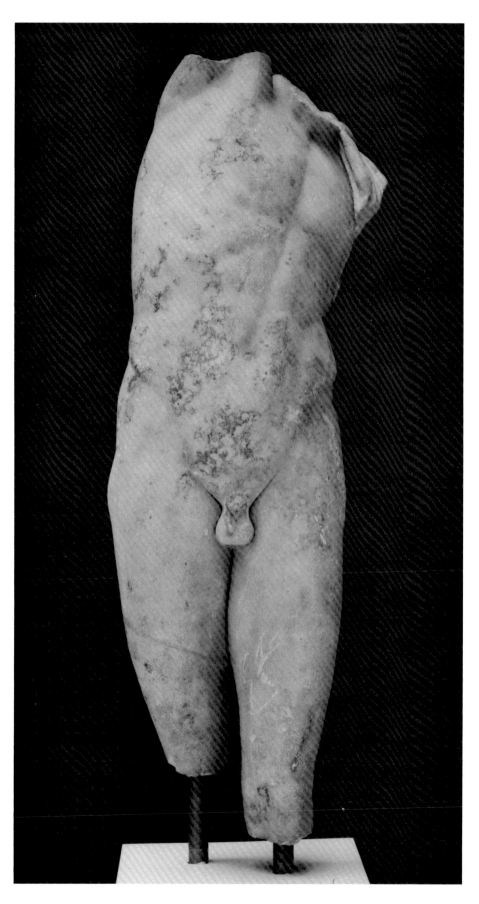

130
TORSO OF A SATYR
Carnegie Institute, Museum of Art,
Pittsburgh, Pennsylvania
(72.42.1)
Formerly in the collection of R. A. McKinnon
Parian (?) marble, H: 0.98 m.
Similar to no. 129 above, reversed. A cloak,
perhaps filled with fruits of the woodlands,
was attached to the satyr's left shoulder.

Parke-Bernet (5 November 1970) lot 297; *ArtQ*
(1973) 112, ill., 121; J. M. Carder, *Carnegie Magazine*
(May 1974) 198–203; E. L. Fundaburk and T. G.
Davenport, *Art in Public Places in the United States*
(1975) no. 292, ill.

131

SATYR AND NYMPH

Santa Barbara Museum of Art,
Santa Barbara, California

Gift of Wright S. Ludington (78.4.8)

Said to have come from Asia Minor

Marble, H: 1.08 m.

Roman copy after a popular Hellenistic creation. It has been proposed by F. Causey-Frel
that the satyr's head in Providence (no. 132)
may join.

M. A. Del Chiaro, *The Collection of Greek and*
Roman Antiquities at the Santa Barbara Museum of
Art (1962) no. S-9.

132
HEAD OF A SATYR
GRASPED BY THE HAIR
Rhode Island School of Design, Museum of Art,
Providence, Rhode Island
(26.165)
Marble, H: 0.272 m.
From the group of a seated satyr and a strug-
gling nymph. Graeco-Roman copy after a
Hellenistic original.

B. S. Ridgway, *Catalogue of the Classical Collection,*
Classical Sculpture (1972) 63–64, 178–180, no. 23.

133
TORSO OF A FAUN OR SATYR
Sterling and Francine Clark Art Institute,
Williamstown, Massachusetts
(970)
Marble, H: 0.635 m.
Graeco-Roman copy after a Hellenistic type.

Unpublished.

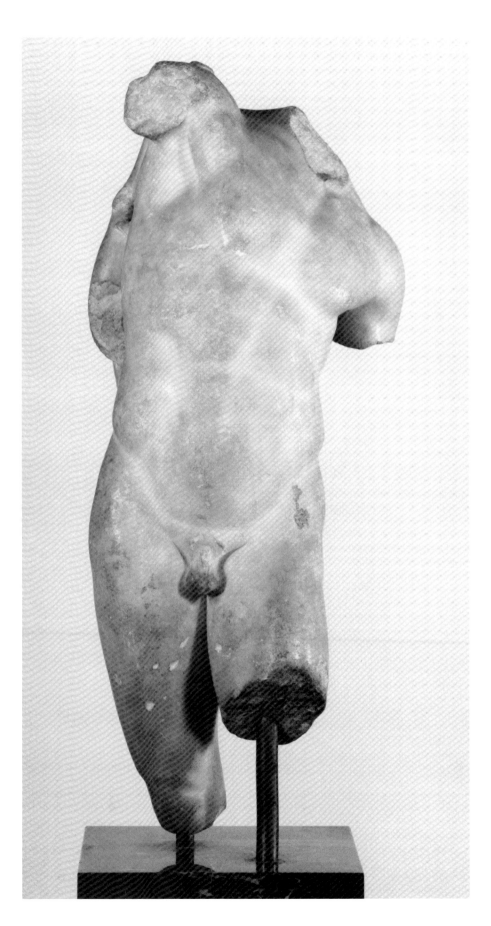

134
NEREID
Norton Simon Museum, Pasadena, California
Marble, H: ca. 1.5 m.
Identified as a Nereid because she is running
on water and has no wings. Head inserted.
Ca. 100 B.C. (J. Frel)

Unpublished.

135
HERMES
Milwaukee Art Center,
Milwaukee, Wisconsin
Gift of the Milwaukee Art Center Garden
Club (SM 1967.23)
In the Giustiniani collection, Rome, from the
seventeenth century; later in the collection
of Williams College
Marble, H: 2.46 m. (as restored)
Only the torso is ancient; the rest is
seventeenth-century restoration.

Galleria Giustiniani 1 (1631) pl. 83; Reinach, *Rép. stat.* 1 (1897) 363, pl. 657, no. 1511; M.N. Beniso-vich, *ArtBull* 35 (1953) 295–8, figs. 4–5.

136 (See colorplate 13.)
ARTEMIS HUNTING
Albright-Knox Art Gallery, Buffalo, New York
George B. and Jenny R. Mathews Fund (53:1)
From Italy
Bronze, H (of Artemis): 0.92 m.
Late Hellenistic.

C. C. Vermeule, *Michigan Daily* (May 22, 1955)
15; E. Schenk, P. Kelleher, The Buffalo Fine Arts
Academy, *Gallery Notes* 18, no. 2 (1954) 2–19, ill.;
Bieber, *Ancient Copies* 75, 82, figs. 287–289; Vermeule, *Greek Art* 86, 133, fig. 113.

137

APHRODITE AFTER HER BATH

The Corcoran Gallery of Art, Washington, D.C.
Gift of W. W. Corcoran (86.9)
Said to have been excavated at Città Lavinia
near Rome; formerly in the collection of Sir
Moses Ezekial (known there as the "Venus
Sallusti")
Marble, H: 1.79 m.
Lower legs and other details restored. Anto-
nine copy after a late-Hellenistic version of the
famous Aphrodite of Knidos by Praxiteles.

   Unpublished.

138
HEAD OF APHRODITE
The Baltimore Museum of Art, Baltimore,
Maryland
(31.34.1)
Found on Lemnos
Parian marble, H: 0.19 m.
Ca. 300 B.C.

BMA News Record (May 1931) cover.

139
FRAGMENTS OF A STATUE OF
APHRODITE PUDICA
Dayton Art Institute, Dayton, Ohio
Purchased with funds provided by Mr. and
Mrs. Ralf Kircher
Marble, H (torso): 1.03 m.; H (base): 0.89 m.
First-century A.D. version of the Capitoline
Venus.

Art of the Ancients: Greeks, Etruscans and Romans,
Andre Emmerich Gallery, New York (February 7–
March 13, 1968) 45, no. 56; M. Bieber, B. H. Evans,
DAI Bulletin 28 (September 1969) 2–17.

140
TORSO OF APHRODITE
North Carolina Museum of Art,
Raleigh, North Carolina
Gift of the North Carolina State Art Society,
Phifer bequest, in memory of Katherine
Clark Pendleton Arrington (G.69.34.1)
Marble, H: 0.84 m.
Capitoline type. Late Hellenistic.

C. W. Stanford, *NCMA Bulletin* 11 (July 1969–
June 1971) 6, 32, ill.; C. C. Vermeule, *NCMA
Bulletin* 10 (September 1970) 2–11, ill.

141
TORSO OF APHRODITE
National Gallery of Art, Washington, D.C.
Gift of Barbara Harrison Wescott in memory
of the Hon. Francis Burton Harrison, 1969
(A-1745)
Pentelic (?) marble, H: 0.981 m.
Copy after the Medici Venus type.

   Unpublished.

142
TORSO OF APHRODITE OR A NYMPH
Santa Barbara Museum of Art,
Santa Barbara, California
Gift of Wright S. Ludington (73.52)
Marble, H: 0.952 m.
Late Hellenistic.

C. C. Vermeule, *Museum Calendar* (May 1974)
3–4, ill.

143

APHRODITE OR FOUNTAIN NYMPH
The Virginia Museum of Fine Arts,
Richmond, Virginia
Beulah Gould Branch bequest (53-1-89)
Marble, H: 1.14 m.
Roman copy of a late Hellenistic type ulti-
mately derived from the Venus of Arles.
Compare G. Lippold, *Handbuch* 3 (1950)
1, p. 83, no. 2.

   Unpublished.

144

HEAD OF APHRODITE

North Museum, Franklin and Marshall College,
Lancaster, Pennsylvania

White coarse marble with high quartz
content, H: 0.245 m.

Roman copy after the Doidalsas Crouching
Aphrodite of the second half of the third
century B.C.

L. E. Roller, *AJA* 79 (1975) 279–281, pl. 49.

145 ←

CROUCHING APHRODITE

The J. Paul Getty Museum, Malibu, California

(71.AA.455)

Evidently from Italy

Marble, H: 0.978 m.

Roman copy of a Hellenistic original of

ca. 100 B.C.

    C. C. Vermeule, N. Neuerburg, *Catalogue of the Ancient Art* (1973) 11–12, no. 20; D. Brinkerhoff, Getty *MJ* 6–7 (1978–79) 86–87, no. 3, figs. 7–9.

146

APHRODITE

The Detroit Institute of Arts, Detroit, Michigan

Gift of Mr. and Mrs. Henry Ford II (74.53)

Marble, H: 1.689 m.

First- or second-century-A.D. variant after a late-first-century-B.C. version of the late-fifth-century-B.C. prototype, the so-called "Venus Genetrix"; perhaps the body for a portrait statue of an empress.

    W. H. Peck, *DIA Bulletin* 53 (1974) 52–53, ill.; idem, *ibid.* 54 (1976) 124–132, cover.

147

MUSE OR MYTHOLOGICAL FEMALE

The Minneapolis Institute of Arts,
Minneapolis, Minnesota

John R. Van Derlip Fund (56.12)

Said to have been found in 1885 during construction in the Tiber; formerly in the collection of D. Vitali, Rome.

Greek-island marble, H: 1.23 m.

Hellenistic original of the first century B.C.

R. Lanciani, *Ancient Rome in the Light of Recent Excavations* (1888) 258; B. Neutsch, *RM* 63 (1956) 46–55, pls. 13–17 (on art market); *MIA Bulletin* (Spring 1957) 1; A. M. Clark, S. Sachs, *Archaeology* 19 (1966) 4, ill.

148
FRAGMENT OF A STATUE OF THE
SLEEPING HERMAPHRODITUS
Carnegie Institute, Museum of Art,
Pittsburgh, Pennsylvania
(72.42.2)
Formerly in the Kevorkian collection
Marble, L: 0.68 m.; W: 0.87 m.
Late Julio-Claudian or Flavian copy after the
Hellenistic original best known in the Louvre
(Borghese) and Museo Nazionale Romano
copies. There are two poppies in the left hand.

Sotheby's (8 December 1970) lot 35; J. N.
Carder, *Carnegie Magazine* (May 1974) 198–203.

149 (See colorplate 14.)
INFANT HERAKLES (?)
The St. Louis Art Museum, St. Louis, Missouri
(36.26)
Allegedly found at Daib el Guirza in the
Fayum
Bronze, H: 0.622 m.
The eyes and teeth inlaid in silver. First-
century-B.C. creation after Hellenistic types.

S. Reinach, *GBA* 16 (1927) 300–301; *CAMSL
Bulletin* 13 (April 1928) 22–24, ill.; *ibid.* 28 (De-
cember 1943) 41–44 (describing cleaning); *Small
Bronzes of the Ancient World*, Detroit Institute of
Arts (1947) 11, no. 85; D. K. Hill, *GBA* 4 (1948)
20, n. 3; *Master Bronzes* 127, no. 128, ill.; *SLAM
Handbook* (1975) 15, ill.

150
CHILD
The Art Institute of Chicago, Chicago, Illinois
Katherine Keith Adler Fund (1976.426)
Crystalline island marble, H: 0.62 m.
Roman copy after a Hellenistic creation
loosely based on Lysippan work.

Unpublished.

151

CHILD WITH GRAPES

The J. Paul Getty Museum, Malibu, California

(73.AA.6)

Marble, H: 0.405 m.

The tombstone of Amynthus from Smyrna
(Izmir) in the Louvre (M. Bieber, *Sculpture*, fig. 539) shows that the child is holding the grapes away from his pet cock.

Graeco-Roman copy after a Hellenistic type.

   Vermeule, *Greek Art* 93–94, 135, fig. 132; *JPGM
Guidebook* (1980) 26, ill.

152
"SPINARIO"
(BOY EXTRACTING A THORN)
The Baltimore Museum of Art, Baltimore,
Maryland
(37.124)
From Daphne-Yakto
Marble, H: 0.442 m.
Second-century-A.D. Roman copy after the
Hellenistic original.

Antioch-on-the-Orontes: II: The Excavations
1933–1936 (1938) 170, no. 104, pl. 2 (before
cleaning).

153
SLEEPING EROS
Fogg Art Museum, Harvard University,
Cambridge, Massachusetts
David M. Robinson Fund (1963.24)
Marble, L: 0.69 m.; W: 0.445 m.
Ca. A.D. 75

   Acquisitions 1962–1963 (1964) 114, ill.

154
FALLING NIOBID
The J. Paul Getty Museum, Malibu, California
(72.AA.126)
Seemingly from Italy
Pentelic marble, H: 1.187 m.; H (with base):
1.467 m.
First century B.C. variant recalling a creation of
ca. 400 B.C.

C. C. Vermeule, N. Neuerburg, *Catalogue of the Ancient Art* (1973) 12–13, no. 22; *JPGM Checklist of Antiquities* 1 (1979) 27, no. 107.

155
STATUE WITH HEAD OF HERMES
Los Angeles County Museum of Art,
Los Angeles, California
William Randolph Hearst collection
(48.24.15)
From Rome. Formerly at Shobden
Court, collection of Lord Bateman
Marble, H: 1.93 m.
Mid-second-century-A.D. work after a Greek
type of the fourth century B.C.

   C. C. Vermeule, *AJA* 60 (1956) 342–343.

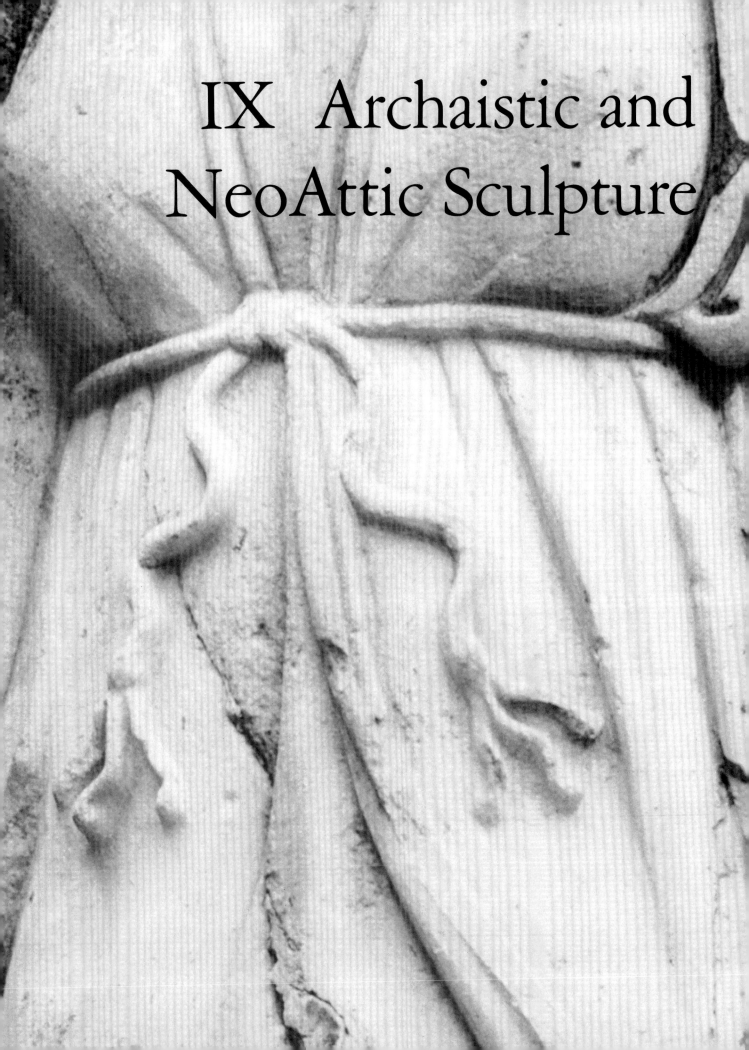

IX Archaistic and NeoAttic Sculpture

156
HEAD OF A YOUTH
Kresge Art Gallery, Michigan State University,
East Lansing, Michigan
(65.56)
Formerly in the Rogers and V. L. Simkhovich
collections
Marble, H: 0.343 m.
Archaistic work of the second century B.C.,
probably for a herm. The hollow eyes were
originally inset.

   B. S. Ridgway, *MSU Bulletin* 1 (November 1967)
no. 2.

157 →
HEAD OF A DIVINITY
The Brooklyn Museum, Brooklyn, New York
Gift of Carl H. DeSilver (03.285)
Seemingly from Rome; formerly in the
Borghese collection
Marble, H: 0.188 m.
An archaizing work of ca. A.D. 75; compare
the statues of Artemis from the school of
Pasiteles in Venice and Naples (A. Giuliano,
ArchCl 5 [1953] 48–54).

   BM Quarterly 17, no. 2 (1930) 43, 47, ill.;
W. Deonna, *Genava* 9 (1931) 92, fig. 8, no. 2.

158

PEPLOPHOROS

The Walters Art Gallery, Baltimore, Maryland
(23.87)

Formerly in the Hope collection, Deepdene

Large-grained island marble, H: 1.43 m.

The head, although ancient, does not belong
(Ridgway). Archaizing work of the first century B.C.–A.D.

Michaelis, *Marbles in Great Britain* 285, no. 13;
Christie's (July 23, 1917) no. 234, pl. 12; Reinach,
Rép. stat. 5 (1924) 367, no. 6; E. Paribeni, *ASAtene*
8–10 (1946–1948) 104 f., fig. 1; E. Langlotz, *JdI*
61–62 (1946–47) 105, pl. 26.2, fig. 1; C. C. Vermeule, *AJA* 59 (1955) 134; B. Ridgway, *Hesperia* 38
(1969) 213–222, pls. 54–7.

159
ODYSSEUS CREEPING FORWARD
DURING THE THEFT OF
THE PALLADION
Isabella Stewart Gardner Museum,
Boston, Massachusetts
(S5s23)
Found in 1885 in the Gardens of Sallust, Rome
Pentelic marble, H: 0.65 m.; L: 1.13 m.
Graeco-Roman imitation of ca. A.D. 75 of an
archaic pedimental sculpture.

R. Lanciani, *NotScavi* (1885) 341 (discovery);
idem, *BullComm* 34 (1906) 183; V. Poulsen, *ActaA*
25 (1954) 301–304; E. Lessing, *The Voyages of Ulysses*
(1965) 85, col. pl. 23 and cover; W. B. Stanford,
J. V. Luce, *The Quest for Ulysses* (1974) 158, no. 128,
ill.; *Sculpture in the ISGM* (1977) 12, no. 14; Ridgway, *Archaic Style*, 314, 321, fig. 69.

160

VOTIVE RELIEF OF A HORSEMAN

The Metropolitan Museum of Art,
New York, New York

Bequest of Walter C. Baker (1972.118.107)

Said to be from Athens

Marble, H: 0.405 m.; W: 0.46 m.

Early-first-century-B.C. work inspired by the
art of the later fifth century.

    Baker Collection no. 55; *American Collections*
no. 153, pl. 42; Bieber, *Sculpture* 152, no. 123; F. Eckstein, *Gnomon* 31 (1959) 643; *New York Private
Collections* 26–27, no. 109, pl. 34; *The Horses of
San Marco,* checklist (1980) no. 6.

161 (See colorplate 15.)

RELIEF WITH PROCESSION OF GODS

Yale University Art Gallery,
New Haven, Connecticut

Leonard C. Hanna, Jr., B.A. 1913, Fund
(1965.132)

Formerly in the collection at Athelhampton
Hall, Dorset (known as the Puddletown
Relief)

Marble, H: 0.64 m.; W: 1.25 m.

The gods are Zeus, Hera, Athena, Aphrodite,
and Apollo. Artemis may have completed
the group and another panel may have shown
the remainder of the twelve gods. The archaizing style suggests a date ca. 50 B.C.

C. C. Vermeule, *AJA* 60 (1956) 322; *YUAG
Bulletin* 31 (1966) 42, ill.; Vermeule, *Greek Art* 109,
139, fig. 153.

162
RELIEF OF APOLLO AND ARTEMIS
The Walters Art Gallery, Baltimore, Maryland
(23.7)
Purchased by Mr. Walters
Marble, H: 0.425 m.; W: 0.317 m.
Graeco-Roman work of ca. 50 B.C. in the
archaistic manner.

   The Ruins of Rome, The University Museum,
Philadelphia (1960–61) no. 225.

163
FRAGMENT OF A RELIEF
WITH FOUR DIVINITIES
Wellesley College Museum, Jewett Arts Center,
Wellesley, Massachusetts
Marble, H: 0.565 m.; W: 0.805 m.
From the preserved left edge: Artemis, Hermes,
Aphrodite, part of Ares.
First century B.C.

H. Philippart, "Collections d'antiquités classiques
aux Etats-Unis," *Revue de l'Université de Bruxelles*
(1928) 49.

164 ←

HERMES AND THE INFANT DIONYSOS
Fogg Art Museum, Harvard University,
Cambridge, Massachusetts
David M. Robinson Fund (1970.25)
From Rome, formerly in the Palazzo Albani
Marble, H: 0.69 m.; W: 0.465 m.
Neo-Attic relief panel.

G. Zoega, *Li Bassirilievi antichi di Roma* (1808)
20–22, pl. III; G. M. A. Hanfmann, C. B. Moore,
Acquisitions, 1969–1970 (1971) 41–49; C. C. Vermeule, *AJA* 68 (1964) 333, n. 89; G. M. A. Hanfmann, D. Mitten, *Apollo* 107 (1978) 366, 368 n. 30.

165

MAENAD OR HORA
Isabella Stewart Gardner Museum,
Boston, Massachusetts
(S5s19)
Found in Rome before 1897
Pentelic (?) marble, H: 1.435 m.; W: 0.585 m.
Part of a series of eight reliefs found in 1908
near the Via Praenestina; the other seven now
in the Museo delle Terme, Rome. Graeco-
Roman work of about A.D. 100 after
Pergamene models of the late fifth–early
fourth century B.C.

Sculpture in the Isabella Stewart Gardner Museum
13–14, no. 15.

166
HEAD OF A WOMAN
*Collection of the Carolina Art Association, Gibbes
Art Gallery, Charleston, South Carolina*
Gift of C. H. Winn (58.44.1)
One of five pieces given to the donor by Pro-
fessor Madris of the University of Athens in
1919; found long before on the Acropolis near
the Porch of the Maidens of the Erechtheum.
Pentelic marble, H: 0.14 m.
Nose restored. Neoclassical creation of the
first century B.C.

 Classical Art from Carolina Collections 20, no. 27.

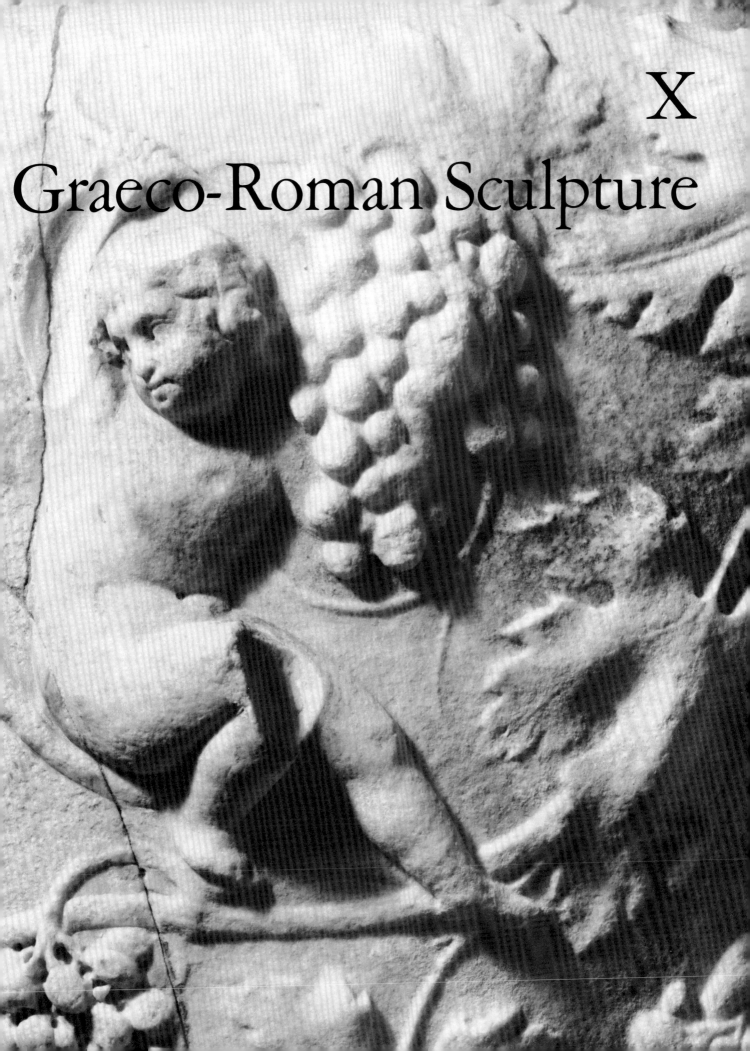

X

Graeco-Roman Sculpture

167

GRAVE STELE OF APOLLONIA,
DAUGHTER OF ARISTANDROS
AND THEBAGENEIAS

The J. Paul Getty Museum, Malibu, California
(74.AA.13)

Pentelic marble, H: 1.11 m.; W: 0.615 m.
The date, ca. 100 B.C., is based not only on the
forms of the stele and its lettering but also on
the hair of the girl with a braid across the top
of the head.

J. Frel, *Recent Acquisitions* (1974) no. 11, ill.;
JPGM Checklist of Antiquities 1 (1979) 24, no. 92.

168

HEAD OF A MAN FROM A VOTIVE
OR FUNERARY RELIEF
Allen Memorial Art Museum, Oberlin College,
Oberlin, Ohio
R. T. Miller, Jr. Fund (41.42)
White (Pentelic?) marble, H: 0.216 m.
Greek work of ca. A.D. 125.

   Catalogue of Paintings and Sculpture (1967) 190,
335, fig. 224.

169

VASE WITH EROTES IN FOLIAGE
Los Angeles County Museum of Art,
Los Angeles, California
William Randolph Hearst collection (51.18.8)
Found at Hadrian's Villa near Tivoli; formerly
in the Buckingham collection, Stowe
Marble, H: 1.15 m.
Ca. A.D. 130.

   Drawn by Piranesi; Michaelis, *Marbles in Great
Britain* 103 (vases brought from Italy in 1774); C.
C. Vermeule, *AJA* 59 (1955) 147; 60 (1956) 344; E.
Feinblatt, *LACMA Bulletin* 7 (Fall 1955) 3 ff.

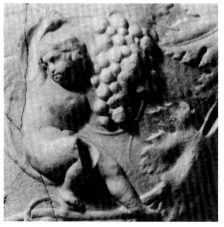

170

PEDIMENT FRAGMENT WITH HELIOS

The Brooklyn Museum, Brooklyn, New York

Charles Edwin Wilbour Fund (62.148)

From Behnesa (ancient Oxyrhynchos)

Limestone, H: 0.246 m.; W: 0.28 m.

Ca. A.D. 150–200.

H. Hoffmann, *JARCE* 2 (1963) 117–124, pls. 20–21; C. C. Vermeule, *Bulletin, Museum of Fine Arts, Boston* 64 (1966) 30, fig. 17b; A. Krug, *AA* 84 (1969) 189 ff.

171

BACCHUS OR SATYR ON A DONKEY
The Minneapolis Institute of Arts,
Minneapolis, Minnesota
John R. Van Derlip Fund (63.41)
Formerly in the collection at the Villa Mattei,
Rome, and Marbury Hall, Cheshire
Marble, H: 0.54 m.; L: 0.45 m.
Extensively restored in eighteenth century.
Ca. A.D. 125.

J. Dallaway, *Catalogue of Painting, Statues, etc. at
Marbury Hall* (1814) no. 13; C. Clarac, *Musée de
sculpture antique et moderne* 4 (1832–1841) 696,
1610a; Michaelis, *Marbles in Great Britain* 505–506,
no. 11; S. Howard, *MIA Bulletin* 52 (March 1964)
2–11; *A Guide to the Galleries* (1970) 56–57, no. 18.

172

TORSO OF PAN

The Bowdoin College Museum of Fine Arts,
Brunswick, Maine

Gift of Nathan Dane, II (1961.97)

Marble, H: 1.035 m.

Hadrianic creation in the Polykleitan tradition.

K. Herbert, *Ancient Art in Bowdoin College* (1964)
40–41, no. 97, pl. 14.

173
DIOSKOUROS
William Rockhill Nelson Gallery of Art–Atkins
Museum of Fine Arts, Kansas City, Missouri
Nelson Fund (33–1533)
Marble, H: 0.76 m.
Compare C. C. Vermeule, *Greek Sculpture and*
Roman Taste (1977) 90, fig. 76, from Perge
in Pamphylia.

   Unpublished.

174
DRUNKEN HERAKLES
North Carolina Museum of Art,
Raleigh, North Carolina
Gift of Mr. and Mrs. Jack Linsky, New York
(GL.55.11.2)
Found in the Roman Forum in 1771, formerly
in the collection at Margam Park, Wales
Marble, H: 1.65 m.
Roman copy of ca. A.D. 150 after a Hellenistic
prototype.

Michaelis, *Marbles in Great Britain* 517–518,
no. 4; C. C. Vermeule, *AJA* 59 (1955) 143; *ibid.* 63
(1959) 337, pl. 78, fig. 14; W. R. Valentiner,
NCMA Bulletin 1 (Spring 1957) 21, 26; M. D. Hill,
NCMA Bulletin 2 (Summer 1958) 31, ill.

175 (See colorplate 16.)
WEARY HERAKLES
The Detroit Institute of Arts, Detroit, Michigan
Gift of Dr. and Mrs. Irving F. Burton (68.65)
From Asia Minor
Marble, H: 0.392 m.
Second-century-A.D. copy of the so-called
"Farnese Herakles."

V. Karageorghis, C. C. Vermeule, *Sculptures from
Salamis* 2 (1966) 18–19, fig. 6; C. C. Vermeule, *AJA*
79 (1975) 326, pl. 53, fig. 5; Vermeule, *Greek Art*
22–23, 119, fig. 27.

176
FRAGMENTARY HEAD
OF A MYTHOLOGICAL FIGURE,
PERHAPS A GIANT OR BARBARIAN
Fogg Art Museum, Harvard University,
Cambridge, Massachusetts
Gift of E. P. Warren (1913.13)
Marble, H: 0.45 m.
Roman copy ca. A.D. 100 of a late Hellenistic
type.

   G. H. Chase, *ArtBull* 3 (1917) 112 ff., fig. 2;
idem, *American Collections* 90; *Catalogue of Ancient
Sculpture* (1950) no. 39; Vermeule, *Greek Art* 81–82,
131, fig. 104A.

177 (See colorplate 17.)
BARBARIAN QUEEN OR
GEOGRAPHICAL PERSONIFICATION
Fogg Art Museum, Harvard University,
Cambridge, Massachusetts
Gift of Edward W. Forbes (1905.7.(1))
Said to have been found at Ostia in the late
eighteenth or early nineteenth century;
formerly in the "Jones" and Ponsonby col-
lections, on loan to the South Kensington
Museum, London, in the late nineteenth
century
Marble, H: 0.345 m.
Late-first–early-second-century-A.D. copy after
a Hellenistic prototype.

Michaelis, *Marbles in Great Britain* 484, no. 18;
Burlington Exhibition 21, no. 29, pl. 28; J. Six, *RM*
27 (1912) 86–93; Chase, *American Collections* 98,
fig. 115; C. Picard, *La sculpture antique* 2 (1926)
198 ff.; Lawrence, *Later Greek Sculpture* 12, 95, pl. 8;
Catalogue of Ancient Sculpture 14, no. 38; R. Calza,
Scavi di Ostia 5: *I ritratti* (1964) 16, no. 5, pl. 3;
Romans and Barbarians, Museum of Fine Arts, Boston
(1976) 7, no. 8 (with previous bibl.); G. M. A. Hanfmann, D. G. Mitten, *Apollo* 107 (1978) no. 195.

178

HEAD OF ZEUS-AMMON

The Brooklyn Museum, Brooklyn, New York
(37.1522)

Formerly in the collection of the New-York
Historical Society

Marble, H: 0.26 m.

Head made for insertion in a statue body. Ca.
A.D. 75–150 copy of a late Hellenistic type.

Late Egyptian and Coptic Art (1943) 16, pls. 5, 6;
T. Kraus, *JdI* 75 (1960) 97; A. Adriani, *Repertorio
d'arte dell'Egitto greco-romano* A, II (1961) 49,
no. 179, pl. 84, fig. 279; G. Grimm, *MDIK* 28
(1972) 143, pl. 31; Vermeule, *Greek Art* 84, fig. 109.

179
TERMINAL OR HERM BUST
OF AFRICA OR ALEXANDRIA
*Formerly in the Cooper-Hewitt Museum for
the Decorative Arts and Design, New York*
(1953-29-1) (sold 1962, present whereabouts
unknown)
Marble, H: 0.36 m.
Graeco-Roman adaptation of ca. 50 B.C. to
A.D. 50 of a Greek fifth-century-B.C. goddess,
perhaps Demeter or Kore.

C. C. Vermeule, *AJA* 61 (1957) 204; idem, *ibid.*
63 (1959) 141.

180
HEAD OF TYCHE
The Detroit Institute of Arts, Detroit, Michigan
Founders Society purchase (41.9)
Marble, H: 0.51 m.
The turreted crown suggests Cybele or a city
Tyche.

DIA Bulletin (May 1941) no. 8; *Masterpieces of
Painting and Sculpture* (1949) 22; *Sculpture in the
DIA, Checklist* (1967) 12; W. H. Peck, *DIA Bulletin*
53 (1974) 54 (as Aristaeus).

181

HEAD OF TYCHE

Memorial Art Gallery of the University of
Rochester, Rochester, New York

R. T. Miller Fund (49.73)

Marble, H: 0.343 m.

Roman copy after a Hellenistic type.

Kevorkian, Anderson Galleries (January 26,
1921) no. 150; *Joseph Brummer Collection* 2 (Parke-
Bernet, April 20–23, 1949) lot 163.

182
HEAD OF SERAPIS
University of Michigan, Kelsey Museum of Archaeology, Ann Arbor, Michigan
(8526)
Excavated at Karanis (Egypt), a surface find.
Serpentine, H: 0.133 m.
Ca. A.D. 150.

Gods of Egypt in the Greco-Roman Period, Kelsey Museum (1977) 55, 94, no. 39, ill.; *Guardians of the Nile: Sculptures from Karanis in the Fayoum* (1978) 37, no. 28.

183
HEAD OF ARES
Museum of Fine Arts, Boston, Massachusetts
Gift of Mr. and Mrs. Cornelius C.
Vermeule III (1977.712)
Probably from southwestern Asia Minor
Crystalline white marble, H: 0.44 m.
A Hadrianic copy, probably after the colossal
fourth-century-B.C. cult image attributed to
Leochares or Timotheos in the temple of Ares
at Halikarnassos.

   Art in Bloom, Museum of Fine Arts (1979) 46,
ill.; C. C. Vermeule, *Berytus* 26 (1978) 86–88, fig. 1;
Vermeule, *Greek Art* 19, 25, 119, fig. 22c.

184

HEAD OF CYBELE OR FORTUNA

R. H. Lowie Museum of Anthropology, University
of California, Berkeley, California
(8–4267)

Marble, H: 0.33 m.

Hadrianic creation after early Hellinistic type.

Del Chiaro, *West Coast Collections* 27–28, no. 23, ill.

185

HEAD OF ISIS–TYCHE

The Brooklyn Museum, Brooklyn, New York

Charles Edwin Wilbour Fund (62.45)

From near Alexandria

Marble, H: 0.336 m.

Ca. A.D. 150.

N. Aimé-Giron, *BIFAO* 23 (1924) 16 ff., 21–25;
BM Annual 2–3 (1960–1962) 109.

186
HEAD OF THE GODDESS ROMA
Royal Ontario Museum,
Toronto, Ontario, Canada
(925.23.25)
Formerly in the Donaldson collection
Parian(?) marble, H: 0.724 m.
Nose, crest, and other small areas
restored.

  Sotheby's (July 6–10, 1925); C. C. Vermeule, *The Goddess Roma*, 2nd ed. (1974) 105, no. 36A.

187
CYBELE OR CARTHAGE
RIDING ON HER LION
The Virginia Museum of Fine Arts,
Richmond, Virginia
Gift of Mr. and Mrs. Arthur Glasgow
(49-10-31)
Alabaster, H: 0.28 m.
Ca. A.D. 200. For the iconography, see under
Museum of Fine Arts, Boston, *Greek and*
Roman Sculpture in Gold and Silver (1974)
24–25, no. 77.

    Ancient Art in the Virginia Museum (1973) 126,
no. 145.

188
SHEPHERD
The Wadsworth Atheneum,
Hartford, Connecticut
Gift of the Hartford Foundation for Public
Giving (1949.176)
Said to be from Ravenna
Marble, H: 0.38 m.
The statue is one of at least five replicas of a
Hellenistic rustic image of an old farmer. It
could have been carved late enough, in the
third or fourth century A.D., to be considered
Christian; but it may have been purely decora-
tive and Theocritan, the male equivalent
of the Antonine old market-woman in the
Metropolitan Museum of Art, New York.

Joseph Brummer Collection, part 2, Parke-Bernet
(New York, 1949) no. 343; *Early Christian and
Byzantine Art*, The Walters Art Gallery (1947)
no. 27; *WA Handbook* (1958) 22; *Romans and
Barbarians* 121–122, no. 134.

189 (See colorplate 18.)
GROUP OF EARLY CHRISTIAN
SCULPTURES
The Cleveland Museum of Art, Cleveland, Ohio
John L. Severance Fund (65.237-246)
From central Asia Minor, said to have been
found together in a huge pithos
Marble
The group consists of five Christian sculptures
and six portraits to be dated in the late third
century A.D., ca. 270–290.

CMA Handbook (1970) 36; W. D. Wixom,
CMA Bulletin of the CMA 54 (March 1967) 66–88;
P. du Bourguet, *Early Christian Art* (1971) 116, 118,
ill.; M. Gough, *The Origins of Christian Art* (1973)
39, 206, pls. 36, 37; *Metropolitan Museum of Art
Bulletin* (Autumn 1977) 60–63, ill.; *Age of Spirituality* 406–411, nos. 362–368; three portrait pairs discussed in Inan-Rosenbaum, *Porträtplastik* 323–327,
nos. 320–325, pls. 226–234.

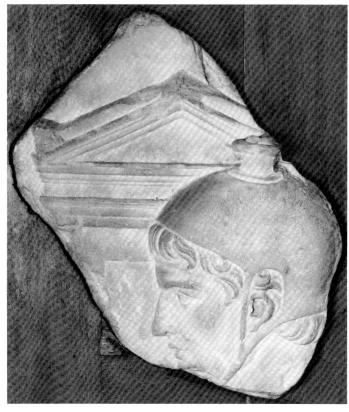

190
RELIEF FRAGMENT
WITH FEMALE PROFILE
Vassar College Art Gallery,
Poughkeepsie, New York
(23.97)
From Rome
Marble, H: 0.178 m.
The style is comparable to that of the Ara
Pacis Augustae.

The Arts of Antiquity: Greece, Etruria, Rome, The
College Art Gallery, State University at New Paltz,
New York (1971) no. 7; J. Uhlenbrock, *The Female*
Image in the Greco-Roman World (n.d.) no. 24; E. I.
Cormack, *The Image of Women from the Classical*
Collection, Vassar College Art Gallery (197–) no. 15.

191
FRAGMENT OF A JULIO-CLAUDIAN
HISTORICAL RELIEF WITH
HEAD OF A FLAMEN
Yale University Art Gallery,
New Haven, Connecticut
Bequest of Adra M. Newell (1967.34.25)
Said to be from Rome
Marble, H: 0.275 m.

Unpublished.

192 (See colorplate 19.)
SECTION OF THE BASE
OF A TRIUMPHAL MONUMENT
The University Museum, University of
Pennsylvania, Philadelphia, Pennsylvania
(MS4916)
From Pozzuoli (Puteoli)
Marble, H: 1.63 m.
An officer, a legionary, and a northern bar-
barian auxiliary. Ca. A.D. 95.

NotScavi (1909) 212; *AJA* 14 (1910) 391; *ibid.* 16
(1912) 101, no. 6; 18 (1914) 526, fig. 2; *University*
Museum Journal 4 (December 1913) 142 ff., fig. 126;
J. Sieveking, *Sitz. Bayer. Akad.* (1919) ill.; S. B.
Luce, *Catalogue of the Mediterranean Section* (1921)
170–172, no. 20; H. Kähler, *Studies . . . D. M.*
Robinson 1 (1951) 430 ff.; *Guide to the Collection: The*
Mediterranean World (1965) 66–67, ill.; *Expedition*
12 (1970) 9.

193
SECTION OF ARCHITECTURAL PANEL
WITH ANIMAL EMERGING FROM AN
ACANTHUS SCROLL
R. H. Lowie Museum of Anthropology, University
of California, Berkeley, California
Gift of Mrs. Phoebe A. Hearst (8-4281)
From the Flavian shops in front of the Basilica
Aemilia or the Domus Flavia, Palatine Hill,
Rome
Marble, H (max.): 0.64 m.; W (max.):
0.57 m.; Th (average): 0.11 m.
Ca. A.D. 90. Compare J. M. C. Toynbee, J. B.
Ward Perkins, *PBSR* 18 (1950) 15, pls. 8–12.

 Unpublished.

194 →
RELIEF WITH STILL LIFE
Museum of Fine Arts, Boston, Massachusetts
Classical Department Exchange Fund
(1979.613)
From an English private collection
Marble, H: 0.295 m.; W: 0.195 m.
The spiny lobster/crayfish and the murex
brandaris (source of the famous purple
murex dye) are unusual in ancient sculp-
ture, as is the combination of landscape and
still-life elements. Compare the fragment
of a Dionysiac landscape in the Fogg Art
Museum, 1949.47.145.

 M. Grant, *Cities of Vesuvius* (1971) 119, ill.;
R. Brilliant, *Pompeii A.D. 79* (1979) xiv, ill.

233

195

PASTORAL RELIEF

The St. Louis Art Museum, St. Louis, Missouri
(75:42)

Yellowish marble, H: 0.34 m.; W: 0.467 m.
Perhaps Paris watching his herd on Mt. Ida.
Late first or early second century A.D. Compare Munich Glyptothek *Beschreibung* (1900)
257, no. 251.

L. A. Brokaw, *Marsyas* 2 (1942) 17 ff.; *SLAM
Handbook* (1975) 44, ill.

196

COMPOSITE CAPITAL WITH
DIONYSOS AND CENTAURS,
ONE OF A PAIR
Isabella Stewart Gardner Museum,
Boston, Massachusetts
(S10s6)
Purchased in Florence, 1897; perhaps from the
eastern shore of the Adriatic
 Pentelic marble, H: 0.395 m.; W: 0.46 m.
The other three sides show Maenads with
tympanum and a vine-crowned satyr.
Ca. A.D. 230–280.

Sculpture in the Isabella Stewart Gardner Museum
(1977) 55–56, no. 80.

197

MITHRAS SLAYING THE BULL

The Virginia Museum of Fine Arts,
Richmond, Virginia

Glasgow Fund (67-58)

Probably found in Rome

Marble, H: 0.79 m.; W: 0.99 m.

Ca. A.D. 275.

P. L. Near, *Arts in Virginia* 11 (1971) 16, ill.;
M. J. Vermaseren, *Hommages à Marcel Renard* 3 (*Col-*
lection Latomus 103) (1969) 646–647, fig. 5; *Ancient*
Art in the Virginia Museum (1973) 130–131, no. 148.

198
MITHRAS SLAYING THE BULL
Cincinnati Art Museum, Cincinnati, Ohio
Gift of Mr. and Mrs. Fletcher E. Nyce
(1968.112)
From the Via Praeneste, Rome, where it was
reused as a doorstep
Marble, H: 0.625 m.; W: 0.952 m.
Second half of the second century A.D.

R. L. Gordon, *Journal of Mithraic Studies* 1 (1976)
166–178, 186; *Sculpture Collection of the CAM* (1970)
53; *MMA Bulletin* (Autumn 1977) 34–35; *Age of
Spirituality* 193–195, no. 173.

199
FRAGMENT OF A PEDIMENT
WITH OCEANUS
M. H. de Young Memorial Museum,
San Francisco, California
Gift of Mrs. Phoebe A. Hearst
Found near Rome
Marble, H (max): 0.64 m.; W (max): 0.57 m.
Compare P. Hommel, *Studien zu den römischen*
Figurengiebeln der Kaiserzeit (1954) 49–51,
fig. 10. Ca. A.D. 225.

   Unpublished.

XI Roman Sarcophagi

200 (See colorplate 20.)
SARCOPHAGUS WITH ORESTES
AND THE FURIES
The Cleveland Museum of Art, Cleveland, Ohio
Gift of the John Huntington Art and Poly-
technic Trust (28.856)
Greek marble, H: 0.80 m.; L: 2.11 m.
Hadrianic work related to a sarcophagus in
the Lateran dated by inscription A.D. 134.

   CMA Bulletin 15 (April 1928) 90-91, ill.;
J. M. C. Toynbee, *The Hadrianic School* (1934)
183 f.; C. C. Vermeule, *Matz Festschrift* 101-102;
G. M. A. Hanfmann, *Roman Art* (1964) 113, no. 119.

201 (See colorplate 21.)
SARCOPHAGUS
WITH EROTES AND VICTORIAE SUP-
PORTING A GORGONEION SHIELD
SYMBOLIC OF A DIONYSIAC TRIUMPH
The Walters Art Gallery, Baltimore, Maryland
(23.36)
From Rome, via Salaria, a tomb complex of
the Licinii
Marble, H (max.): 1.20 m.; L: 2.24 m.
Ca. A.D. 210.

Reinach, *Rép. rel.* 2 (1912) 198, no. 3; *AJA*
(1915) 23, fig. 10; K. Lehmann-Hartleben, E. C.
Olsen, *Dionysiac Sarcophagi in Baltimore* (1942)
19–20; V. H. Poulsen, *JWAG* 11 (1948) 9; D. K.
Hill, *Archaeology* 10 (1957) 21; F. Matz, *Ein römisches
Meisterwerk: Der Jahreszeitensarkophag Badminton–
New York* (1958) 152, 156; R. Brilliant, *The Arch of
Septimius Severus in the Roman Forum, MAAR* 29
(1967) 111, n. 20, fig. 34; J. B. Ward-Perkins,
RendPontAcc 48 (1975–76) 191–238, fig. 10.

202
FRONT OF A SARCOPHAGUS
WITH THE LIFE OF DIONYSOS

The Art Museum, Princeton University,
Princeton, New Jersey
John Maclean Magie and Gertrude Magie
Fund (49-110)
From Rome
Proconnesian marble, H: 0.385 m.; L (as pre-
served): 1.50 m.
The right side is at Woburn Abbey; another
fragment in Arezzo belongs on the left.
Ca. A.D. 190–200.

L. Curtius, *JOAI* 36 (1946) 42 ff.; F. F. Jones,
Archaeology 7 (1954) 242; J. S. Held, *Rubens Draw-
ings* 1 (1959) 129, fig. 39; C. C. Vermeule and D. von
Bothmer, *AJA* 63 (1959) 347; F. F. Jones and
R. Goldberg, *Ancient Art in the Art Museum* (1960)
62–63; M. Bieber, *The History of the Greek and Roman
Theater* (1961) fig. 93; E. Simon, *RM* 69 (1962)
136 ff.; R. Turcan, *Les sarcophages romains à representations dionysiaques* (1966) 51, 164, 167–168, 381, 384,
407, 412 ff., 524; *ArtJ* 26 (1967) 172, fig. 2; F. Matz,
Die dionysischen Sarkophage 3 (1969) 354 ff., no. 202;
Antiquity in the Renaissance, Smith College Museum
of Art (1978) no. 15.

203
ATHENIAN SARCOPHAGUS WITH DIONYSIAC REVELS
Isabella Stewart Gardner Museum,
Boston, Massachusetts
(S12e3)
From Tivoli (according to Aldroandi) and
Rome, the Farnesina (1556) and the Palazzo
Farnese; purchased from the Sciarra collec-
tion 1898
Pentelic marble, H: 1.05 m.; L: 2.24 m.
Late Severan work, ca. A.D. 225.

F. Matz, *Die antiken Sarkophagreliefs* 4.1; *Die
dionysischen Sarkophage* 1 (1968) 106–110, no. 9, pls.
13–15; *Sculpture in the Isabella Stewart Gardner Museum* (1977) 44–46, no. 61 (with previous bibl.); *The
Connoisseur* (May 1978) 46–47.

204

FRAGMENT OF A HORSE

The Ackland Art Museum, The University of
North Carolina, Chapel Hill, North Carolina
Whitaker Fund (77.66.1)
Marble, H: 0.794 m.; W: 0.381 m.
From a lion-hunt sarcophagus of the late
second century A.D.

Unpublished.

205
SARCOPHAGUS
WITH THE DRAGGING OF HECTOR
AROUND THE WALLS OF TROY
Rhode Island School of Design, Museum of Art,
Providence, Rhode Island
(21.074)
From Rome
Marble, H (max.): 1.404 m.; L: 2.329 m.
Asia Minor workshop, ca. A.D. 190.

Vermeule, *Roman Imperial Art* 61, fig. 24; B. S.
Ridgway, *Catalogue of the Classical Collection, Classical Sculpture* (1972) 96–98, 212–216, no. 38.

206

FRAGMENT OF A SARCOPHAGUS
OR ARCHITECTURAL RELIEF
WITH MYTHOLOGICAL
OR ALLEGORICAL SCENE:
ALEXANDER THE GREAT
AS MELEAGER (?)

The Art Institute of Chicago, Chicago, Illinois
Lent by the Alsdorf Foundation (57.1968)
From near Antioch in Syria
Pentelic marble, H: 0.95 m.; L: 1.20 m.
Ca. A.D. 200.

C. C. Vermeule, *Studies Presented to George M. A.
Hanfmann* (1971) 176, pl. 45; G. Koch, *AA* (1978)
116–135; *Search for Alexander* 119, no. 40.

207
FRAGMENTARY SARCOPHAGUS
WITH THE RETURN OF MELEAGER'S
BODY TO KALYDON
The Museum of Fine Arts, Houston, Texas
Agnes Cullen Arnold Endowment Fund
(76.228)
From Italy
Marble, H: 0.62 m.; L: 2.10 m.
The late Severan style is very strongly in the
classical mode, perhaps reflecting a Hadrianic
relief; ca. A.D. 220–230. The young man in the
chariot at left has portrait features and may
represent the deceased.

Houston (magazine) (August 1976) 50; *ArtJ* 36
(1976–77) 162; *A Guide to the Collection* (1981) 14,
no. 24.

208
SARCOPHAGUS
WITH EROTES PARODYING
DIONYSOS AND HERAKLES
The Virginia Museum of Fine Arts,
Richmond, Virginia
Williams Fund (60-1)
Formerly in the Lanckoronski collection,
Vienna
Asia Minor marble, H: 0.99 m.; L: 2.30 m.
Pamphylian sarcophagus; the reliefs have
been sawed apart for mounting on a wall.
Ca. A.D. 150.

Palais Lanckoronski (1903) 10; C. C. Vermeule,
Matz Festschrift 109; H. Wiegartz, *Kleinasiatische*
Säulensarkophage (1965) 168, pl. 42 a, b; *Ancient Art*
in the Virginia Museum (1973) 110–111, no. 129.

209

FRAGMENT OF A SARCOPHAGUS,
CAPTIVE BARBARIAN

Allen Memorial Art Museum, Oberlin College,
Oberlin, Ohio

R. T. Miller, Jr. Fund (40.39)

From Smyrna

White (Proconnesian?) marble, H: 0.508 m.;
W: 0.875 m.

The man with the Phrygian cap may well be
Odysseus, from a representation of the Theft
of the Palladion by him and Diomedes, in-
stead of a Parthian prisoner. Sarcophagus of
Lydian or western Asia Minor type, to be
dated in the late Severan period, ca. A.D. 225.

J. Strzygowski, *BZ* 10 (1901) 726; G. Mendel,
BCH 33 (1909) 333, no. 12; E. Weigand, *JdI* 29
(1914) 37 ff., no. 73; C. R. Morey, *Sardis* 5.1 (1924)
43; E. Capps, *AMAM Bulletin* 2 (1945) 53 ff.;
M. Lawrence, *MAAR* 20 (1951) 147–148, fig. 34;
C. C. Vermeule, *Matz Festschrift* 98 ff., no. 104;
H. Wiegartz, *Kleinasiatische Säulensarkophage, Ist.*
Forsch. 26 (1965) 76, 125, 165–166; Vermeule, *Ro-*
man Imperial Art 60–61, 87, 415.

210
SARCOPHAGUS FRAGMENT WITH
NEREIDS, TRITONS, AND SEAHORSES
Dartmouth College Museum and Galleries,
Hanover, New Hampshire
(S.977.21)
Formerly in Wilton House
Marble, H: 0.37 m.; L: 0.85 m.
Late second century A.D.

O. Alvarez, "The Dartmouth Sarcophagus," *The*
Celestial Brides (Stockbridge, Mass., 1978) 143, 274,
ill.; *Acquisitions 1974–1978* (1979) 18, ill.

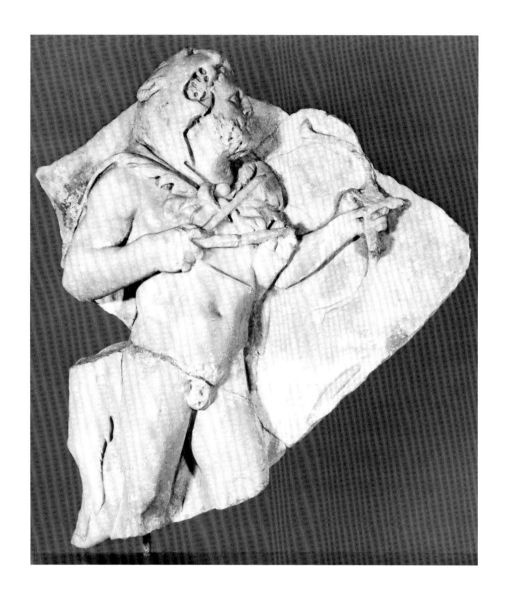

211

FRAGMENT OF A LABORS-OF-
HERAKLES SARCOPHAGUS

Honolulu Academy of Arts, Honolulu, Hawaii
Gift of Mrs. Charles M. Cooke (3602)
Formerly in the S. Pozzi collection, Paris
Marble, H: 0.56 m.; W: 0.51 m.
Mature, bearded Herakles originally between
columns with drawn bow and arrow, prob-
ably part of the labor of the Stymphalian
Birds. Mid-second century A.D.

Collection S. Pozzi, G. Petit (June 25–27, 1919),
no. 363, no ill.; Del Chiaro, *West Coast Collections* 31,
no. 32, ill.

212 →

FRAGMENT OF A LABORS-OF-
HERAKLES SARCOPHAGUS

Honolulu Academy of Arts, Honolulu, Hawaii
Gift of Mrs. Charles M. Cooke (3601)
Formerly in the collection of M. Couchoud,
Versailles and said to be from Nikopolis;
formerly in the S. Pozzi collection, Paris
Marble, H: 0.725 m.
Youthful, beardless Herakles in frieze depic-
tion of three of the Labors: Erymanthean
Boar, Hydra of Lerna, and Nemean lion.
Mid-second century A.D.

Collection S. Pozzi, G. Petit (June 25–27, 1919)
no. 363 ill. (said to have been found at Previsa in
Albania); T. Philadelpheus, *ArchEph* (1922) 79,
fig. 27; A. Giuliano, *StArch* 4 (1962) 42, no. 200;
C. C. Vermeule, *Matz Festschrift* 109; Del Chiaro,
West Coast Collections 31, no. 31, ill.

253

213

FRAGMENT OF A SARCOPHAGUS
WITH CHILD OR EROS

Los Angeles County Museum of Art,
Los Angeles, California
William Randolph Hearst collection
(49.14.2)
Asia Minor marble, H: 0.50 m.
Third century A.D.

  H. Wiegartz, *Kleinasiatische Säulensarkophage*
(1965) 135, 164, pl. 19, fig. f; Del Chiaro, *West Coast*
Collections 31, 71, no. 29.

214
SARCOPHAGUS WITH THE
THREE GRACES, GENII, EROTES, ETC.
Carnegie Institute, Museum of Art,
Pittsburgh, Pennsylvania
Gift of Baroness Cassel van Doorn
(58.4.2)
Presumably from Italy, via France
Marble, H: 0.47 m.; L: 1.83 m.
Ca. A.D. 225.

C. C. Vermeule, *Matz Festschrift* 104, pl. 29, fig. 2;
H. Sichtermann, *RM* 76 (1969) 271–272, pl. 89,
fig. 2.

215
SARCOPHAGUS WITH A LADY
AS A MUSE, FOUR MUSES,
AND A PHILOSOPHER
The J. Paul Getty Museum, Malibu, California
(72.AA.90)
White fine-grained Thasian (?) marble,
H (max.): 1.375 m.; W (approx.): 2.24 m.
Ca. A.D. 250–275.

   Magna Graecia, Galerie Kamer, New York
(1967) no. 29; C. C. Vermeule, N. Neuerburg,
Catalogue of the Ancient Art (1973) 40–41, no. 90;
JPGM Checklist of Antiquities 2 (1979) 25, no. V40.

216

FRAGMENT OF A SARCOPHAGUS LID
WITH RECLINING SEASON

Wellesley College Museum, Jewett Arts Center,
Wellesley, Massachusetts
(1970.12)

Marble, H: 0.26 m.; W: 0.465 m.

Ca. A.D. 175.

    Kunstwerke der Antike, Auktion 34, Münzen und
Medaillen AG, Basel (6 May 1967) 111, no. 210,
pl. 73; *ArtQ* 33 (1970) 454.

217
SARCOPHAGUS WITH TONDO BUST
SUPPORTED BY EROTES
SYMBOLIC OF THE FOUR SEASONS
Elvehjem Museum of Art, University of Wisconsin,
Madison, Wisconsin
Max W. Zabel Fund (69.13.1)
From Italy, via England
Marble, H: 0.71 m.; L: 1.83 m.
Ca. A.D 280.

Progress Report Second Semester (1969–70) 3, ill.;
Bulletin (1970–71) 45; Sotheby's (London, 1 July
1969) 65, no. 121, ill.; C. C. Vermeule, D. von
Bothmer, *AJA* 63 (1959) 344–345, pl. 85, figs.
37–38; *ArtQ* (Autumn 1970) 319, ill.

218 (top)
SARCOPHAGUS WITH SEASONS
AND DIONYSIAC ATTRIBUTES
M. H. de Young Memorial Museum,
San Francisco, California
(54662)
From Rome, via Florence
Marble, H: 0.51 m.; L: 1.78 m.
Ca. A.D. 280.

C. C. Vermeule, *Matz Festschrift* 106, pl. 30, fig. 1;
Del Chiaro, *West Coast Collections* 30, 70, no. 27.

219
EARLY CHRISTIAN STRIGILAR
SARCOPHAGUS WITH ORATOR
FLANKED BY ORANT
AND GOOD SHEPHERD
The Detroit Institute of Arts, Detroit, Michigan
(26.138)
From Florence
Marble, H: 0.65 m.; L: 2.15 m.
The short sides are enriched with baskets
containing produce.

Bulletin of the DIA 18 (1926) 8, 9, ill.; *Masterpieces
of Painting and Sculpture* (1949) 27; *Sculpture in the
DIA* (1966) 34; C. C. Vermeule, *Matz Festschrift* 102.

220

SARCOPHAGUS WITH CHILDREN
The Walter P. Chrysler Museum,
Norfolk, Virginia
(77.1276)
From the Villa Carpegna; formerly in the
collection of William Boyce Thompson,
Yonkers (Elizabeth Seton College)
Marble, H: 1.54 m.; L: 2.13 m.; W: 0.81 m.
The sarcophagus body is Tetrarchic; the lid
with the reclining woman is earlier but possi-
bly reused in antiquity (G. Koch).

F. Matz, F. von Duhn, *Antike Bildwerke in Rom*
(1881–82) no. 2208; J. Jüthner, *RM* 43 (1928) 17,
pl. 3; H. Wiegartz, *Mélanges Mansel* 1 (1974) 349,
n. 17.

221

FRAGMENT OF A SARCOPHAGUS
WITH CHRIST BLESSING THE LOAVES
AND FISHES

The Dumbarton Oaks Collection, Harvard
University, Washington, D.C.
(59.3)
Marble, H: 0.305 m.; W: 0.26 m.
Probably from Rome, carved A.D. 320–340.

   Handbook of the Byzantine Collection (1967) 6, no.
18; G. Vikan, *Catalogue of Sculpture* (forthcoming).

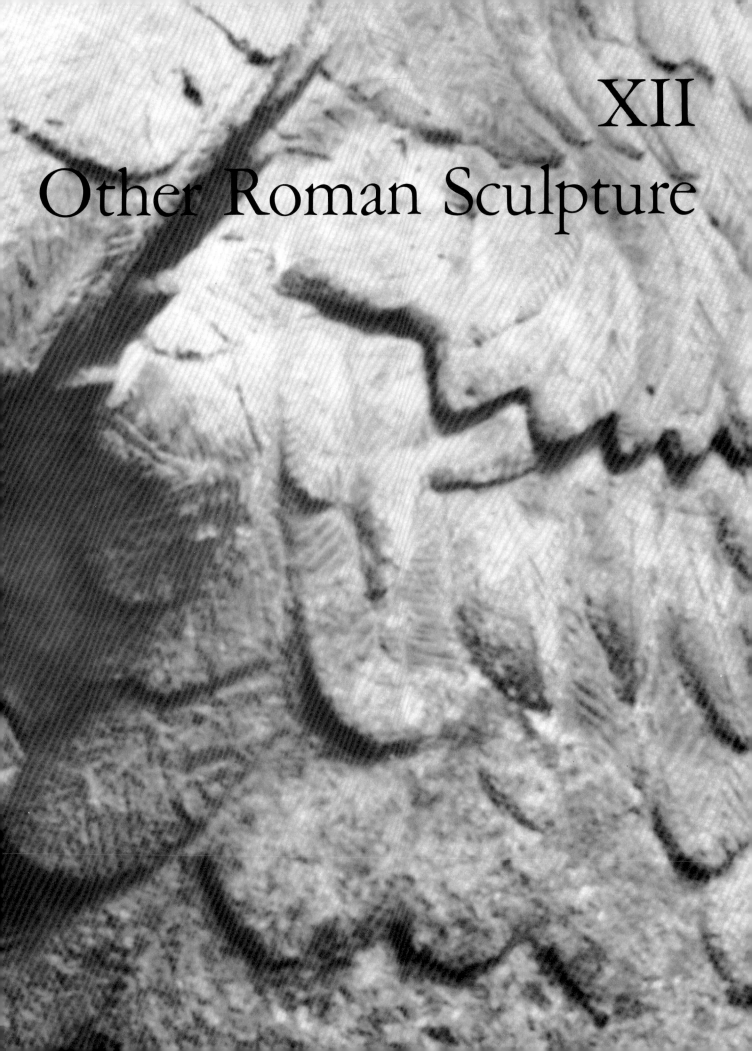

222

ROMAN CINERARY CHEST

The Minneapolis Institute of Arts,
Minneapolis, Minnesota

John R. Van Derlip Fund (62.20 a-b)

Marble, H (lid and chest): 0.48 m.; W: 0.28 m.;

D: 0.195 m.

Ca. A.D. 75. The lid does not belong.

   ArtQ 25 (1962) 262, 265; *Bulletin de Musée*
National de Varsone 3 (1962) 43, fig. 6, no. 2.

223
CINERARIUM OR GRAVE ALTAR
Isabella Stewart Gardner Museum,
Boston, Massachusetts
(S27e29)
Said to have been found near S. Paolo fuori
le Mura, Rome
Pentelic marble, H: 0.65 m.; W: 0.465 m.
Ca. A.D. 50.

  Sculpture in the Isabella Stewart Gardner Museum
(1977) 35, no. 46.

224
STATUE BASE OR GRAVE ALTAR
Villa Vizcaya Museum and Gardens,
Miami, Florida
(B166 (M0 14))
From Rome; formerly in the Borghese
collection
Greek island marble, H: 0.90 m.; L (at base):
1.525 m.
Roman work in the East Greek style of the
Hadrianic period.

C. C. Vermeule, *Matz Festschrift* 103.

225

FRAGMENT OF AN ALTAR
WITH VICTORIA

*R. H. Lowie Museum of Anthropology, University
of California, Berkeley, California*
Gift of Mrs. Phoebe A. Hearst (8–4283)
Found near Rome; formerly in the Comin
collection, Rome
Marble, H: 0.45 m.; W: 0.50 m.; D: 0.33 m.
Severan work, ca. A.D. 200.

Selection 1966, The University Art Collections
(1966) 38–40, no. 31.

226

THRONE

Isabella Stewart Gardner Museum,
Boston, Massachusetts

(S5c4)

Said to be from Telesina, South Italy (or near
Benevento?)

Pentelic (?) marble, H: 0.64 m.; W: 0.665 m.

Late-second-century-A.D. copy of a work of the
late Hellenistic period with symbolic figure
in Near Eastern garb between sphinxes.

G. M. A. Richter, *The Furniture of the Greeks,*
Etruscans and Romans (1966) 33, figs. 160–161;
Sculpture in the Isabella Stewart Gardner Museum
(1977) 53–54, no. 78 (with previous bibl.).

227
TABLE SUPPORT WITH GRIFFINS
Villa Vizcaya Museum and Gardens,
Miami, Florida
(463 (MO 18))
From the regions of Pompeii and
Herculaneum
Marble, H: 0.795 m.; W (at base): 0.82 m.
Compare G. M. A. Richter, *The Furniture of*
the Greeks, Etruscans and Romans (1966) 113,
figs. 578, 579. Before A.D. 79.

C. C. Vermeule, *Studies in Ancient Egypt, the Ae-*
gean, and the Sudan. Essays in Honor of Dows Dunham
(1981) 185–186.

228
EAGLE
The J. Paul Getty Museum, Malibu, California
(72.AB.151)
Said to be from Ibidjick, ancient Bubon,
in southwest Asia Minor
Bronze, H: 1.04 m.
Ca. A.D. 200.

   B. Fredericksen, ed., *The J. Paul Getty Museum*
(1975) 39, ill.; *JPGM Guidebook* (1976) 45, ill.; C. C.
Vermeule, *Festschrift Jucker* 188, no. M, pl. 62.2;
JPGM Checklist of Antiquities 2 (1979) 38, no. V80.

XIII Roman Portraits

229
SEATED FUNERARY STATUE
OF A MAN IN THE GUISE OF
A HELLENISTIC POET
Albright-Knox Art Gallery, Buffalo, New York
Charles W. Goodyear Fund (36:1)
Found outside Rome along the Via Appia
Marble, H: 1.37 m.
New research has raised doubts that the head,
much reworked, belongs to the body.
Ca. 80–50 B.C.

K. Lehmann-Hartleben, *AJA* 46 (1942) 204–216,
figs. 6–12, pls. 11, 12; *Paintings and Sculpture in the
Permanent Collection* (1949) 172–173, 204, no. 83, ill;
R. Wünsche, *MJb* 31 (1980) 26, figs. 20, 21.

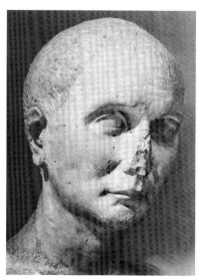

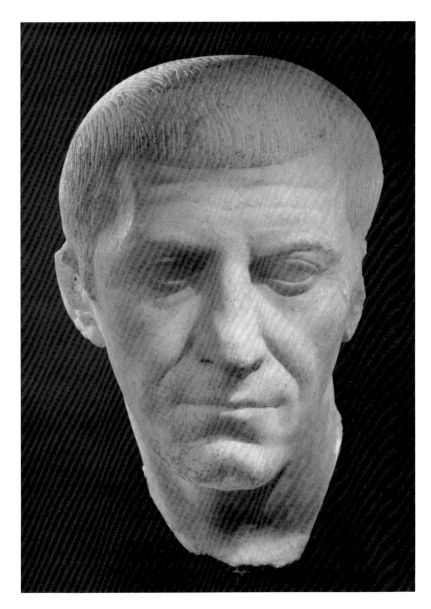

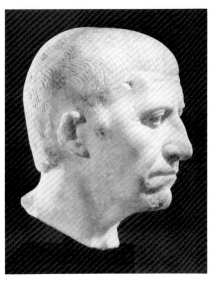

230

PORTRAIT HEAD OF A MAN
Montreal Museum of Fine Arts,
Montreal, Quebec, Canada
(974.55)
Marble, H: 0.275 m.
Said to be a replica of ca. A.D. 100 of a Re-
publican portrait, possibly L. Domitius
Ahenobarbus (90–48 B.C.) or C. Cassius
Longinus (90/85–42 B.C.).

   H. Jucker, *Apollo* 103 (1976) 350–357, figs. 1–5;
MMFA Guide (1977) 42, fig. 27; J. M. C. Toynbee,
Roman Historical Portraits (1978) 61–62, fig. 85.

231

PORTRAIT HEAD OF A MAN

The University Museum, University of
Pennsylvania, Philadelphia, Pennsylvania
(32–36–64)
From Minturnae, temple of Julius Caesar
Marble, H: 0.20 m.
Ca. 45 B.C.

A. Adriani, *NotScavi* 16 (1938) 198–199; *University Museum Bulletin* 22 (June 1958) cover; C. C.
Vermeule, *PAPS* 108 (1964) 109, fig. 4; *Guide to
the Collection: The Mediterranean World* (1965)
64–67.

232
PORTRAIT BUST OF A MAN
The Detroit Institute of Arts, Detroit, Michigan
(27.211)
From Rome
Marble, H: 0.41 m.
Perhaps a retrospective portrait of an original
of ca. 40 B.C.

Bulletin of the DIA 9 (1927) 5; C. C. Vermeule,
PAPS 108 (1964) 104; *DIA Illustrated Handbook*
(1971) 37, ill.; W. H. Peck, *Bulletin of the DIA* 50
(1971) 53, 57.

233

PORTRAIT HEAD OF A ROMAN,
PERHAPS MARK ANTONY

The Brooklyn Museum, Brooklyn, New York

Charles Edwin Wilbour Fund (54.51)

Said to have come from Alexandria

Green schist, H: 0.205 m.

Ca. 30 B.C.

Five Years of Collecting, The Brooklyn Museum
(1956) 21 ff., no. 24, pls. 43–44; O. Brendel, *Collection Latomus* 58 (1962) 366–367; F. Johansen,
Meddelelser fra Ny Carlsberg Glyptotek 35 (1978) 70,
76, fig. 23; G. Grimm, *JdI* 85 (1970) 162; J. M. C.
Toynbee, *Roman Historical Portraits* (1978) 45, fig. 52.

234
PORTRAIT BUST OF A MAN
Cincinnati Art Museum, Cincinnati, Ohio
William Hayden Chatfield collection
(1957.485)
Marble, H: 0.457 m.
Perhaps a Trajanic copy of a Republican
portrait of ca. 40 B.C.

   Sculpture Collection of the CAM (1970) 50–51.

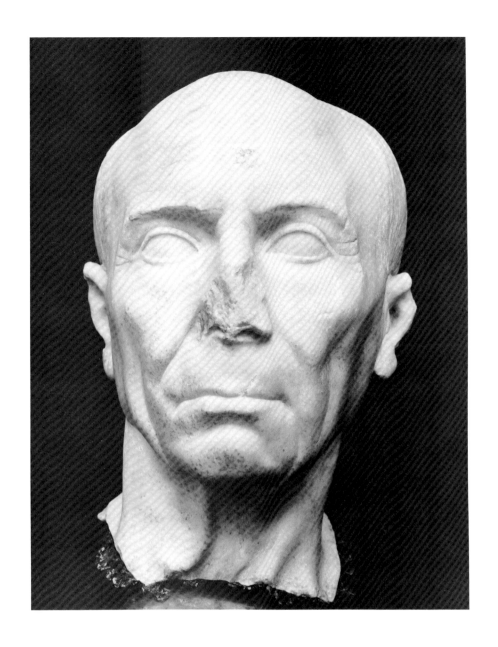

235
PORTRAIT HEAD OF A MAN, PERHAPS
A RETROSPECTIVE PORTRAIT
Rhode Island School of Design, Museum of Art,
Providence, Rhode Island
(25.063)
Presumably from Italy; formerly in the col-
lection of E. P. Warren
Marble, H: 0.336 m.
A later copy of a Republican original of
ca. 30 B.C.

A. M. Davidson, *AJA* 44 (1940) 114; *Greek and*
Roman Portraits, Museum of Fine Arts, Boston
(1959) no. 32; B. S. Ridgway, *Catalogue of the*
Classical Collection, Classical Sculpture (1972) 80–81,
195–196, no. 30.

236
PORTRAIT STATUE OF A LADY
Worcester Art Museum, Worcester, Massachusetts
(1978.78)
Marble, H: 2.006 m.
Perhaps Octavia, the sister of Octavian, later
the emperor Augustus, ca. 40–30 B.C.

   WAM Journal 1 (1977–78) 61, ill. 47.

237
PORTRAIT HEAD OF A MAN
The Cleveland Museum of Art, Cleveland, Ohio
J. H. Wade Fund (66.20)
From Egypt
Marble, H: 0.327 m.
Mid-first-century-A.D. copy after a portrait of
ca. 30 B.C., perhaps C. Cornelius Gallus.

CMA Bulletin (September 1966) 185, no. 5;
Archaeology 19 (1966) 278, ill.; R. Burton, *The Connoisseur* 163 (1966) 128–129, ill.; *CMA Handbook*
(1969) 24; J. D. Cooney, *CMA Bulletin* (January
1967) 17–21, ill.

238
PORTRAIT HEAD
OF THE EMPEROR AUGUSTUS
The Detroit Institute of Arts, Detroit, Michigan
Gift of Mr. and Mrs. James S. Holden (24.101)
Found in Rome in 1914
Marble, H: 0.483 m.
Heroic-scale portrait of the early part of
Augustus's reign.

   Bulletin of the DIA 6 (1925) 636, no. 6 ill.; *ibid.* 11
(1930) 29, ill.; D. M. Robinson, *AJA* 30 (1926)
127–128, fig. 2; R. Montoni, *Civiltà Romana* 5
(1938) 59, 88, no. 32; C. C. Vermeule, *PAPS* 108
(1964) 104.

239
PORTRAIT HEAD
OF THE EMPEROR AUGUSTUS
Kelsey Museum of Archaeology, University of
Michigan, Ann Arbor, Michigan
(75.1.1)
Fine-grained white marble, H: 0.30 m.
An early replica of the Prima Porta type,
perhaps from the eastern empire.

Kelsey, *Roman Portraiture* 14–15, no. 3, ill.

240

PORTRAIT HEAD
OF THE EMPEROR AUGUSTUS

The Walters Art Gallery, Baltimore, Maryland
(23.21)

Marble, H: 0.403 m.

From a draped statue; the top and sides of the head were made of different material and attached with clamps. Ca. A.D. 5.

Handbook (1936) 39, fig.; D. K. Hill, *AJA* 41 (1937) 112; C. C. Vermeule, *PAPS* 108 (1964) 101; D. K. Hill, *Bulletin WAG* 22 (1970); P. Zanker, *Studien zu den Augustus-Porträts*, 1: *Der Actium Typus* (1973) no. 34a; G. Grimm, *Römische Mummienmasken aus Aegypten* (1974) 110, n. 87.

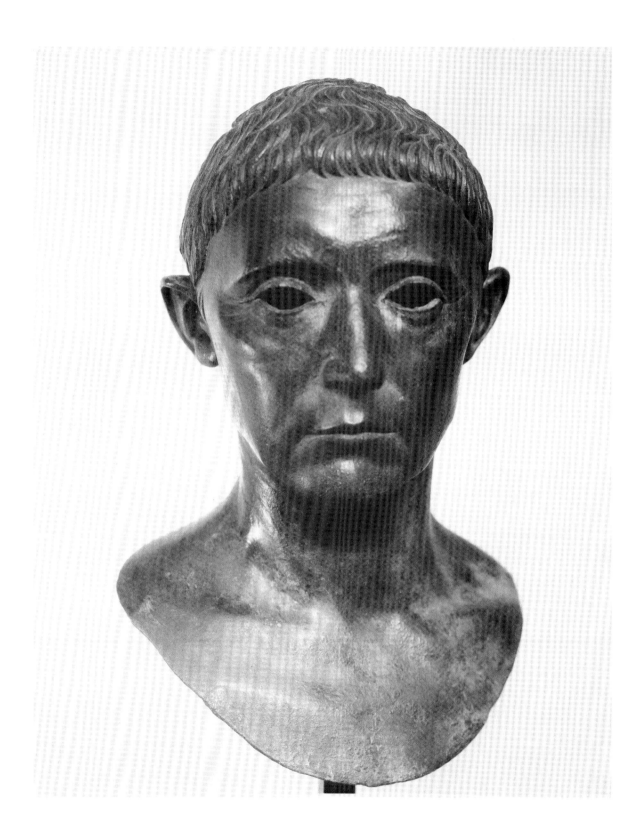

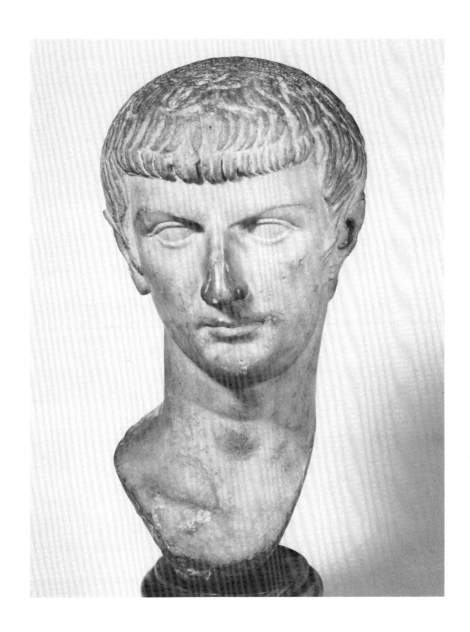

241 ←

PORTRAIT BUST OF A MAN

The Cleveland Museum of Art, Cleveland, Ohio

Gift of the John Huntington Art and
Polytechnic Trust (28.860)

Seemingly from the region of Naples

Bronze, H: 0.38 m.

Probably to be dated to the reign of Augustus.
The eyes were originally inlaid. Compare the
bronze bust in Leningrad (B. Schweitzer, *Die
Bildniskunst der römischen Republik* [1948] 120,
no. J5, figs. 190–191).

M. Bieber, *Art in America* (April 1944) 65–83,
fig. 4; Worcester, *Roman Portraits* 18–19, no. 5;
G. M. A. Hanfmann, *Roman Art* (1964) 171, pl. 69;
Master Bronzes 234–235, no. 228; *CMA Handbook*
(1969) 24; Ackland, *Ancient Portraits* no. 15.

242

PORTRAIT HEAD OF A MAN

*Sterling and Francine Clark Art Institute,
Williamstown, Massachusetts*

(1007)

Marble, H: 0.47 m.

Nose restored. Second quarter of the first
century A.D.

Unpublished.

243
PORTRAIT HEAD OF
THE EMPEROR TIBERIUS
Fogg Art Museum, Harvard University,
Cambridge, Massachusetts
David M. Robinson Fund, jointly with The
Department of Classics McDaniel Fund
(1963.54)
From near Rome
Marble, H: 0.31 m.
Ca. A.D. 22

   Acquisitions, 1962–1963 (1964) 114, ill.; C. C.
Vermeule, *PAPS* 108 (1964) 102, figs. 10 a, b.

244
PORTRAIT OF DRUSUS MAJOR,
BROTHER OF TIBERIUS
The University Museum, University of
Pennsylvania, Philadelphia, Pennsylvania
(32-33-66)
From Minturnae
Marble, H: 0.43 m.
Posthumous copy of a type of ca. A.D. 41–45,
made for insertion into a statue body. Com-
pare L. Fabbrini, *Boll. d'Arte* (October–
December 1964) 315–326.

A. Adriani, *NotScavi* 16 (1938) 208, no. 55,
pl. 15.1–2; H. Fuhrmann, *AA* 55 (1940) 510–512,
fig. 45; K. Matthews, *Expedition* 1.4 (1959) 36–37.

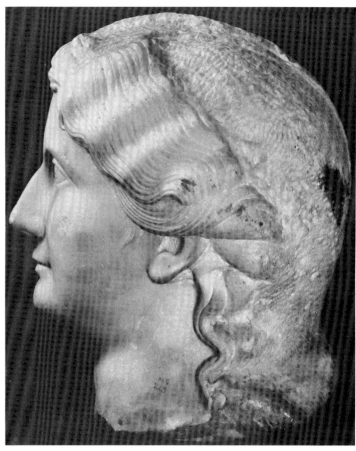

245

PORTRAIT HEAD OF
AGRIPPINA THE ELDER

The University Museum, University of
Pennsylvania, Philadelphia, Pennsylvania
(MS 213)

From Troy

Marble, H: 0.40 m.

From a posthumous statue of ca. A.D. 38.

S. B. Luce, *Catalogue of the Mediterranean Section*
(1921) 190, no. 58 (the body in the Berlin Museum); C. C. Vermeule, *PAPS* 108 (1964) 110,
fig. 14; idem, *Roman Imperial Art* 192–193, fig. 122;
V. Poulsen, *MJb* 19 (1968) 21, n. 61; K. Fittschen,
GGA 225 (1973) 55, no. 12; Inan-Rosenbaum,
Porträtplastik 150–152, no. 98, pl. 86.

246

PORTRAIT HEAD OF A WOMAN

The Hispanic Society of America,
New York, New York

(D.203)

From Spain

White Italian marble, H: 0.39 m.

Perhaps the empress Livia, for insertion in a
statue body.

J. Pijoan, *Antique Marbles in the Collection of the
HSA* (1917) 22–26, ill.; *HSA Handbook* (1928) 61,
ill.; A. García y Bellido, *Esculturas romanas de España
y Portugal* (1949) 47–49, no. 36, pl. 32 (as Agrippina
Minor); *A History of the HSA, 1904–1954* (1954) 99,
fig. 66; J. de C. Serra-Ràfols, *Cuadernos de Arqueología
e Historia de la Ciudad* 6 (1964) 55–57; K. Polaschek,
StArch 17 (1973) 30, pls. 12.2, 15.1, 18.1 (as possibly
deified Drusilla).

247

PORTRAIT HEAD OF A BOY

The Lyndon Baines Johnson Library,

Austin, Texas

Gift to President Johnson from His Excellency
Antonio Segni, President of the Italian
Republic, January 16, 1964

Marble, H: 0.30 m.

The rounded neck base is for insertion into a
statue.

Unpublished.

248
PORTRAIT HEAD OF
THE EMPEROR CALIGULA
Worcester Art Museum, Worcester, Massachusetts
(1914.23)
Found near Marino at Lake Albano at the
same time and place as the marble bust of
Caligula in the Metropolitan Museum of
Art (14.37)
Marble, H: 0.488 m.
Ca. A.D. 40.

WAM Bulletin 5.3 (1914) 12, ill.; *ibid.* 23 (1932)
4, 17, ill.; E. H. Swift, *AJA* 25 (1921) 356; Chase,
American Collections 179, fig. 217; F. P. Johnson,
AJA 30 (1926) 162; R. West, *Römische Porträt-
plastik* 1 (1933) 201; V. Poulsen, *Meddelelser fra Ny
Carlsberg Glyptotek* 14 (1957) 34–35, figs. 7, 8; idem,
ActaA 29 (1958) 185–186, figs. 13–14; Worcester,
Roman Portraits 26–27, no. 9.

249 (See colorplate 22.)
TOGATE STATUE OF
THE EMPEROR CALIGULA
The Virginia Museum of Fine Arts,
Richmond, Virginia
(71-20)
From Rome
Marble, H: 2.09 m.
Ca. A.D. 38

   Ancient Art in the Virginia Museum (1973)
122–123, no. 139; H. Jucker, *Arts in Virginia* 13
(1973) 16–25, figs. 1–8.

250

PORTRAIT OF A ROMAN LADY
AS CYBELE

The J. Paul Getty Museum, Malibu, California
(57.AA.19)
From Rome; formerly in the Mattei collection, Rome, and the collection of Lowther Castle
Marble, H: 1.62 m.
Ca. A.D. 50–60.

M. Bieber, *The Statue of Cybele in the J. Paul Getty Museum* (1968); C. C. Vermeule, N. Neuerburg, *Catalogue of the Ancient Art* (1973) 27–28, no. 58; *Roman Portraits in the JPGM*, Philbrook Art Center (1981) 42–43, 123, no. 28 (with full bibl.).

251
PORTRAIT OF A CHILD,
POSSIBLY NERO
The Metropolitan Museum of Art,
New York, New York
Gift of various donors (66.11.5)
Formerly in the collections of Sir Francis Cook
(Doughty House) and Alfred Gallatin
Bronze, H: 0.29 m.
Early first century A.D., possibly a portrait of
the young Nero.

A. Conze, *AA* (1903) 144; Burlington Exhibition 14–15, no. 15, pl. 15; C. Harcourt Smith, *The
Cook Collection* (1908) no. 37, pl. 33; Christie's
(14 July 1925) lot 118, ill.; Arndt-Bruckmann, 107
(1927) nos. 1066–1067; F. Poulsen, *Probleme der
römischen Ikonographie* (1937) 10–13, pl. 12; V. H.
Poulsen, *ActaA* 22 (1951) 122–125, fig. 12; Sotheby's
(13 June 1966) lot 58, ill.; A. Oliver, *MMA Bulletin*
(1967) 264–272.

252

TOGATE STATUE
OF THE YOUNG NERO

The Detroit Institute of Arts, Detroit, Michigan
Gift of the Founders Society (69.218)
Said to have been found in southwest Asia
Minor
Marble, H: 1.40 m.
Probably to be dated ca. A.D. 52, shortly before
the emperor Claudius died and Nero suc-
ceeded him.

C. C. Vermeule, *MFA Bulletin* 67 (1969)
120–128; W. H. Peck, *Bulletin* 50 (1971) 52–58,
figs. 1, 3, 5, 7; *DIA Illustrated Handbook* (1971) 38;
Archaeology (1971) 54, ill.; U. W. Hiesinger, *AJA*
79 (1975) 116, 118, pl. 21, figs. 30, 31.

253
PORTRAIT HEAD
OF THE EMPEROR NERO
University of Missouri Museum of Art and
Archaeology, Columbia, Missouri
Gift of Mr. and Mrs. T. E. Bachman (62.46)
From Egypt
Marble, H: 0.42 m.
The picked beard is secondary, probably mod-
ern. Inserted in a togate statue. Ca. A.D. 69.

Missouri Alumnus (March 1963) 7 (as young
Titus); H. Jucker, *Jahr. d. Bernischen Historischen
Museums* 43–44 (1963–64) 292; C. C. Vermeule,
PAPS 108 (1964) 104, 128, fig. 22; M. Wegner, *Die
Flavier* (1966) 85 (not Titus); C. C. Vermeule, *AJA*
68 (1964) 337; idem, *Roman Imperial Art* 233, fig. 130.

254
PORTRAIT HEAD
OF THE EMPEROR NERO
Worcester Art Museum, Worcester, Massachusetts
(1915.23)
From Rome
Marble, H: 0.38 m.
Broken from a statue. There are iron pins on
the back of the head as if fitted with a sep-
arate crown.

WAM Bulletin 5.4 (1915) 7–9, ill.; *Art through
Fifty Centuries* (1948) 16, fig. 16; *Greek and Roman
Portraits*, Museum of Fine Arts, Boston (1959)
no. 46; Worcester, *Roman Portraits* 28–29, no. 10;
V. Poulsen, *Les Portraits romains* 1 (1962) 34–35;
WAM Handbook (1973) pl. 25; U. W. Hiesinger,
AJA 79 (1975) 113, 120–124, pl. 25, figs. 45–47.

255

PORTRAIT HEAD OF A PRIEST

The St. Louis Art Museum, St. Louis, Missouri

(7:22)

Found in Rome

Marble, H: 0.26 m.

Second half of the first century A.D.

CAM Bulletin 9 (October 1924) 52–53; ill.; Worcester, *Roman Portraits* no. 36 (called late fourth century A.D.); *SLAM Handbook* (1975) 44, ill.

256
COLOSSAL PORTRAIT HEAD OF
THE EMPEROR VESPASIAN
The Walters Art Gallery, Baltimore, Maryland
(23.119)
From Pergamon; formerly in the collections
of J. P. Lambros, Athens, and G. Dattari,
Cairo.
Marble, H: 0.66 m.
The neck fitted a statue draped in the Greek
manner. Compare the colossal Domitian from
Ephesus now in Izmir. Ca. A.D. 75.

J. Hirsch and A. Sambon, Auction (Paris, 1912)
no. 268, pl. 33; G. Daltrop et al., *Die Flavier* (1966)
72–73; Vermeule, *Roman Imperial Art* 229–230,
fig. 129; idem, *PAPS* 108 (1964) 101, 127, fig. 19.

257 →
PORTRAIT HEAD OF
THE EMPEROR DOMITIAN
Museum of Fine Arts, Boston, Massachusetts
Frank B. Bemis Fund (1978.227)
From the region around Rome (?)
Greek island marble, H: 0.205 m.
The emperor is idealized as Hercules, with the
heavy wreath and cauliflowered ears of the
Genzano type. Ca. A.D. 90.

G. Daltrop et al., *Die Flavier* (1966) 105 (Rome
art market); *The Museum Year, 1978–79* (1979) 21,
ill., *Iconographic Studies* (1980) 7–13, figs. 6–7, 20–21.

258

PORTRAIT STATUE OF
THE EMPEROR TRAJAN
Fogg Art Museum, Harvard University,
Cambridge, Massachusetts
Alpheus Hyatt Fund (1954.71)
From Italy, via England
Marble, H: 1.91 m.
Posthumous dedication of ca. A.D. 120.

G. M. A. Hanfmann, *Fogg Art Museum Annual*
Report, 1953–54, 6–7, ill.; idem, C. C. Vermeule,
AJA 61 (1957) 223–253, pls. 68–71, 72, fig. 8; *Greek*
and Roman Portraits, Museum of Fine Arts, Boston
(1959) no. 49; E. Simon, *Latomus* 21 (1962) 175,
pl. 48.

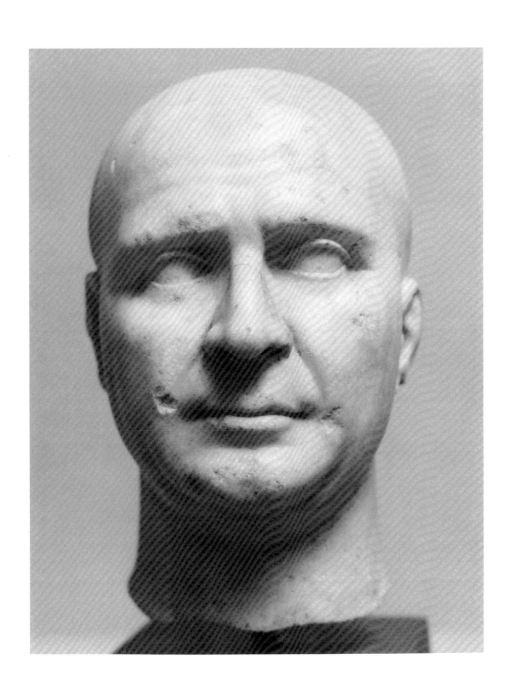

259
PORTRAIT HEAD OF AN ISIS PRIEST
Allen Memorial Art Museum, Oberlin College,
Oberlin, Ohio
Gift of Mrs. Joseph Cook (1902.1)
White (Pentelic?) marble, H: 0.305 m.
The smoothly shaven head and small X
above the right forehead both identify a
priest serving the cult of Isis. Early second
century A.D.

W. Dennison, *AJA* 9 (1905) 11 ff.; C. C. Vermeule, *AMAM Bulletin* 17 (1959–60) 6 ff.; *European
and American Paintings and Sculpture in the AMAM*
(1967) 213, 336, fig. 226.

260
PORTRAIT BUST OF A MAN
John and Mable Ringling Museum of Art,
Sarasota, Florida
(5354)
Ultimately from Italy
Marble, H(max.): 0.705 m.
Considerably damaged by later recutting.
Compare G. Daltrop, *Privatbildnisse*, figs. 11,
17, 20, and 25. Ca. A.D. 115–120.

   Unpublished.

261
PORTRAIT HEAD OF A YOUNG MAN
WEARING A WREATH
Royal Ontario Museum,
Toronto, Ontario, Canada
(959.17.12)
Marble, H: 0.278 m.
Trajanic work of ca. A.D. 110, although some-
times identified as fourth century A.D.

S. Stucchi, *ArchCl* 2 (1950) 204–208, pls. 40.1–2,
41.1–2; C. C. Vermeule, *PAPS* 108 (1964) 115,
fig. 45; W. von Sydow, *Zur Kunstgeschichte des
spätantiken Porträts in 4. Jahr. n. Chr.* (1969) 148–
149; N. Leipen, *AJA* 82 (1978) 109–114, figs. 1–6.

262

PORTRAIT BUST OF A MAN
University of Mississippi Art Gallery,
Oxford, Mississippi
Gift of David M. Robinson (77.3545)
Found at Hadrian's Villa near Tivoli in 1775
by Gavin Hamilton; formerly in the collection
at Margam Park, Wales
Marble, H: 0.64 m.
Ca. A.D. 120.

 Michaelis, *Marbles in Great Britain* 520, no. 10;
F. Poulsen, *Greek and Roman Portraits in English
Country Houses* (1923) 67, no. 48; Daltrop, *Privat-
bildnisse* 118, fig. 18; L. Turnbull, *Archaeological
News* (Fall 1973) 37–40, fig. 4.

263
BUST OF A LADY
William Rockhill Nelson Gallery of Art–Atkins
Museum of Fine Arts, Kansas City, Missouri
Nelson Fund (48-9)
From Egypt, possibly Alexandria
Marble, H: 0.635 m.
The lightly engraved pupils and the acanthus
leaf suggest a date ca. A.D. 115–120, although
the hairstyle follows older fashions in the
capital.

Graindor, *Bustes et statues-portraits d'Égypte ro-*
maine (1937) 109–111, no. 53, pls. 45, 46; *Handbook*
(1959) 37; Worcester, *Roman Portraits* 34–35, no.
13; H. Jucker, *Das Bildnis im Blätterkelch* (1961)
83–84, no. St 26, pl. 32.

264
PORTRAIT
OF THE EMPEROR HADRIAN
Rhode Island School of Design, Museum of Art,
Providence, Rhode Island
Gift of Mrs. Murray S. Danforth (59.050)
From Italy; formerly in the collection of Lord
Melchett
Marble, H: 0.409 m.
The restored bust has been removed. The
head was made for insertion in a statue. Ca.
A.D. 127.

Worcester, *Roman Portraits* 40–41, no. 16; B. S.
Ridgway, *Catalogue of the Classical Collection, Classical
Sculpture* (1972) 88–89, no. 34.

265
PORTRAIT HEAD
OF THE EMPEROR HADRIAN
The Art Institute of Chicago, Chicago, Illinois
Kate S. Buckingham Fund (1979.350)
Marble, H: 0.36 m.
Later portrait type of the 130s.

AIC Bulletin 74 (January–March 1980).

309

266

STATUE OF THE EMPEROR HADRIAN
Iberia Savings and Loan Association,
New Iberia, Louisiana
Formerly in the collections of the Villa
Montalto–Negroni–Massimi, Rome, and
Cobham Hall, Kent
Marble, H: ca. 2 m.
Ca. A.D. 130.

C. C. Vermeule, *AJA* 59 (1955) 133, pl. 42, fig. 9;
Wegner, *Hadrian* (1965) 95.

267 →

BUST OF THE EMPEROR HADRIAN
William Rockhill Nelson Gallery of Art–Atkins
Museum of Fine Arts, Kansas City, Missouri
Nelson Fund (31–96)
Marble, H: 0.66 m.
Hadrian wears a cuirass with a high relief
gorgoneion and a large *paludamentum* over
the left shoulder; there are no restorations.
Ca. A.D. 130.

Handbook (1959) 39; *Bulletin* 3 (1960) 6–7, fig. 6.

268
PORTRAIT HEAD OF A BOY
AS THE RESTING DIONYSOS
Museum of Fine Arts, Boston, Massachusetts
Classical Department Exchange Fund
(1980.30)
Crystalline marble from the Greek islands
(Naxos?) or perhaps Asia Minor, H (with
hand): 0.245 m.
A variant of the Lycian Apollo, carved ca. A.D.
120 for private, presumably funerary, use.

Unpublished.

269 →
BUST OF ANTINOUS
William Rockhill Nelson Gallery of Art–Atkins
Museum of Fine Arts, Kansas City, Missouri
Nelson Fund (59-3)
From Egypt
Marble, H: 0.70 m.
Ca. A.D. 135.

Handbook (1959) 39, ill.; *Bulletin* 3 (1960) 1 ff.,
ill.; Worcester, *Roman Portraits* 42–43, no. 17; C. W.
Clairmont, *Die Bildnisse des Antinous* (1966) 54,
no. 48, pl. 31.

313

270 (See colorplate 23.)
PORTRAIT STATUE OF VIBIA SABINA
Museum of Fine Arts, Boston, Massachusetts
Classical Department Purchase Fund
(1979.556)
Greek island marble, H: 2.02 m.
Numerous traces of polychromy. Ca. A.D.
130–134, hence a posthumous image.

Unpublished.

271
PORTRAIT STATUE OF A WOMAN
The J. Paul Getty Museum, Malibu, California
(72.AA.94)
Marble, H: 1.143 m.
Ca. A.D. 120 or slightly later. The head was
carved separately and inserted.

C. C. Vermeule, N. Neuerburg, *Catalogue of the
Ancient Art* (1973) 29, no. 61; *Greek and Roman
Portraits from the JPGM*, Fine Arts Gallery, Califor-
nia State University, Northridge (1973) 24, no. 29;
Inan-Rosenbaum, *Porträtplastik* 331, no. 330,
pls. 237.3, 239; *Roman Portraits in the JPGM*,
Philbrook Art Center (1981) 66–67, 126, no. 51.

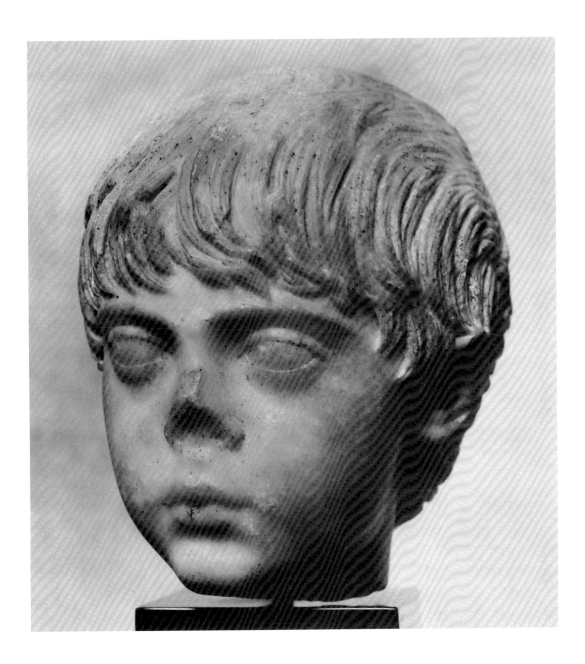

272
PORTRAIT OF A BOY
The Detroit Institute of Arts, Detroit, Michigan
Bequest of Mr. and Mrs. Edgar B. Whitcomb
(53.366)
From near Frascati
Marble, H: 0.21 m.
Ca. A.D. 140.

 Paintings and Sculpture Given by E. B. and A. S. Whitcomb (1954) 131.

273
STATUE OF A YOUTH
REPRESENTED AS APOLLO
William Rockhill Nelson Gallery of Art–Atkins
Museum of Fine Arts, Kansas City, Missouri
Nelson Fund (34-91/1)
From Hadrian's Villa near Tivoli; formerly
in the collection at Lansdowne House,
London
Island marble, H: 1.65 m.
Ca. A.D. 140.

Michaelis, *Marbles in Great Britain* 445, no. 34;
C. C. Vermeule, *AJA* 58 (1954) 255; idem, *ibid.* 59
(1955) 139; idem, *The Nelson Gallery and Atkins
Museum Bulletin* 3 (1960) 7, fig. 5; *Handbook* (1974)
48; E. K. Gazda, *Bulletin: Museums of Art and
Archeology*, University of Michigan 3 (1980) 6, figs.
9–10.

274 (See colorplate 24.)

PORTRAIT HEAD OF POLYDEUKION

Kelsey Museum of Archaeology, University of
Michigan, Ann Arbor, Michigan
(74.6.1)

Marble, H: 0.29 m.

Portrait of the favorite pupil of Herodes
Atticus, ca. A.D. 150.

Kelsey Museum, *Roman Portraiture* 20–21, no. 6;
Eighty Works in the Collection . . . A Handbook (1979)
no. 30; E. K. Gazda, *Bulletin: Museums of Art and
Archaeology*, University of Michigan 3 (1980) 1–14.

275
PORTRAIT HEAD OF A MAN
The Museum, United States Naval Academy,
Annapolis, Maryland
(*92.1.35)
Reported to have been presented by Matthew
C. Perry to the U.S. Naval Lyceum in Brook-
lyn in 1834 after he had acquired it in Turkey
during a tour of duty; said to be from Ephesus
Marble, H: 0.247 m.
Ca. A.D. 145.

   O. Oliver, *Beyond the Shores of Tripoli*, Fogg Art
Museum (1979), unpaged, ill.

276

PORTRAIT OF A PRIEST

The University Museum, University of
Pennsylvania, Philadelphia, Pennsylvania
(MS 215)

Acquired in 1895 from a native of Caesarea in
Cappadocia

Fine-grained white marble, H: 0.323 m.

The diadem has eleven heads of divinities in
high relief.

S. B. Luce, *Catalogue of the Mediterranean Section*
(1921) 173, no. 28; V. Müller, *Museum Journal* 23
(1932) 45–54, figs. 3–4; C. C. Vermeule, *PAPS* 108
(1964) 110, fig. 25, 128; Inan-Rosenbaum, *Porträtplastik* 275–276, no. 264, pls. 188, 275.4.

277

PORTRAIT HEAD
OF ANTONINUS PIUS

The Bowdoin College Museum of Fine Arts,
Brunswick, Maine

E. P. Warren collection (1906.1)

From Rome

Marble, H: 0.38 m.

Ca. A.D. 140–150.

M. Wegner, *Antoninischer Zeit* 126; K. Herbert,
Ancient Art in Bowdoin College (1964) 42, no. 100,
pl. 15; Worcester, *Roman Portraits* 48–49, no. 20.

278
BUST OF A MAN
The St. Louis Art Museum, St. Louis, Missouri
(299.23)
Said to have been found in a well in Athens;
formerly in the collection of Frederich L. von
Gans, Frankfurt
Marble, H: 0.80 m.
Beard somewhat recut. Cleaned to remove
water stains. From the Greek imperial world
in the reign of Commodus.

   C. C. Vermeule, *PAPS* 108 (1964) 113, fig. 27;
SLAM Handbook (1975) 16, ill.

279 →
BUST OF A WOMAN
The Newark Museum, Newark, New Jersey
Charles W. Engelhard Fund (71.79)
Said to be from Syria
Marble, H: 0.64 m.
Hair style and bust type of the early Antonine
period.

   ArtQ 35 (1972) 186, 197; S. H. Auth, *Archaeology*
29 (1976) 105.

280 (See colorplate 25.)
VEILED PORTRAIT STATUE
OF A WOMAN
Dallas Museum of Fine Arts, Dallas, Texas
Gift of Mr. and Mrs. Cecil H. Green (1973.11)
Marble, H: 1.75 m.
Ca. A.D. 160.

Unpublished.

281
PORTRAIT HEAD OF THE EMPEROR
MARCUS AURELIUS
Kimbell Art Museum, Fort Worth, Texas
(AP 67.11)
Marble, H: 0.365 m.
Ca. A.D. 170, or possibly a posthumous Severan
commemoration, ca. A.D. 195.

    Kunstwerke der Antike, Auktion 34, Münzen und
Medaillen A.G., Basel (6 May 1967) 109–110, no.
208, pl. 74; *KAM Catalogue* (1972) 12–14; *KAM
Handbook of the Collection* (1981) 12.

282
PORTRAIT HEAD OF THE EMPEROR
MARCUS AURELIUS
Indiana University Art Museum,
Bloomington, Indiana
William Lowe Bryan Memorial (62.2)
From Ostia or Portus, possibly made in Egypt
Marble, H: 0.46 m.

A posthumous portrait, ca. A.D. 200. The
rough carving would suit a decorative statue
in an architectural setting. The top of the
head was made separately, probably to attach
a large wreath, and the statue was therefore
perhaps cuirassed.

C. C. Vermeule, *MFA Bulletin, Boston* 60 (1962)
14–15, figs. 5–6; idem, *Roman Imperial Art* 281,
fig. 149 B; J. Balty, *Latomus* 85 (1966) 38, no. 8;
A. M. McCann, *The Portraits of Septimius Severus,*
MAAR 30 (1968) 198–199, no. V B, pl. 102 (as
Clodius Albinus).

283
PORTRAIT OF AN EMPRESS,
POSSIBLY FAUSTINA MINOR
The J. Paul Getty Museum, Malibu, California
(72.AA.117)
Marble, H: 0.275 m.
Ca. A.D. 150–155.

C. C. Vermeule, N. Neuerburg, *Catalogue of the
Ancient Art* (1973) 32–33, no. 70; B. Fredericksen,
ed., *The J. Paul Getty Museum* (1975) 65; *Greek and
Roman Portraits from the JPGM*, Fine Arts Gallery,
California State University, Northridge (1973)
27–28, no. 37; *Roman Portraits in the JPGM*, Philbrook Art Center (1981) 72–73, 127, no. 55.

284
PORTRAIT OF AN EMPRESS,
FAUSTINA MINOR
The Cleveland Museum of Art, Cleveland, Ohio
Gift from J. H. Wade (25.161)
From Rome
Marble, H: 0.255 m.
Ca. A.D. 165.

M. Bieber, *Art in America* 32 (1944) 73, fig. 9,
75–76; M. Wegner, *Antoninischer Zeit* 2.4, 211–212.

285 →
PORTRAIT OF A WOMAN,
POSSIBLY FAUSTINA MINOR
Kimbell Art Museum, Fort Worth, Texas
(AP 69.18)
From southwestern Asia Minor
Marble, H: 0.336 m.
Three imperial busts grace the diadem. The
small-scale head has been broken from a
draped statue, probably showing the empress
as a priestess of the imperial cult. Ca. A.D. 175,
the year of her death.

C. C. Vermeule, *Museum of Fine Arts Bulletin,
Boston* 67 (1969) 120–128; *KAM Catalogue* (1972)
14–15; Inan-Rosenbaum, *Porträtplastik* 327–329,
no. 326, pls. 235, 275.1–3; *KAM Handbook of the
Collection* (1981) 13.

286

HEAD OF VENUS
The Toledo Museum of Art, Toledo, Ohio
Gift of Edward Drummond Libbey (76.21)
From Asia Minor
Marble, H: 0.416 m.
Found together with no. 287. Sometimes
called an idealized portrait of Lucilla.

   Kelsey, *Roman Portraiture* no. 8; E. Gazda, *Toledo
Museum News* 20 (1978) 43–55.

287
PORTRAIT HEAD
OF THE EMPEROR LUCIUS VERUS
The Toledo Museum of Art, Toledo, Ohio
Gift of Edward Drummond Libbey (76.20)
From Asia Minor
Marble, H: 0.363 m.
Found together with 286.

 Kelsey, *Roman Portraiture* no. 7; E. Gazda, *Toledo Museum News* 20 (1978) 43–55.

288

PORTRAIT HEAD

OF THE EMPEROR LUCIUS VERUS

The Cleveland Museum of Art, Cleveland, Ohio

J. H. Wade Fund (52.260)

From Alexandria

Marble, H: 0.38 m.

A posthumous portrait, ca. A.D. 175.

Worcester, *Roman Portraits* 54–55, no. 23;
Vermeule, *Roman Imperial Art* 286–287, fig. 152;
CMA Handbook (1970) 25.

289 (See colorplate 26.) →

BUST OF A LADY

Worcester Art Museum, Worcester, Massachusetts

In part from the Sarah C. Garver Fund
(1966.67)

Said to have been found in Lycia

Bronze, H: 0.54 m.

Head and bust hollow cast separately and
soldered together with lead; eyes originally
inlaid. Perhaps Lucilla or Crispina.

WAM Annual Report (1967) cover, x, xv; *The
Connoisseur* 167 (1968) 131, fig. 15; *Master Bronzes*
240–241, no. 233; C. C. Vermeule, *BurlMag* 110
(1968) 167, fig. 57; V. Poulsen, *BurlMag* 111 (1969)
150 ff., figs. 57–59; *Handbook to the WAM* (1973) 30,
ill.; J. Inan, *IstM* 27–28 (1977–78) 276, no. 4, pl.
83.1–3; *Antiquity in the Renaissance*, Smith College
(1978) no. 66; Inan-Rosenbaum, *Porträtplastik*
339–340, no. 339, pls. 247–248.

290
FRAGMENTARY PORTRAIT HEAD
OF THE EMPEROR COMMODUS
James Alsdorf Collection, Winnetka, Illinois
From Beirut (and therefore Sidon? or possibly
Tyre)
Marble, H: 0.406 m.
Ca. A.D. 192.

Vermeule, *Roman Imperial Art* 289–290, fig. 154.

291
PORTRAIT HEAD
OF A BEARDED MAN
Memorial Art Gallery of the University of
Rochester, Rochester, New York
R. T. Miller Fund (46.39)
Said to have been found along the Appian
Way
Asia Minor marble, H: 0.274 m.
Severan work, possibly a portrait of a
kosmetos.

The Dark Ages, Worcester Art Museum (1937)
no. 41, ill.; E. G. Suhr, *AJA* 53 (1949) 258–260, pls.
37–38; idem, *ibid.* 59 (1955) 322, fig. 3;
C. C. Vermeule, *PAPS* 108 (1964), 112.

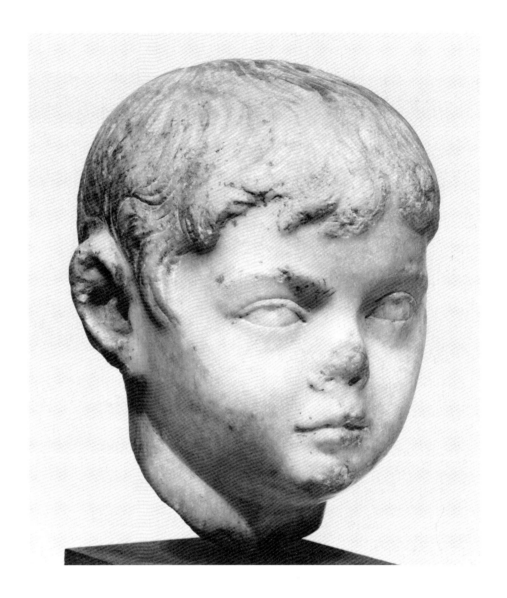

292
PORTRAIT OF A BOY
The Detroit Institute of Arts, Detroit, Michigan
Gift of Mrs. Edsel B. Ford (62.160)
Marble, H: 0.215 m.
Late second century A.D.; the subject may
have been the young baby princeling Geta
ca. A.D. 193.

   Sculpture in the DIA (1966) 14; Kelsey, *Roman
Portraiture* 28–29, no. 10.

293 →
PORTRAIT BUST OF A MAN
The Denver Art Museum, Denver, Colorado
Gift of various donors (1965.22)
Marble, H: 0.75 m.
Severan work of ca. A.D. 195.

   Roman Sculpture and Coins, Worcester Art
Museum (1961); *Guide to the DAM* (1976) 16, ill.

294
PORTRAIT OF A MAN
Santa Barbara Museum of Art,
Santa Barbara, California
Gift of Wright S. Ludington (71.51.2)
From southern Asia Minor
Bronze, H: 0.29 m.
This is possibly one of the bronzes from
the group identified with a city (Bubon) in
northeast Lycia or eastward toward Kremna
in Pisidia. Ca. A.D. 200.

Vermeule, *Roman Imperial Art* 401, 548; M. A.
Del Chiaro, *AJA* 78 (1974) 69–70, pl. 20, figs. 7–9
(as Gallienic); *West Coast Collections* 24, no. 11, ill.
p. 64; Inan-Rosenbaum, *Porträtplastik* 336–337,
no. 337, pl. 245; C. C. Vermeule, *Festschrift Jucker*
186, no. F.

295
STATUE OF THE EMPEROR
SEPTIMIUS SEVERUS
The Virginia Museum of Fine Arts,
Richmond, Virginia
The Williams Fund (67–50)
From Rome; formerly in the Giustiniani
collection, Rome, and the collection of Wil-
liams College, Williamstown, Massachusetts
Marble, H: 2.18 m.
Much restored, but the head is ancient and
(in my opinion) belongs. The garb is that of a
general on the eastern frontier. Ca. A.D. 200, a
type made popular in the Antonine period.

C. C. Vermeule, *PAPS* 108 (1964) 116–117,
fig. 38; Bieber, *Ancient Copies* 242, 262, fig. 869.

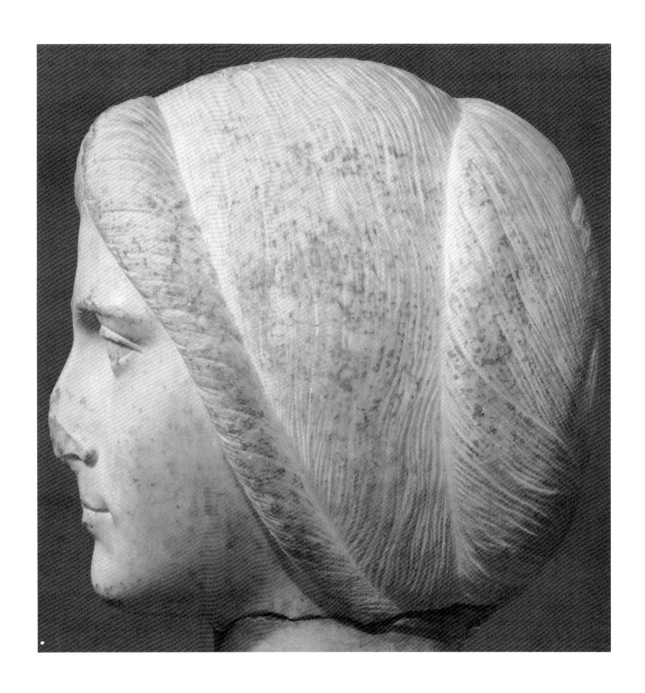

296 (See colorplate 27.)

PORTRAIT HEAD OF A LADY

Cincinnati Art Museum, Cincinnati, Ohio
(1946.5)

Possibly from Syria

Marble, H: 0.25 m.

Perhaps Didia Clara or the young Julia
Domna, ca. A.D. 190–200.

Wilatham, *Art of the Late Antique* 46, no. 1, pl. 1;
Ancient Civilizations: Egypt, Greece, Rome. CAM
(1961) no. 27; C. C. Vermeule, *PAPS* 108 (1964)
103; *Sculpture Collection of the CAM* (1970) 52–53;
G. M. A. Hanfmann, *Roman Art* (1975) 97–98, 179,
no. 84.

297 (See colorplate 28.)
BUST OF THE EMPEROR
SEPTIMIUS SEVERUS
Indiana University Art Museum,
Bloomington, Indiana
Gift of Thomas T. Solley (75.33.1)
Marble, H: 0.77 m.
A pair with the bust of Julia Domna (no.
298). A later portrait of the emperor, ca. A.D.
201–210.

   Art Journal (Winter 1975–76) 153–154, ill.;
K. Fittschen, *IUAM Bulletin* 1.2 (1978); *Guide to the
Collections* (1980) 60, ill.

298
BUST OF THE EMPRESS JULIA DOMNA
Indiana University Art Museum,
Bloomington, Indiana
Gift of Thomas T. Solley (75.33.2)
Marble, H: 0.675 m.
A pair with the bust of Septimius Severus
(no. 297). Ca. A.D. 200–210.

   Art Journal (Winter 1975–76) 153–154, ill.;
K. Fittschen, *IUAM Bulletin* 1.2 (1978); *Guide to the
Collections* (1980) 60, ill.

299
PORTRAIT OF THE EMPRESS
JULIA DOMNA
Fogg Art Museum, Harvard University,
Cambridge, Massachusetts
Gift of C. Ruxton Love, Jr. (1956.19)
Found at or near Selimiyeh (ancient Sala-
minias) in Syria
Bronze, H: 0.36 m.
A late type of ca. A.D. 205.

American Private Collections 29, no. 178, pl. 54;
G. M. A. Hanfmann, *FAM Annual Report*
(1955–56) 42, 43; *ArtQ* 19 (1956) 302; Vermeule,
Roman Imperial Art 299, 304, fig. 158; U.W.
Hiesinger, *AJA* 73 (1969) 39–44, pls. 15, 16, fig. 5.

348

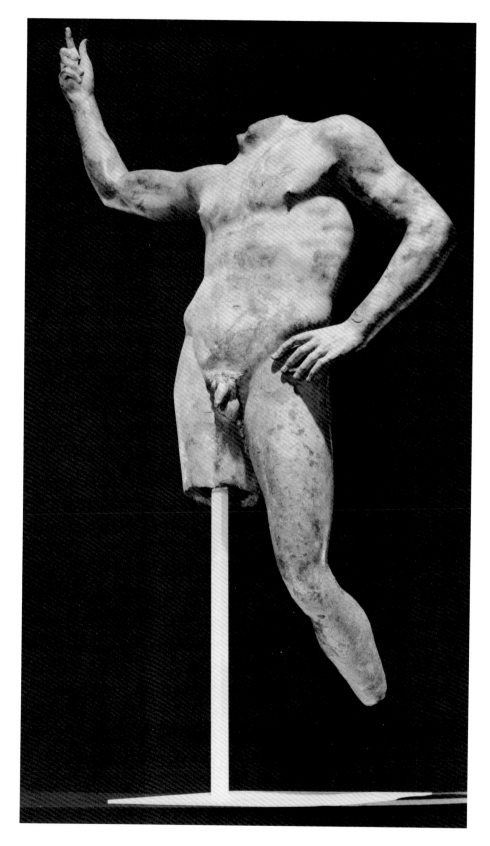

300
STATUE OF A SEVERAN EMPEROR
The Museum of Fine Arts, Houston, Texas
Gift of D. and J. de Menil in memory of
Conrad Schlumberger (62-19)
Said to be from the region of ancient Pisidia
Bronze, H: 2.083 m.
Severan work, perhaps the emperor Septimius
Severus.

M. L. d'Otrange Mastai, *The Connoisseur* 152
(1963) 203; Vermeule, *Roman Imperial Art* 300, 401,
fig. 164; H. Hoffmann, *Ten Centuries That Shaped the
West: Greek and Roman Art in Texas Collections*
(1970) 233-242, no. 111; E. Berger, *AK* 14 (1971)
139, no. 3; P. Oliver-Smith, *AntPl* 15 (1975)
95-108, pls. 42-46; Inan-Rosenbaum, *Porträtplastik*
48, 108, 121 n. 1; *A Guide to the Collection* (1981) 13,
no. 22, pl. 3.

301

TORSO OF AN EMPEROR (?)
IN CEREMONIAL ARMOR
The Detroit Institute of Arts, Detroit, Michigan
Matilda R. Wilson Fund (72.273)
From Italy or North Africa, via Ireland and
France
Marble, H: 1.11 m.
The small, semicircular *pteryges* with rosettes,
floral stars, and Medusa heads are clearly
Severan or later. The statue may have repre-
sented the young emperor Caracalla and may
be dated ca. A.D. 210.

    M. Dunmez-Onof, *Ancient Works of Art* (1970)
no. 14; *ArtQ* 35 (1972) 435, fig. 1; *Bulletin* 52
(1973) 48; C. C. Vermeule, *Berytus* 23 (1974) 21–23,
no. 298A, figs. 6–8.

302 →

PORTRAIT OF THE EMPEROR
CARACALLA
*William Rockhill Nelson Gallery of Art–Atkins
Museum of Fine Arts, Kansas City, Missouri*
(47–66)
From Rome
Fine Greek island marble, N: 0.48 m.
Copy after the first official portrait-type of
Caracalla as sole emperor, A.D. 212.

    C. C. Vermeule, *PAPS* 108 (1964) 105 f., fig. 40;
Wegner, *Caracalla* 64; C. C. Vermeule, *Apollo* 99
(1974) 315, 317, figs. 6, 6a.

351

303
PORTRAIT HEAD
OF THE EMPEROR CARACALLA
The University Museum, University of
Pennsylvania, Philadelphia, Pennsylvania
(E 976)
Found at Koptos in Egypt in 1894 by W. M.
Flinders Petrie near the steps of the temple of
Isis
Syenite (red granite), H: 0.51 m.
Early third century A.D.

W. M. Flinders Petrie, *Koptos* (1896) 23; Graindor, *Bustes et statues-portraits d'Égypte romaine*
145–146, pl. 71; Waltham, *Art of the Late Antique*
46, no. 2; *Romans and Barbarians*, 25, no. 31.

304

PORTRAIT HEAD OF A YOUNG MAN,
POSSIBLY GETA

*R. H. Lowie Museum of Anthropology, University
of California, Berkeley, California*

(8–4258)

Found near Rome

Marble, H: 0.28 m.

Version of the portrait-type of A.D. 195–206.

Joseph Brummer sale catalogue 1 (20–23 April,
1949) lot 171; Del Chiaro, *West Coast Collections* 24,
no. 10, ill.; S. Nodelman et al., *Roman Portraits;
Aspects of Self and Society* (1980) 104, no. D.

305 (See colorplate 29.)
BUST OF THE EMPEROR ELAGABALUS
Museum of Fine Arts, Boston, Massachusetts
Mary S. and Edward J. Holmes Fund
(1977.337)
From the Mediterranean, via Central Europe
Highest-quality white marble, H (max.): 0.7 m.
Ca. A.D. 219.

    C. C. Vermeule, *Roman Art* (1978) cover; idem,
Iconographic Studies (1980) 35–51, pl. I.

306

PORTRAIT HEAD OF PLAUTILLA
The Museum of Fine Arts, Houston, Texas
Laurence H. Favrot Fund (70-39)
Translucent marble, H: 0.355 m.
Type of 202-203, the years of Plautilla's mar-
riage to Caracalla. Compare also the Pentelic
marble copy in the Getty Museum.

ArtQ 34 (Autumn 1971) 370-371, ill.; *Bulletin* 2
(November 1971) 85-86, ill.; J. L. Schrader, *Bulletin*
2 (February 1972) 168-173, cover (as Julia Paula);
C. C. Vermeule, *Iconographic Studies* (1980) 37-42,
52, pl. II; S. Nodelman et al., *Roman Portraits:
Aspects of Self and Society* (1980) no. 15, *passim* (as
Plautilla); *A Guide to the Collection* (1981) 14, no. 23.

307
PORTRAIT OF A MAN
The Ackland Art Museum, The University of
North Carolina, Chapel Hill, North Carolina
Ackland Fund (69.9.1)
Marble, H: 0.32 m.
Early third century A.D.

Ackland, *Ancient Portraits* no. 22; *Classical Art*
from Carolina Collections 46–47, no. 68.

308
PORTRAIT OF A LADY
The Detroit Institute of Arts, Detroit, Michigan
Gift of P. S. Nesi (38.41)
Marble, H: 0.248 m.
Removable stone wig of a different marble;
late Severan period, ca. A.D. 230.

    P. T. Rathbone, *Bulletin of the DIA* 17 (1938)
68–70; Worcester, *Roman Portraits* 62–63, no. 27;
C. C. Vermeule, *PAPS* 108 (1964) 104; Waltham,
Art of the Late Antique 46, no. 3, not ill.; Kelsey,
Roman Portraiture 26–27, no. 9 as late Antonine re-
worked in the Severan period.

309

PORTRAIT HEAD OF A MAN

Montreal Museum of Fine Arts,
Montreal, Quebec, Canada

Horsley and Annie Townsend bequest
(68.1600)

Marble, H: 0.28 m.

Close to portrait types of the emperor
Alexander Severus of the 230s.

   ArtQ 32 (1969) 69, ill. 71, 3; D. G. Carter, *Vie des*
Arts 20 (1976) 17, fig. 12.

310
PORTRAIT OF THE EMPEROR
BALBINUS
The Cleveland Museum of Art, Cleveland, Ohio
Gift from J. H. Wade (25.945)
Marble, H: 0.185 m.
The head belongs to the famous sarcophagus
of the emperor Balbinus in the museum of the
Catacomb of Praetextatus. Ca. A.D. 238.

CMA Handbook (1966) 26; H. Jucker, *AA*
(1966) 501–514; idem, *CMA Bulletin* 54 (January
1967) 11–16; *Curator's Choice from the Ancient World*,
The Newark Museum (1968) ill.; Waltham, *Art of
the Late Antique* 47, no. 6, pl. 3; Wegner, *Caracalla*
247.

311
SARCOPHAGUS FRAGMENT
WITH A PORTRAIT OF A MAN
R. H. Lowie Museum of Anthropology, University
of California, Berkeley, California
Gift of Mrs. Phoebe A. Hearst (8-4274)
Formerly in the Comin collection, Rome
White Carrara marble, H (max.): 0.16 m.
Second quarter of the third century A.D.

Selection 1966: The University Art Collections
(1966) 40–41; Waltham, *Art of the Late Antique* 47,
no. 7, pl. 4; S. Nodelman et al., *Roman Portraits;*
Aspects of Self and Society (1980) 102–103, no. C.

312
PORTRAIT HEAD OF A GIRL
The Art Museum, Princeton University,
Princeton, New Jersey
(55.3228)
From Paris
Marble, H: 0.215 m.
Ca. A.D. 250.

Parke-Bernet (9 April 1953) 19, lot 117; *ArtQ* 18
(1955) 301 ff., ill.

313
PORTRAIT BUST OF A MAN
The Walters Art Gallery, Baltimore, Maryland
(54.1148)
From the house of Laberius Gallus, Bolsena;
formerly in the Massarenti collection, Rome
Bronze, H: 0.193 m.
Fine Gallienic work of ca. A.D. 260–268.

NotScavi (1882) 315 f.; *AnnInst* (1882) 180 f., pl. S;
*Catalogue du Musée de Peinture, Sculpture et Archéologie
au Palais Accoramboni* 2 (1897) 8 ff., no. 14; *CIL* 2702;
D. K. Hill, *Catalogue of Classical Bronze Sculpture in the
WAG* (1949) 51–52, no. 106, pl. 21; *Master Bronzes*
247, no. 236; H. Hoffmann, *Apollo* 86 (1967) 338, fig.
16.

314 →
PORTRAIT HEAD
OF A BEARDED MAN
The J. Paul Getty Museum, Malibu, California
(73.AA.7)
Italian marble, H: 0.35 m.
A.D. 240–250.

Greek and Roman Portraits from the JPGM, California State University, Northridge (1973) 30,
no. 43, ill.; Vermeule, *Greek Art* 85, 132, fig. 110B;
JPGM Guidebook (1980) 27, ill; *Roman Portraits in
the JPGM*, Philbrook Art Center (1981) 108–109,
132, no. 89.

315
PORTRAIT HEAD
OF A BEARDED MAN
Royal Ontario Museum,
Toronto, Ontario, Canada
(959.17.13)
Formerly in the Ludwig Curtius collection
Marble, H: 0.28 m.
Ca. A.D. 250.

   Art Treasures of the ROM (1961) 105, ill.; C. C.
Vermeule, *PAPS* 108 (1964) 115, 134, fig. 43.

316

PORTRAIT HEAD OF A MAN
The Detroit Institute of Arts, Detroit, Michigan
Gift of Mr. and Mrs. James S. Holden (27.212)
From Rome
Marble, H: 0.317 m.
Ca. A.D. 250.

DIA Bulletin 9 (1927) 30, no. 3, ill.; *Masterpieces of Painting and Sculpture from the DIA* (1949) 25, ill. (as Philippus Arabs); *AJA* 63 (1959) 109; Worcester, *Roman Portraits* 68–69, no. 30; C. C. Vermeule, *DOP* 15 (1961) 6, fig. 8; idem, *PAPS* 108 (1964) 104; *Treasures from the DIA* (1963) 35, ill. (as Philippus Arabs); Kelsey, *Roman Portraiture* 30–31, no. 11, ill. (with previous bibl.).

317 ←

PORTRAIT BUST
OF THE EMPEROR GALLIENUS
John and Mable Ringling Museum of Art,
Sarasota, Florida
(SN5013)
From Rome, by way of Dresden and Munich
Marble, H: 0.73 m.; H (of head only): 0.30 m.
Ca. A.D. 260. Compare Felletti Maj, *Icono-*
grafia, 222, no. 289, though much reworked,
and the bust does not belong.

C. C. Vermeule, *PAPS* 108 (1964) 113; M. Berg-
mann, *Studien zum römischen Porträt des 3. Jarhun-*
derts n. Chr. (1977) 53, pl. 14.5–6.

318

PORTRAIT HEAD OF THE EMPEROR
GALLIENUS AS DIONYSOS
The Art Institute of Chicago, Chicago, Illinois
Katherine Keith Adler Fund (1975.328)
Crystalline island marble, H: 0.34 m.
The back of the head was made separately
and attached with a large tenon. Ca. A.D.
260–270.

J. Maxon, *Annual Report, 1974–1975* 7, 12, ill, 31.

319

PORTRAIT HEAD OF A PRIEST

R. H. Lowie Museum of Anthropology, University
of California, Berkeley, California

Gift of Mrs. Phoebe A. Hearst (8-4266)

Formerly in the collection of conte Marini,
Rome

Large-grained white marble, H: 0.35 m.

Gallienic.

C. C. Vermeule, *PAPS* 108 (1964) 110, fig. 44;
Selection 1966: The University Art Collections (1966)
37 f., no. 30; Inan-Rosenbaum, *Porträtplastik*
322–323, no. 319; pl. 225; S. Nodelman et al., *Roman*
Portraits; Aspects of Self and Society (1980) 100–101,
no. B (as Antonine).

320
PORTRAIT HEAD OF A PRIEST
Cincinnati Art Museum, Cincinnati, Ohio
Bequest of William H. Chatfield (1973.292)
From Greece or Asia Minor
Marble, H: 0.36 m.
Ca. A.D. 260–280.

Romans and Barbarians 102, no. 111.

321
PORTRAIT HEAD
OF A BEARDED MAN
Fogg Art Museum, Harvard University,
Cambridge, Massachusetts
Alpheus Hyatt Fund (1949.47.138)
Marble, H: 0.28 m.
Ca. A.D. 270–280.

Ancient Sculpture Exhibition, Fogg Art Museum
(1950) no. 50; G. M. A. Hanfmann, *Latomus* 11
(1953) 17–23, pl. III, figs. 5–6; Waltham, *Art of the*
Late Antique 48, no. 10, pl. 5; Ackland, *Ancient*
Portraits no. 23.

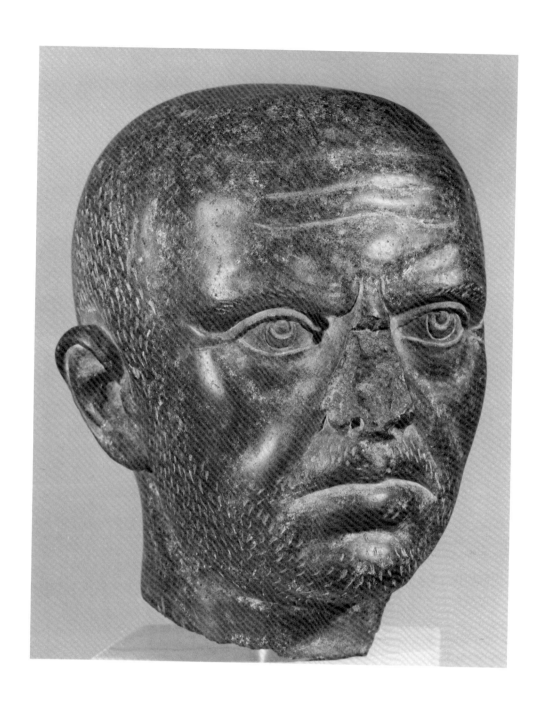

322
PORTRAIT HEAD OF A MAN
(DIOCLETIAN?)
Worcester Art Museum, Worcester, Massachusetts
Alexander H. Bullock Fund (1974.297)
Roman (Egypto-Roman?)
Seemingly from Italy and Egypt, via a British
collection
Black basalt, H: 0.203 m.
Ca. A.D. 302–305.

R. S. Teitz, *WAM Bulletin* 4 (February 1975)
cover and 15–16; *WAM Annual Report* (1975) 18;
Age of Spirituality 10–11, no. 3.

323

PORTRAIT HEAD OF CONSTANTIA

The Art Institute of Chicago, Chicago, Illinois

Edward E. Ayer Fund (1960.64)

From Athens, the Roman Agora

Translucent white marble, H: 0.225 m.

The type is based on models of the end of the
reign of Hadrian into the first decade of Antoninus Pius's rule, revived for ladies of the
Flavian house. Ca. A.D. 313.

C. C. Vermeule, *AIC Quarterly* 54 (December
1960) 9–10, fig. 8; Worcester, *Roman Portraits*
76–77, no. 34; C. C. Vermeule, *PAPS* 108 (1964)
103; Hanfmann, *Roman Art* 103, 187, no. 98;
E. B. Harrison, *DPO* 21 (1967) 87–88, fig. 31 (as
early Antonine); Vermeule, *Roman Imperial Art*
356, 364–365, fig. 179; W. von Sydow, *Zur Kunstgeschichte des spätantiken Porträts im 4. Jahr. n. Chr.*
3.8 (1969) 152; Calza, *Iconografia* 268–269, figs.
331–332; H. von Heintze, *Jahr. für Antike und
Christentum* 14 (1971) 78–83; *Romans and Barbarians* 110–111, no. 118; *Age of Spirituality*
289–290, no. 268.

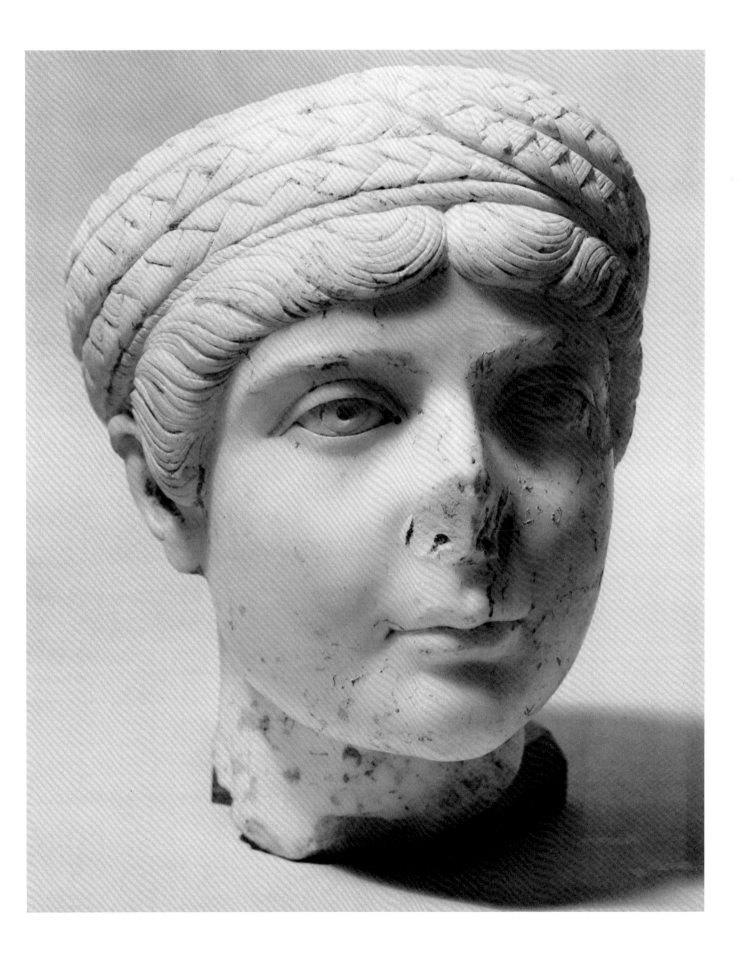

324
PORTRAIT OF A LADY
William Rockhill Nelson Gallery of Art–Atkins Museum of Fine Arts, Kansas City, Missouri
Nelson Fund (34–200)
Marble, H: 0.27 m.

From the same workshop as the head of the young Fausta (Calza, *Iconografia* 268–269, no. 182, pl. 94). On the other hand, the difficulties of chronology and style may be resolved if the head is thought of as one of the two daughters of Constantine the Great, perhaps Helena the Younger, and dated ca. A.D. 325. At least one other replica, on the London art market in 1973, exists.

C. C. Vermeule, *PAPS* 108 (1964) 105, 131, fig. 35 (as late Antonine); idem, *Apollo* 99 (1974) 318–319, figs. 10, 10a.

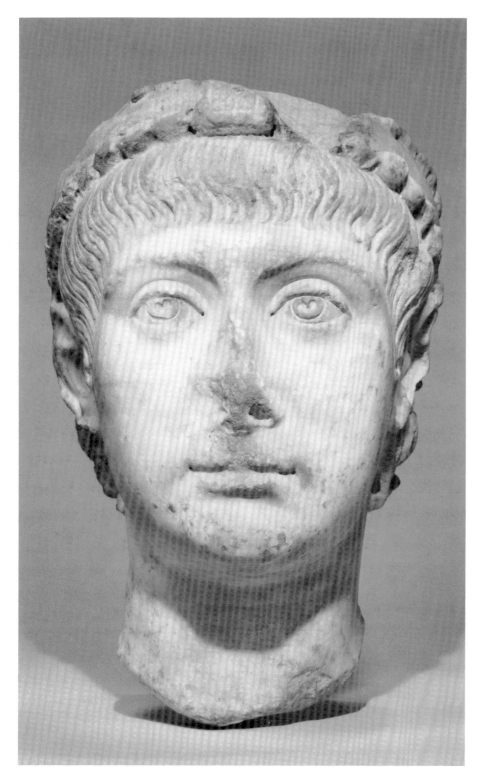

325
PORTRAIT OF A PRINCE
The Metropolitan Museum of Art,
New York, New York
Rogers Fund (67.107)
Formerly in a private collection in Istanbul
Marble, H: 0.26 m.
The hair and diadem identify the young man
as probably one of Constantine's sons.
Ca. A.D. 325–340.

G. Bruns, *Jdl* 47 (1932) 135 ff., fig. 103, pls. 5–6;
R. Delbrueck, *Spätantike Kaiserporträts* (1933)
154–155, pls. 58–59; Calza, *Iconografia* no. 233;
Romans and Barbarians 110–113, no. 119; *Age of*
Spirituality 22, no. 15.

326
PORTRAIT HEAD
OF THE EMPEROR HONORIUS
The Detroit Institute of Arts, Detroit, Michigan
Gift of Dr. W. R. Valentiner (37.157)
Marble, H: 0.101 m.
Five small holes in the diadem would have
anchored a metal wreath. Ca. A.D. 395–400
(younger than Honorius on the Rothschild
cameo).

P. T. Rathbone, *DIA Bulletin* 17 (1938) 70, no. 8;
E. P. Richardson, *Small in Size, Great in Art* (1946)
7, ill.; Walters, *Early Christian and Byzantine Art*
23, no. 4, pl. 8; R. Delbrueck, *MdI* 4 (1951) 7–9,
pls. 1–3; C. C. Vermeule, *PAPS* 108 (1964) 104;
Waltham, *Art of the Late Antique* 49, no. 17, pl. 9;
Romans and Barbarians 151, no. 188; *Age of Spirituality* 27–28, no. 21.

327
PORTRAIT HEAD OF A MAN
Museum of Fine Arts, Boston, Massachusetts
Gift of Heinz Herzer (1977.656)
From northern Europe, and, ultimately,
probably Italy
Coarse-grained marble from Proconnesus or
northwest Asia Minor, H: 0.43 m.
Ca. A.D. 475–500. Compare the head in the Ny
Carlsberg Glyptotek no. 775 (Poulsen, *Les
Portraits romains* 203, no. 209, pl. 342).

Romans and Barbarians 154, no. 191; C. C. Vermeule, *Iconographic Studies* (1980) 3–9, figs. 1, 3 (as
retrospective Titus).

328 (See colorplate 30.)
BUST OF A LADY
The Metropolitan Museum of Art,
New York, New York
The Cloisters Fund (66.25)
Probably from Istanbul
Marble, H: 0.53 m.
Justinianic work from Constantinople.

E. Alföldi-Rosenbaum, *MMA Journal* 1 (1968)
19–40; *The Middle Ages: Treasures from the Cloisters
and the Metropolitan Museum of Art*, Los Angeles
County Museum of Art (1970) no. 18; H. von
Heintze, *Berl Mus* 20 (1970) 51–61 and idem,
JAC 14 (1971) 61–69 (as forgery); E. Alföldi-
Rosenbaum, *JAC* 15 (1972) 174–178; S. Sande,
ActaIRN 6 (1975) 95, n. 3 (as Theodosian); *Age of
Spirituality* 292, 294–295, no. 272; Inan-Rosen-
baum, *Porträtplastik* 335–336, no. 335, pl. 268.

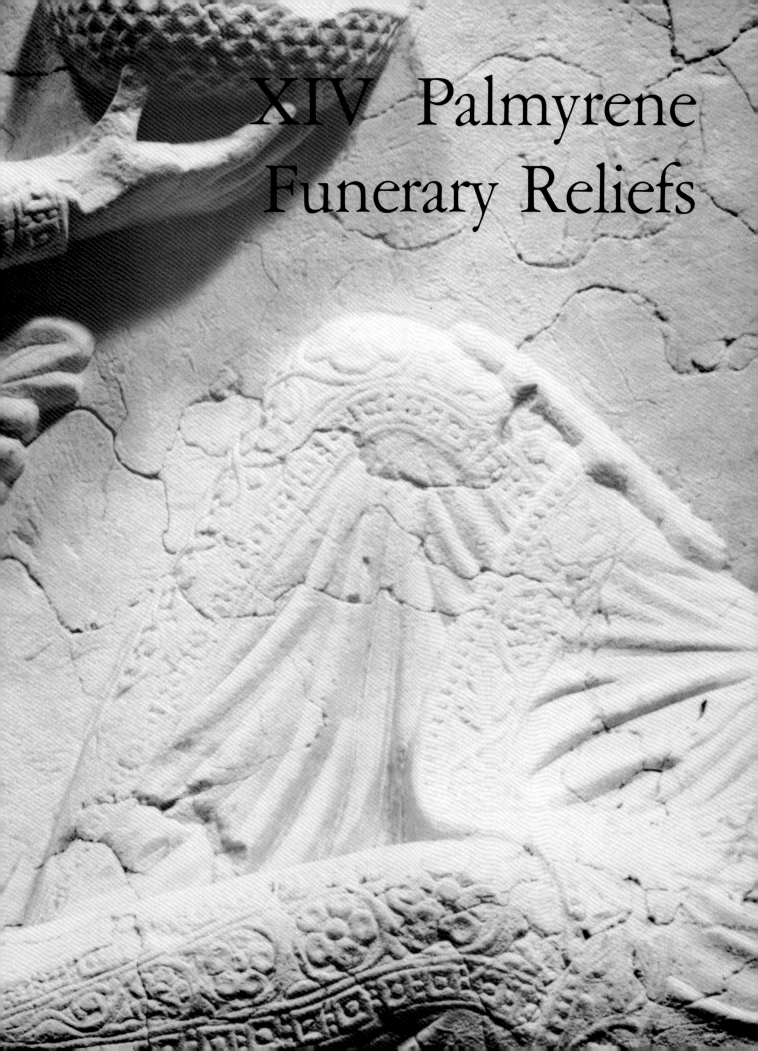

XIV Palmyrene Funerary Reliefs

329
FUNERARY RELIEF OF A WOMAN
Fogg Art Museum, Harvard University,
Cambridge, Massachusetts
Gift of Alden Sampson, Richard Norton, and
Edward Forbes (1908.3)
From Palmyra
Limestone, H: 0.70 m.
Ca. A.D. 150.

W. Deonna, *Genava* 1 (1923) 52; idem, *Syria* 4
(1924) 231; Chase, *American Collections* 190–191, fig.
242; Ingholt, *Palmyrensk Skulptur* 132, PS 374, 158.

330 →
FUNERARY RELIEF OF UMMABI,
DAUGHTER OF MAQQI
The Toledo Museum of Art, Toledo, Ohio
Gift of Edward Drummond Libbey (62.18)
From Palmyra
Limestone, H: 0.584 m.; W: 0.483 m.
Ca. A.D. 175.

D. Mackay, *Iraq* 11 (1949) 160–187, pl. 60.1 and
drawing of armlet fig. 6a; Sotheby's (18 June 1961)
lot 152, ill.; *Toledo Museum News* 7 (Winter 1964)
81, ill.; C. C. Vermeule, *PAPS* 108 (1964) 114; A.
Frankfurter, *Art News* 63 (1965) 25, ill.; *GBA* 65
(1965) 11, ill.; E. Spaeth, *American Art Museums*
(1969) 205; V. Hoke, *Toledo Museum News* 17
(1974) 51–53, ill.

331

FUNERARY PORTRAIT OF MALOCHA,
SON OF NUR-BEL

Cincinnati Art Museum, Cincinnati, Ohio

Gift of E. S. David (1958.257)

From Palmyra

Limestone, H: 0.527 m.

Ca. A.D. 150.

    Sculpture Collection of the CAM (1970) 54.

332

FUNERARY RELIEF OF A PRIEST

The Berkshire Museum, Pittsfield, Massachusetts

Gift of Zenas Crane (03.7.1)

From Palmyra

Limestone, H: 0.585 m.; W. 0.445 m.

He wears the modius and holds an alabastron and an incense bowl. One of six Palmyrene reliefs donated to the Pittsfield Museum. Second half of the second century A.D.

Ingholt, *Palmyrensk Skulptur* 106, 159, PS 150; idem, *Palmyrene and Gandharan Sculpture*, Yale University Art Gallery (1954) no. 4, ill.; Faison, *New England* 142, fig. 1; C. C. Vermeule, *PAPS* 108 (1964) 111.

333

FUNERARY RELIEF

OF YARKHAI, SON OF OGGA,

AND HIS DAUGHTER BALYA

The Portland Art Museum, Portland, Oregon

Gift of Mr. Aziz Atiyeh (54.3)

From Palmyra

Limestone, H: 0.56 m.; W: 0.83 m.

Second half of the second century A.D.

Ronzevalle, *RBibl* 11 (1902) 413–416, no. 3;
Lidzbarski, *Ephemeris für semitische Epigraphik* 2
(1910) 78C; Ingholt, *Palmyrensk Skulptur* 95, PS65
(private collection in Homs); Portland Art Association *Bulletin* 15 (March 1954) no. 7; *Archaeology*
7 (1954) 121, no. 2; Worcester, *Roman Portraits* no.
24; Del Chiaro, *West Coast Collections* 32, no. 37.

334
FUNERARY RELIEF OF A PRIEST
William Rockhill Nelson Gallery of Art–Atkins
Museum of Fine Arts, Kansas City, Missouri
Nelson Fund (65–2)
From Palmyra
Limestone, H: 0.445m.
No. 335 may be a pendant from the same
tomb complex.

   Handbook (1974) 55, ill.

335

FUNERARY RELIEF

The Cleveland Museum of Art, Cleveland, Ohio

Leonard C. Hanna, Jr. Bequest (64.359)

From Palmyra

Limestone, W: 0.737 m.

Compare *Fasti A* 20 (1965) 251–252, no. 3784, pl. 21, fig. 58. The figure, presumably a goddess rather than a priestess, lies on a couch in the "Ariadne" pose. No. 334 may be a pendant from the same tomb complex.

J. D. Cooney, *CMA Bulletin* 53 (February 1966) 34–37; *CMA Handbook* (1966) 26.

336
FUNERARY RELIEF OF BON'AM
SON OF AQUL
Stanford University Museum of Art,
Stanford, California
(17205)
From Palmyra
Limestone, H: 0.965 m.; W: 0.76 m.
The young man holds a flower in his left hand.
Mid-second century A.D.

Del Chiaro, *West Coast Collections* 32, no. 36, ill.

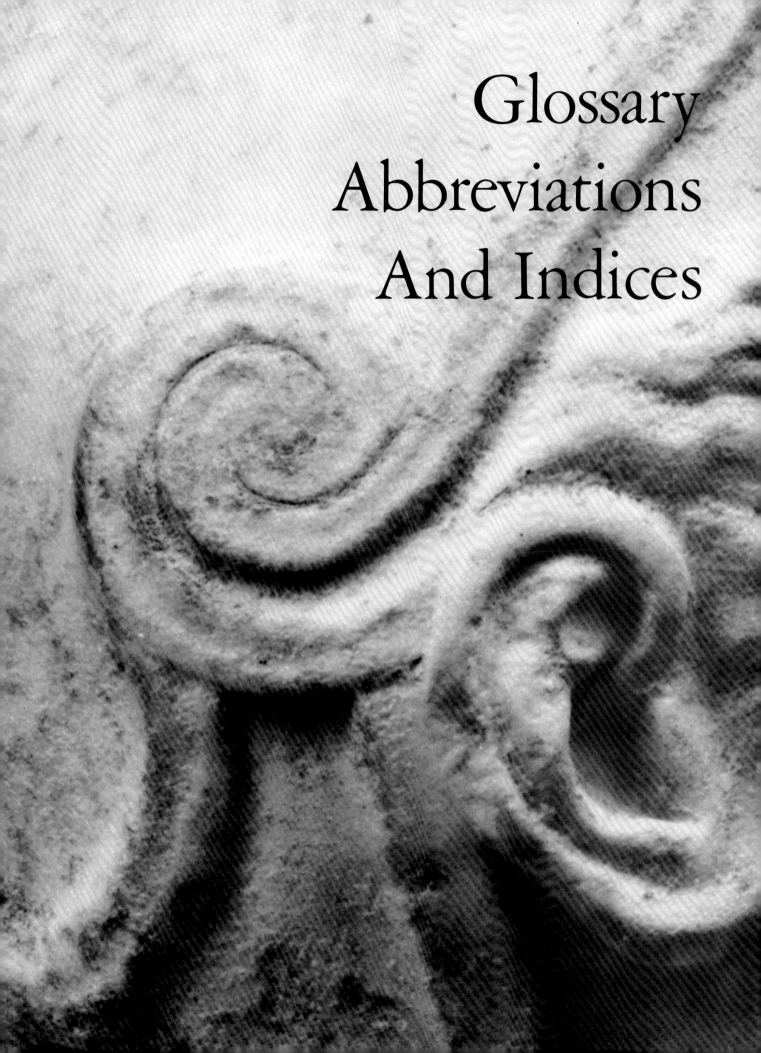

Glossary
Abbreviations
And Indices

Glossary

Akroterion (plural: akroteria). Ornament(s) and figure(s) on the corners and apex of a Greek pedimental or triangular roof.

Alabastron (plural: alabastra). A small, cylindrical or ball-shaped vase, often represented on funerary reliefs.

Amazonomachy. Battle between Greeks and Amazons.

Archaic. Phase of Greek art from about 620 to 480 B.C.

Attic. Athenian or pertaining to (the art of) Attica and the Attic peninsula.

Caryatid. A female figure used as an architectural support.

Cinerarium. A rectangular or circular stone chest in which the Romans placed the ashes of the deceased. Sometimes cineraria doubled as funerary altars in the columbaria or underground cemeteries of Rome.

Codex. A book with pages, the ancient forerunner of the modern format.

Cycladic. Pertaining to (the art of) the Cycladic (Aegean) islands.

Dark Age. Phase of Greek art from about 1000 to 800 B.C.

Diadoumenos. An athlete binding a diadem or fillet around his head.

Diskophoros. An athlete holding a discus.

Dorian. The civilization and art of the Dark Ages and, later, of the Greeks in the Peloponnesus.

Geometric. Phase of Greek art from about 800 to 650 B.C.

Gigantomachy. Battle between the Olympian divinities and the giants.

Glyptic. Carved in stone, sculptural.

Golden Age. Phase of Greek art from about 450 to 400 B.C.

Gorgoneion. Stylized head or mask of the Gorgon Medusa.

Griffin. A mythological beast, part eagle and part lion.

Hellenistic. Phase of Greek art from about 330 to 30 B.C.

Herm. A head of a divinity (Hermes, hence the name) or a portrait of a person (often a famous man of letters) carved onto a rectangular bust or shaft extending to the ground.

Himation. A long outer garment worn by Greek men and women, particularly from the fourth century B.C. onwards.

Hora. A female personification of time or the seasons; a woodland divinity seen in contexts suggesting the passage of life.

Kore (plural: korai). The Greek word for maiden, from specific use as the name of Demeter's daughter Persephone.

Kouros (plural: kouroi). The Greek word for a youth or young man.

Lekythos. A tall, cylindrical vase, sometimes represented in marble as a funerary marker or tombstone.

Loutrophoros. A tall vase with two (amphora) or three (hydria) handles, represented in marble for funerary purposes.

Maenad. Female follower of Dionysos, usually shown sacrificing animals or participating in revels.

Minoan. The prehistoric civilization and art of Crete.

Modius. A basket for measuring grain, worn as a divine attribute.

Mycenaean. The prehistoric civilization and art of Greece.

Nereid. A sea divinity, one of the daughters of Nereus.

Niobid. Child of Niobe, slain (save for one) by Apollo and Artemis.

Nymph. Female personification of fountains, pools, streams, and other pleasant places in woodland or forest settings.

Orientalizing. Phase of Greek art from about 650 to 610 B.C.

Ottoman. Phase of Eastern European civilization about 1453 to 1919.

Palladion. Sacred image of Pallas Athena at Troy.

Paludamentum. A cloak worn about the shoulders.

Pediment. The triangular area crowning the front and back of a Greek building.

Peplos. A woolen outer garment worn by Greek women, particularly during the Archaic and Classical periods of Greek art.

Pentelic. Pertaining to marble from Mount Pentelicon near Athens.

Peplophoros. A woman wearing a peplos.

Pilaster. A column in flat relief used as decoration on a building or monument.

Pteryges. The semicircular flaps or tabs below the breastplate and above the leather skirt-straps of a Roman suit of armor.

Rotulus. A book in the form of a scroll like a modern diploma.

Sarcophagus. A coffin, in the Hellenistic and Roman periods usually made of stone or, especially in Syria, of lead.

Satyr. Mythological follower of Dionysos having pointed ears and a goat's tail.

Siren. A mythological creature with a woman's head and a bird's body, who played sweet music and lured mortals to their death on rocky shores.

Shawabti. An Egyptian mummiform figure used as a funerary offering.

Sphinx. A mythological creature, with a woman's head, wings, and a lion's body.

Stele. A carved or painted stone set up for funerary or commemorative purposes.

Strigilar. The adjective from *strigil*, used to describe carving in the shape of the S-curved object with which Greek athletes scraped oil from their bodies after exercising.

Tenon. A raised, rectangular section of carved stone over or onto which another block was joined and held together with adhesives or clamps.

Terra cotta. Made of baked or fired clay; a work of Greek art thus produced.

Togate. The adjective from *toga*, a Roman citizen's formal or dress garment worn around the body and legs over a tunic.

Tondo. A carved or painted circle enframing a composition, usually a portrait head or bust.

Trapezophoros (plural: trapezophoroi). The Greek word for a *table support*.

Tyche (as in "city Tyche"): Personification of the spirit or fortune of a city or region; the general goddess of good luck, thus the personification of a living metropolis and its fortunes.

Votary. A person or, here, the image of a person making a dedication at a temple or shrine.

Abbreviations of Book Titles

Ackland, *Ancient Portraits* — *Ancient Portraits*, Ackland Art Center, University of North Carolina, Chapel Hill, April 5–May 17, 1970.

Age of Spirituality — K. Weitzmann, ed., *Age of Spirituality*, The Metropolitan Museum of Art, New York, November 19, 1977–February 12, 1978.

American Private Colls. — *Ancient Art in American Private Collections*. Fogg Art Museum, Cambridge, Massachusetts, 1954.

Arnold, *Polykletnachfolge* — D. Arnold, *Die Polykletnachfolge (JdI Ergänzungsheft 25)*, Berlin, 1969.

Baker Collection — *The Walter C. Baker Collection*, The Metropolitan Museum of Art, New York, 1950.

Beazley, *Lewes House* — J. D. Beazley, *The Lewes House Collection of Ancient Gems*, Oxford, 1920.

Bieber, *Ancient Copies* — M. Bieber, *Ancient Copies: Contributions to the History of Greek and Roman Art*, New York, 1977.

Bieber, *Sculpture* — M. Bieber, *Sculpture of the Hellenistic Age*, rev. ed., New York, 1961.

Burlington Exhibition — Burlington Fine Arts Club, *Exhibition of Ancient Greek Art*, London, 1903, rev. ed., London, 1904.

Calza, *Iconografia* — R. Calza, *Iconografia romana imperiale, 3, Da Carausio a Giuliano*, Rome, 1972.

Chase, *American Collections* — G. H. Chase, *Greek and Roman Sculpture in American Collections*, Cambridge, Massachusetts, 1924.

Classical Art in Carolina Colls. — C. R. Mack, *Classical Art in Carolina Collections*, Columbia Museum of Art, Columbia, South Carolina, 1974.

Comstock, Vermeule, *Sculpture in Stone* — M. B. Comstock and C. C. Vermeule, *Sculpture in Stone; The Greek, Roman and Etruscan Collections of the Museum of Fine Arts, Boston* 1977.

Daltrop, *Flavier* — G. Daltrop, U. Hausmann, M. Wegner, *Die Flavier: Vespasian, Titus, Domitian, Nerva, Julia Titi, Domitilla, Domitia (Das Römische Herscherbild, 2.1)*, Berlin, 1966.

Daltrop, *Privatbildnisse* — G. Daltrop, *Die Stadtrömischen männlichen Privatbildnisse Trajanischer und Hadrianischer Zeit*, Münster, 1958.

Del Chiaro, *West Coast Collections* — M. Del Chiaro, *Roman Art in West Coast Collections*, Santa Barbara, California, 1973.

EA — P. Arndt and W. Amelung, *Photographische Einzelaufnahmen antiker Skulpturen*, Berlin, 1893–1940.

Faison, *New England* — S. L. Faison, *Art Museums of New England*, New York, 1958.

Fuchs, *Skulptur* — W. Fuchs, *Die Skulptur der Griechen*, Munich, 1969.

Furtwängler, Oikonomides, *Masterpieces* — A. Furtwängler, *Masterpieces of Greek Sculpture: A Series of Essays on the History of Art*, ed. E. Sellers, New York, 1895; new and enlarged edition, ed. A. N. Oikonomides, Chicago, 1964.

Gabelmann, *Löwenbild* — H. Gablemann, *Studien zum frühgriechischen Löwenbild*, Berlin, 1965.

Graindor, *Bustes et statues-portraits* — P. Graindor, *Bustes et statues-portraits d'Egypte romaine*, Cairo, n.d.

Hanfmann, *Roman Art* — G. M. A. Hanfmann, *Roman Art*, Greenwich, Connecticut, 1965.

Hekler, *Bildnisse Griechen* — A. Hekler, H. von Heintze, *Bildnisse berühmter Griechen*, 3d ed., Berlin, 1962.

IG — *Inscriptiones Graecae*, Berlin, 1873– .

Inan and Rosenbaum, *Porträtplastik* — J. Inan, E. Alföldi-Rosenbaum, *Römische und frühbyzantinische Porträtplastik aus der Türkei*, Mainz, 1979.

Inan and Rosenbaum, *Portrait Sculpture* — J. Inan, E. Rosenbaum, *Roman and Early Byzantine Portrait Sculpture in Asia Minor*, London, 1966.

Ingholt, *Palmyrensk Skulptur* — H. Ingholt, *Studier over palmyrensk Skulptur*, København, 1928.

Jucker Festschrift — *Eikones: Studien zum griechischen und römischen Bildnis (Antike Kunst 12)*, Bern, 1980.

Kelsey, *Roman Portraiture* — E. Gazda, ed., *Roman Portraiture: Ancient and Modern Revivals*, Kelsey Museum of Archaeology, Ann Arbor, 1977.

Kyrieleis, *Bildnisse der Ptolemäer* — H. Kyrieleis, *Bildnisse der Ptolemäer*, Berlin, 1975.

Lawrence, *Later Greek Sculpture* — A. W. Lawrence, *Later Greek Sculpture and Its Influence on East and West*, London, 1927.

Lippold, *Handbuch*

G. Lippold, *Handbuch der Archäologie: im Rahmen des Handbuchs der Altertumswissenschaft*, 3.1, Munich, 1950.

Lippold, *Vaticanischen Skulpturen*

G. Lippold, *Die Skulpturen des Vaticanischen Museums*, 3.1-2, Berlin, 1936-1956.

Master Bronzes

Master Bronzes from the Classical World, Fogg Art Museum, Cambridge, Massachusetts, 1967.

Matz Festschrift

Festschrift für Friedrich Matz, ed. N. Himmelmann-Wildschutz and H. Biesantz, Mainz, 1962.

Metropolitan, *Chase, Capture*

The Chase, the Capture: Collecting at the Metropolitan Museum of Art, New York, 1975.

Michaelis, *Marbles in Great Britain*

A. Michaelis, *Ancient Marbles in Great Britain*, Cambridge, 1882.

New York Private Collections

Ancient Art in New York Private Collections, The Metropolitan Museum of Art, New York, 1961.

Pandermalis, *Strategenköpfen*

D. Pandermalis, *Untersuchungen zu den Klassischen Strategenköpfen*, Freiburg, 1969.

Picard, *Manuel*

C. Picard, *Manuel d'archéologie grecque*, 1-4, Paris, 1935-1966.

Reinach, *Rép. rel.*

S. Reinach, *Répertoire de reliefs grecs et romains*, 1-3, Paris, 1909-1912.

Reinach, *Rép. stat.*

S. Reinach, *Répertoire de la statuaire grecque et romaine*, 1-6, Paris, 1897-1930.

Richter, *Greek Sculptures*

G. M. A. Richter, *Catalogue of Greek Sculptures in the Metropolitan Museum of Art*, Cambridge, Massachusetts, 1954.

Richter, *Kouroi*

G. M. A. Richter, *Kouroi: A Study of the Development of the Greek Kouros from the Late Seventh to the Early Fifth Century B. C.*, New York, 1960.

Richter, *Portraits of the Greeks*

G. M. A. Richter, *The Portraits of the Greeks*, 1-3, London, 1965.

Ridgway, *Archaic Style*

B. S. Ridgway, *The Archaic Style in Greek Sculpture*, Princeton, New Jersey, 1977.

Ridgway, *Severe Style*

B. S. Ridgway, *The Severe Style in Greek Sculpture*, Princeton, New Jersey, 1970.

Romans and Barbarians

Romans and Barbarians, Museum of Fine Arts, Boston, December 17 1976-February 27, 1977.

Schefold, *Meisterwerke*

K. Schefold, *Meisterwerke griechischer Kunst*, Basel, 1960.

Search for Alexander

The Search for Alexander, National Gallery of Art, Washington, D.C., November 16, 1980-April 5, 1981.

Vermeule, *Greek and Roman Portraits*

C. C. Vermeule, *Greek and Roman Portraits, 470 B.C.-A.D. 500*, Museum of Fine Arts, Boston, 1959, rev. ed. with M. B. Comstock, Boston, 1972.

Vermeule, *Greek Art*

C. C. Vermeule, *Greek Art: Socrates to Sulla*, Museum of Fine Arts, Boston, 1980.

Vermeule, *Polykleitos*

C. C. Vermeule, *Polykleitos: First in a Series of Picture Books on Famous Sculptors*, Museum of Fine Arts, Boston, 1969.

Vermeule, *Roman Imperial Art*

C. C. Vermeule, *Roman Imperial Art in Greece and Asia Minor*, Cambridge, Massachusetts, 1968.

Vermeule, *Roman Taste*

C. C. Vermeule, *Greek Sculpture and Roman Taste*, Ann Arbor, 1977.

Walters, *Early Christian and Byzantine Art*

Early Christian and Byzantine Art, The Walters Art Gallery, Baltimore, Maryland, 1947.

Waltham, *Art of the Late Antique*

Art of the Late Antique from American Collections, Rose Art Gallery, Brandeis University, Waltham, Massachusetts, December 18, 1968-February 16, 1969.

Wegner, *Antoninischer Zeit*

M. Wegner, *Die Herrscherbildnisse in antoninischer Zeit (Das römische Herrscherbild*, 2.4), Berlin, 1939.

Wiggers, *Caracalla*

H. B. Wiggers and M. Wegner, *Caracalla bis Balbinus: Das römische Herrscherbild*, 3.1, Berlin, 1971.

Wegner, *Hadrian*

M. Wegner, *Hadrian, Plotina, Marciana, Matidia, Sabina (Das römische Herrscherbild*, 2.3), Berlin, 1956.

Worcester, *Roman Portraits*

M. Milkovich, *Roman Portraits*, Worcester Art Museum, Worcester, April 6-May 14, 1961.

Abbreviations of Journal Titles

AA	Archäologischer Anzeiger.
ActaA	Acta Archaeologica.
ActaIRN	Institutum Romanum Norvegiae: Acta ad archaeologiam et artium historiam pertinentia.
AJA	American Journal of Archaeology.
AK	Antike Kunst.
AM	Mitteilungen des Deutschen Archäologischen Instituts, Athenische Abteilung.
AnnInst	Annales Institutorum.
AntPl	Antike Plastik.
ArchEph	Archaiologikē Ephēmeris.
ArtBull	Art Bulletin.
ArtQ	Art Quarterly.
ASAtene	Annuario della Scuola Archeologia de Atene.
Atti Lincei	Atti della Accademia Nazionale dei Lincei.
BABesch	Bulletin van de Vereeniging tot Bevordering der Kennis van de Antieke Beschaving.
BAntFr	Bulletin de la Société nationale des antiquaires de France.
BCH	Bulletin de correspondance hellénique.
BerlMus	Berliner Museen, Berichte aus den preussischen Kunstsammlungen
BIFAO	Bulletin de l'Institut français d'archéologie orientale.
BullComm	Bullettino della Commissione archeologica comunale in Roma.
BullMFA	Bulletin of the Museum of Fine Arts, Boston.
BurlMag	Burlington Magazine.

BZ	Byzantinische Zeitschrift.
DOP	Dumbarton Oaks Papers.
GBA	Gazette des Beaux Arts.
Getty MJ	The J. Paul Getty Museum Journal.
GGA	Göttingische gelehrte Anzeigen.
GRBStudies	Greek, Roman, and Byzantine Studies.
IstM	Mitteilungen des Deutschen Archäologischen Instituts, Abteilung Istanbul.
JAC	Jahrbuch für Antike und Christentum.
JARCE	Journal of the American Research Center in Egypt.
JdI	Jahrbuch des Deutschen Archäologischen Instituts.
JHS	Journal of Hellenic Studies.
JOAI	Jahreshefte des Oesterreichischen archäologischen Instituts.
MAAR	Memoirs of the American Academy in Rome.
MdI	Mitteilungen des Deutschen Archäologischen Instituts (1948–1952).
MJb	Münchener Jahrbuch der bildenden Kunst.
MMABulletin	The Metropolitan Museum of Art Bulletin.
MMAJournal	Metropolitan Museum Journal.
MonPiot	Monuments et mémoires publ. par l'Académie des inscriptions et belles lettres, Fondation Piot.
MUSE	MUSE, Annual of the Museum of Art and Archaeology, University of Missouri, Columbia
NotScavi	Notizie degli Scavi di Antichità.

PAPS	Proceedings of the American Philosophical Society.
PBSR	Papers of the British School in Rome.
RBibl	Revue biblique.
RendPontAcc	Atti della Pontificia Accademia Romana di Archeologia: Rendiconti.
RM	Mitteilungen des Deutschen Archäologischen Instituts, Römische Abteilung.
StArch	Studia Archaeologia

Index of Collections (by city)

Fort Worth, Texas			
Kimbell Art Museum	Cycladic idol	2	27
	Cypriote head of a man	45	74
	Head of Meleager	52	82–83
	Funerary statue of a servant girl	82	111
	Head of Marcus Aurelius	281	328
	Head of Faustina Minor	285	332–333
Hanover, New Hampshire			
Dartmouth College Museum	Cypriote head of a man	46	74–75
and Galleries	Front of a Nereid sarcophagus	210	251
Hartford, Connecticut			
The Wadsworth Atheneum	Pair of funerary lions	99	128–129
	Shepherd	188	223
Honolulu, Hawaii			
Honolulu Academy of Arts	Head of Apollo	17	43
	Stele of Xenocrates	67	98
	Head of a satyr	126	159
	Fragment of a columnar Herakles sarcophagus	211	252
	Fragment of a frieze Herakles sarcophagus	212	252–253
Houston, Texas			
The Museum of Fine Arts	Heroic banquet relief	9	34–35
	Grave stele of a woman	78	108
	Sarcophagus with the return of Meleager's body to Kalydon	207	247
	Statue of a Severan emperor	300	349
	Head of Plautilla	306	355
Indianapolis, Indiana			
Indianapolis Museum of Art	Persephone	56	86
	Head of Berenike II	109	140
Kansas City, Missouri			
William Rockhill Nelson Gallery of	Head of a youth	6	30–31
Art–Atkins Museum of Fine Arts	Veiled head of a woman	61	91
	Grave stele of Polystrate of Halai	92	121
	Statuette of Seleucus IV Philopator	112	143
	Head of a Hellenistic ruler	115	146
	Torso of a dancing satyr	125	158
	Dioskouros	173	208
	Bust of a lady	263	307
	Bust of Hadrian	267	310–311
	Bust of Antinous	269	312–313
	Statue of a youth	273	318–319
	Bust of Caracalla	302	350–351
	Head of a Constantinian lady	324	374
	Palmyrene funerary relief	334	385
Lancaster, Pennsylvania			
North Museum	Head of Aphrodite	144	177
Franklin and Marshall College			
Los Angeles, California			
Los Angeles County Museum of Art	Athena	31	58
	Head of a goddess (Demeter?)	34	62
	Hygieia	48	78
	Herakles	49	79
	Athlete	58	87
	Hermes	155	188

Stanford, California			
Stanford University Museum of Art	Torso of Dionysos	41	69
	Palmyrene funerary relief	336	387
Toledo, Ohio			
The Toledo Museum of Art	Young athlete	24	50–51
	Ram	122	155
	Head of Venus	286	334
	Head of Lucius Verus	287	335
	Palmyrene funerary relief	330	380–381
Toronto, Ontario, Canada			
Royal Ontario Museum	Head and torso of Dionysos	37	65
	Stele with seated woman	80	110
	Stele of Iostrate	88	117
	Head of a girl	93	122
	Head of Roma	186	221
	Head of a young man	261	305
	Head of a bearded man	315	364
Washington, D.C.			
The Corcoran Gallery of Art	Aphrodite	137	170
Dumbarton Oaks	Fragment of an Early Christian sarcophagus	221	262
National Gallery of Art	Torso of Aphrodite	141	174
Waterville, Maine			
Colby College Museum of Art	Girl with garland	119	152
Wellesley, Massachusetts			
Wellesley College Museum	Diskophoros	19	45
Jewett Arts Center	Relief with four gods	163	197
	Sarcophagus lid with reclining Season	216	258
Williamstown, Massachusetts			
Sterling and Francine Clark	Torso of a satyr	133	166
Art Institute	Head of a Julio-Claudian man	242	285
Williams College Museum of Art	Head of Zeus (?)	124	157
Winnetka, Illinois			
James Alsdorf Foundation	Sarcophagus with mythological scene	206	246
	Head of Commodus	290	338
Worcester, Massachusetts			
Worcester Art Museum	Cypriote head of a goddess	44	72–73
	Stele of a warrior	63	94
	Old man from a stele	94	123
	Statue of a lady (Octavia?)	236	279
	Head of Caligula	248	291
	Head of Nero	254	298
	Bust of a lady (Lucilla?)	289	336–337
	Diocletian (?)	322	371

Index of Personal Names

Note: References are cited by page number for the Introduction and by catalogue number (here in bold face) for the Catalogue, viz.: Athena, 3, 22; **18, 29, 31, 50, 161**

(Note: names in *italics* are from inscriptions)

Agorakritos, 34
Agrippina the Elder, 245
Alexander the Great, 3, 4, 5, 6, 16; **101, 103, 206**
Alkamenes, 34
Antinous, 13; **123, 269**
Antoninus Pius, 7, 9; **277, 323**
Antony, Mark, 6; **233**
Apollonia, **167**
Aqul, **336**
Aristandros, **167**
Aristonice, **75**
Aristotle, 4
Arsinoe II, **110**
Artemisia, 4
Arundel, Lord, **49, 107**
Ashmole, Bernard, 22
Augustus (see also Octavian), 6, 9, 15; **236, 238, 239, 240, 241**
Aurelius, Marcus, 9; **281, 282**

Baker, W. C., 3, **95, 160**
Balbinus, **310**
Balya, **333**
Barber, Charles E., 14
Bell, Alexander Graham, 15
Berenike II, **109**
Biddle, Nicholas, 13
Bon'am, **336**
Bonaparte, Lucien, 14
Branteghem, van, collection, **98**
Brewer, Mrs. Gardner, 14
Brugsch, Emil, 18
Brummer, Ernest, 16, **87, 96**
Brummer, Joseph, 16
Buckingham collection (Stowe), **169**

Caesar, Julius, 6; **231**
Caligula (Gaius Germanicus), **248, 249**
Canino, Princess of, 14
Caracalla (Marcus Aurelius Antoninus), 9; **301, 302, 303, 306**
Cassius Longinus, C., **230**
Cesnola, Alexander Palma di, 12, 18
Cesnola, Luigi (Louis) Palma di, 11, 12, 17, 18, 20; **46, 47**
Chapman, S.H. and H., 14
Charbonneaux, Jean, 22
Chrysler, Walter P., 15
Cicero, 6
Claudius, **252**
Cleopatra, 5, 6
Clodius Albinus, **282**
Cohen, Mendes I., 18
Comin collection (Rome), **225, 311**

Commodus, 9; **278, 290**
Constantia, 21; **323**
Constantine, 1, 8, 9; **324, 325**
Cook, A.B., 7
Cook, F. (Doughty House), **251**
Cornelius Gallus, C., **237**
Crawford, Thomas, 14
Crispina, **289**
Curtius, Ludwig, 93, **315**

Davis, Norman, 20, **22**
Debbas, Abdo, 14
Deering, James, 15
Dennis, George, 14
Didia Clara, **296**
Diocletian, 9; **322**
Domitian, 9; **256, 257**
Domitius Ahenobarbus, L., **230**
Dresnay, Vicomte, (Paris), **67**
Drusilla, **246**
Drusus Major, **244**

Elagabalus, 9; **305**
Elgin, Lord (Broom Hall), 12
Elliott, Jesse D., 13, 14
Emerson, Ralph Waldo, 13
Epicurus, **105**
Etruscans, 6

Fausta, **324**
Faustina Minor, **283, 284, 285**
Forbes, Edward W., 15

Gallatin, Alfred, **251**
Gallienus, 21; **317, 318**
Gardner, Isabella Stewart, 14, 15
Geta, **292, 304**
Getty, J. Paul, 20, 22
Gordon, C. T. (Cairness House), **63**
Graves, Robert, 9
Greenough, Horatio, **33**
Gridley, Elnathan, 13

Hadrian, 7, 8, 9; **54, 169, 262, 264, 265, 266, 267, 323**
Haker, King, 17
Hamilton, Gavin, **262**
Hartwig, P. (Rome), **28**
Hatshepsut, 17
Hearst, Phoebe Apperson, 15; **193, 197, 199, 225, 311**
Hearst, William Randolph, 15; **23, 34, 48, 49, 58, 155, 169, 213**
Helena the Younger, **324**
Hephaistion, **102**

Herodes Atticus, 7; **274**
Honorius, **326**
Hope, Thomas (Deepdene), **31, 48, 49, 107, 122, 158**
Houdon, J.-A., 13

Iostrate, **88**

Jackson, Andrew, 13
Jarvis, J.J., 14
Julia Domna, 9, 13, 21; **296, 298, 299**
Julia Maesa, 13
Julia Mamaea, 13
Julia Paula, **306**
Julia Soemias, 13

Kalamis, 17
Kallistrate, **69**
Kresilas, **28, 30**

Laberius Gallus, **313**
Lanckoronski collection (Vienna), **208**
Latins, 6
Lawrence, Edwin Henry, 18
Leochares, 4; **183**
Libbey, Edward Drummond, 20
Licinius I, 21
Livia, **246**
Livingston, Robert R., 12
Loring, Charles Greely, 18
Lowell, John, 16
Lucilla, **286, 289**
Lucius Verus, 9; **287, 288**
Ludington, Wright S., 15; **13, 55, 131, 142, 294**
Lysippos, 4; **58, 59, 150**

Malocha, **331**
Maquay, George, 14
Maqqi, **330**
Marini collection (Rome), **319**
Massarenti collection (Rome), **313**
Mattei collection (Rome), **171, 250**
Mausolus, 4
Melchett, Lord, **264**
Menander, 5; **104**
Mengarini collection, **35**
Metrodoros, **105, 106**
Morgan, J. Pierpont, **99**
Mummius, 6
Myron, 7

Napoleon I, 12
Nelson, William Rockhill, 20
Nero, 9, 22; **251, 252, 253, 254**

Norton, Charles Eliot, 15
Nur-Bel, 331

Octavia, 236
Octavian (see also Augustus), 6; 236
Odescalchi collection (Rome), 21; 19
Ogga, 333

Pasha, Ismail, 17
Pasiteles, 157
Patterson, Daniel F., 13
Perikles, 3; 28
Perkins, Charles Callahan, 12, 14
Perry, Matthew Calbraith, 13; 275
Petrie, William Flinders, 303
Pheidias, 3, 4, 7, 21; 18, 29, 31, 34
Philip II of Macedon, 4
Philippus Arabs, 316
Philokydis, 72
Philomelos, 71
Plato, 9
Plautilla, 306
Polydeukes (Polydeukion), 7; 274
Polykleitos, 4, 21; 19, 20, 21, 22, 23, 24, 25, 32, 172
Polystrate, 92

Ponsonby, Ashley G.J., 177
Pozzi, S., collection (Paris), 32, 120, 211, 212
Praxiteles, 4, 7; 35, 36, 38, 40, 41, 57, 74, 89, 93, 137
Ptolemies, 5
Ptolemy III Euergetes, 5; 108, 111

Reed, Horatio Blake, 17
Rowland, Benjamin Jr., 16

Sabina, Vibia, 270
Sabines, 6
Schimmel, Norbert, 10
Seleucus IV Philopator, 112
Severus, Alexander, 309
Severus, Septimius, 9, 21; 295, 297, 298, 300
Simon, Norton, 16, 20
Skopas, 4, 15, 21; 48, 49, 50, 51, 52, 53, 54
Socrates, 4
Suetonius, 9
Sulla, 6; 116
Tacitus, 9
Tetrarchs, 9

Theagenes, 100
Thebageneias, 167
Thorndike, Augustus, 13
Tiberius, 243, 244
Timotheos, 183
Titus, 9, 22; 253, 327
Torlonia family, 12, 14
Trajan, 9; 258

Ummabi, 330

Vanderlyn, John, 12
Vedius, 123
Vespasian, 9; 256
Virgil, 6

Walters, Henry, 20; 162
Warren, Edward Perry, 4, 40, 176, 235, 277
Whitehill, Walter Muir, 16
Wix de Zsolnay collection (Vienna), 8

Xenocrates, 67

Yarkhai, 333

Index of Place Names

Actium, 6
Adriatic Sea, 59, 196
Aegean, 4
    Greek islands of , 2; 1, 4, 12, 114
    Islands of, 19; 115
    Region, 101, 102
Africa, 1, 6, 8; 179, 301
Albano, Lake, 248
Alexandria, 5, 6, 17; 109, 114, 117, 179, 185, 233, 263, 288
American Academy (Rome), 14
American Academy of Fine Arts (New York), 12, 13
Amorgos, 15
Ann Arbor (University of Michigan), 20, 22
Antioch, 12; 206
Aphrodisias, 5
Arabia, 7
Arezzo, 202
Argos, 3, 4
Ariccia, 30
Armenia, 7
Asia Minor, 1, 2, 3, 4, 5, 6, 7, 8, 12, 13; 10, 24, 60, 113, 114, 115, 131, 175, 183, 189, 228, 252, 268, 285, 286, 287, 294, 320
Athelhampton Hall (Dorset), 161
Athens and vicinity, 2, 3, 4, 5, 6, 7, 19; 28, 74, 86, 91, 93, 99, 160, 278
    Acropolis, 3; 11, 27, 84, 166
    Agora, Roman, 323
    Erechtheum, 3; 166
    Kanellopoulos Museum, 64

Kerameikos cemetery, 73, 94
    Parthenon, 3, 4
    Spata, 66
Attica, 2, 4, 7; 4, 12, 32, 42, 62, 63, 67, 68, 69, 70, 72, 73, 75, 76, 79, 80, 81, 85, 86, 92, 94

Baltimore (Johns Hopkins University), 19
Baltimore (Walters Art Gallery), 11, 20, 22
Behnesa (Oxyrhynchos), 170
Beirut, 6, 13, 14; 290
Benevento, 112, 226
Berkeley (University of California), 15
Black Sea, 5
Bloomington (University of Indiana), 11, 21
Boeotia, 83
Bolsena, 313
Borghese, villa (Rome), 157
Boston, 2, 11, 12, 13, 14, 15, 16, 17, 20, 22
Brooklyn, 13, 20
Brunswick, Maine (Bowdoin College), 11
Bubon (see also Ibidjick), 228, 294

Caesarea (in Cappadocia), 276
Cambridge, Massachusetts, 15, 20
Capua, 2
Caria, 2, 5
Carpegna, villa (Rome), 220
Carrara, 1
Carthage, 6, 187
Centocelle, 26, 36
Chalkis, 89

Chapel Hill, North Carolina, 16
Chicago, 21
Cilicia, 14
Città Lavinia, 137
Civitavecchia, 51
Cleveland, 2, 11, 20
Cobham Hall (Kent), 266
Columbia, Missouri (University of Missouri), 22
Constantinople (see also Istanbul), 328
Corinth, 2, 6
Crete, 2, 22
Crimea, 7
Cyclades, 11, 19; 1, 2
Cyprus, 3, 11, 12, 17, 18; 43, 44, 45, 46, 47

Dacia, 9
Dai el Guirza, 149
Daphne-Yakto, 152
Detroit, 20
Dumbarton Oaks, 11
Durham, North Carolina, 16

Egypt: 2, 3, 5, 6, 8, 10, 15, 16, 17, 18, 22; 103, 108, 110, 111, 114, 237, 253, 263, 269, 282, 303, 322
Eleusis, 3, 30
Elis, 2
Ephesus, 4, 13; 123, 256, 275
Epidaurus, 4
Euboea, 89

Farnese, palazzo (Rome), 203

Index of Mythological Names

PHOTOGRAPH CREDITS

Armen Photographers, Newark, 279; Boissonas, Geneva, 164;
Dutro Blocksom, 76; E. Irving Blomstrann, New Britain, 99, 188;
Barney Burstein, Boston, 19; James Edmunds, 266; P. Richard Eels, 135;
Thomas Feist, 10, 42, 153, 206; Raymond Fortt, London, 30, 104, 121, 154, 167, 283;
Greenberg, Wrazen & May, Buffalo, 27, 136; Bartlett Hendricks, Pittsfield, 332;
Hickey & Robertson, Houston, 78, 85; Peter A. Juley, New York, 73;
Ron Kelley, Santa Barbara, 55; Hartwig Koopermann, 123; Balthazar Korab, Troy, 72;
O. E. Nelson, New York, 249   Karl Obert, Santa Barbara, 294;
Nathan Rabin, New York, 197; John D. Schiff, New York, 323;
Ken Strothman, Bloomington, 282; Tierney & Killingsworth, Miami, 224, 227;
Herbert P. Vose, Wellesley, 70; Whitaker Studio, Richmond, 143;
Larry Webster, Boston, 14, 38; Dietrich Widmer, Lindenberg, 106, 216, 228

Design: Patrick Dooley

Typesetting: Dharma Press, Oakland: Fototronic Garamond

Production assistance: Diana Weaver, Lucinda Costin,
Katherine Kiefer, William Kiskadden

Printing: Jeffries Banknote Company, Los Angeles on LOE 80 lb. dull

Binding: Roswell Book Binding, Phoenix

Cover illustration courtesy of
Yale University Art Gallery (see no. 161)